1917.

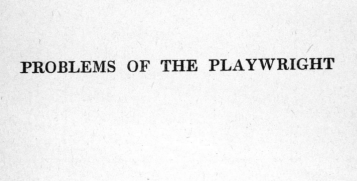

PROBLEMS OF THE PLAYWRIGHT

PROBLEMS OF THE PLAYWRIGHT

BY

CLAYTON HAMILTON

MEMBER OF THE NATIONAL INSTITUTE OF ARTS AND LETTERS

NEW YORK

HENRY HOLT AND COMPANY

1917

TO
William Archer
GREETINGS OVERSEAS

PREFACE

THIS book is a companion volume to THE THEORY OF THE THEATRE and STUDIES IN STAGECRAFT, and should, if possible, be read in association with its predecessors in the series.

We are living in the midst of a great period of the history of the drama—perhaps the very greatest that the world has ever seen; but the general theatre-going and play-reading public is only gradually developing a consciousness of this astounding fact. The reason is not difficult to define. In the evolution of any art, creation always precedes criticism, because criticism is merely an analysis of what has been created; and, since the contemporary drama began to bourgeon only thirty years ago, it is not surprising that contemporary criticism is only now beginning to interpret it. A few books by pioneers have been before the public for half a dozen or a dozen years, to plead, like lone voices in an almost empty auditorium, for adequate appreciation of the modern drama; but it was not until very recently that a sturdy group of books has been prepared to sally forth, shoulder to shoulder, like an army with banners, to conquer the credence of the public in the new era of great drama that is now contributing a glory to the theatre of the world.

Those of us who were in college from fifteen to twenty years ago will remember that we were taught that there were four great periods in the history of the drama—the Greek period of Sophocles, the Spanish period of Calderon, the English period of Shakespeare, and the French period of Molière. We were led to regard the drama as an art that had been dead for several centuries. Our professors were still diffident of Ibsen; and they would have considered it a sacrilege against the dignity of scholarship to advise us to study the works of such untested dramatists as Hauptmann and Pinero and Brieux. In half a generation, this attitude toward the contemporary drama has been rendered obsolete. It is no longer considered necessary, as a requirement for a baccalaureate diploma, to read John Ford in preference to Maurice Maeterlinck. The most popular courses in our colleges to-day are courses in the contemporary drama; and the study has been taken up by every woman's club and literary circle in the land. So swift has been this new development that a large public, crying out for instruction, has outstripped the available supply of teachers; and, for the present, it has become the duty of every one who knows this or that concerning the contemporary drama to write a book about it and pass his knowledge on, at second hand, to the many who are eager to receive it. It is comforting to note that this demand, at last, is being dealt with. So many books about the current drama are, at present, being issued in rapid succession from the press that, in another year or two, the most conservative of readers will no longer be permitted to plead ignorance as an excuse for failing to appreciate the artistic triumphs of the theatre of to-day.

But this new criticism of a new creation has not as yet attained its classic stage. Sophocles achieved his Aristotle; but our great contemporary drama still awaits a great dramatic critic. The task of criticism is more difficult to-day than it has ever been before. For one thing, the drama has become, for the first time, cosmopolitan. In interpreting the periods of Sophocles, Calderon, Shakespeare, and Molière, the critic could confine his attention, in each instance, to a single nationality. But worthy contributions to the contemporary drama have been made by nations so diverse as Scandinavia, Russia, Germany, Austria, France, Belgium, Holland, Hungary, Italy, Spain, England, and America. Aristotle could actually see and study at first hand all the plays that were existent in his world; but, on the same terms, no modern critic could possibly evaluate the best dramatic productions of the last thirty years.

For another thing, the creations of the contemporary period have been more diverse in content, in purpose, and in method, than the creations of any of the other great periods that have been enumerated. The Elizabethan period endured for half a century—from 1590 to 1640, let us say; but all the plays presented in this period display a family resemblance to each other. The difference between Shakespeare and Webster and Fletcher " and the rest " [to quote a phrase from the diary of Philip Henslowe] is a difference merely of degree, and not at all of kind. Similarly [to take another period] the art of Æschylus, Sophocles, and Euripides was the same art, in principle and

method. Such periods can be summed up easily by a
critic who, like Aristotle, is endowed with eyes to see.
But it is much more difficult to interpret a brief period
of thirty years that discloses such diverse products as
*The Weavers, Chantecler, The Thunderbolt, The Blue
Bird, Hindle Wakes, The Dream Play, The Red
Robe, The Cherry Orchard*, and *Sumurûn*. All of
these are great works; but they show no relation
to each other that is immediately recognizable.
They differ not merely in degree, but also in kind;
and the critic who endeavors to interpret all of
them must induce a separate set of principles for
each.

For still another thing, a development of the drama
in recent years toward naturalism has been accompanied by a simultaneous development of the theatre
toward fantastical romance; so that the contemporary
critic is required to deal synchronously with such
utterly different undertakings as those of Elizabeth
Baker and Gordon Craig—or as those of the Granville
Barker who wrote *The Madras House* and the Granville
Barker who produced *The Man Who Married a Dumb
Wife*. Criticism of so chaotic and diverse a period must
necessarily appear, for the present at least, chaotic
and diverse. The same standard that is used in judging Marlowe may be used in judging Shirley; but it
would manifestly be unfair to apply the same standard
in judging *Hedda Gabler* and *Cyrano de Bergerac*. It
should be, I think, apparent to any reasonable mind
that the time has not yet come for coherent and complete and final criticism of that superb and varied

efflorescence of the drama in the very midst of which
we dwell.

The most that can be accomplished by dramatic
critics at the present time is to interpret various trends
and tendencies in and for themselves. Some future
critic, looking back from a distance of a century or
more, may be able to include Shaw and Synge and
Sudermann and Maeterlinck in a single stroke of the
eye; but for the present it seems wiser to approach
these masters separately, in different moods and with
different standards of appreciation. Brieux and Reinhardt, Stanley Houghton and Gordon Craig, D'Annunzio and Pinero, should be treated as the subjects of
different studies in stagecraft. For this reason, a
multiplication of critical studies of the contemporary
drama is greatly to be desired. Each commentator
should contrive to teach us something worthy of remembrance regarding that particular phase of the vast,
kaleidoscopic spectacle which has chiefly attracted his
attention. But no single critic, under these conditions,
can be readily accepted as a final and complete authority on every aspect of so multifarious a phenomenon
as the contemporary drama.

The present volume [which is to be regarded as a
sort of suffix to The Theory of the Theatre and
Studies in Stagecraft] is intended merely as a minor
contribution to an instant need. In this book, the
kaleidoscopic field of the contemporary drama is considered from various points of view,—that of the critic,
the dramatist, the stage-director, the scenic artist, the
manager, and the theatre-going public.

Most of the studies included in this volume have appeared, in earlier versions, in various magazines,— *The Bookman, Vogue, Good Housekeeping,* and *The Theatre.* To the proprietors of these publications I am indebted for the privilege of quoting from my contributions to their pages. It is scarcely necessary to state that these studies have been revised and rearranged and, in many passages, entirely rewritten.

In the process of preparing the present volume for the press, I have encountered certain passages of repetition which I have decided not to delete, because of the advisability of adding emphasis to an important point by iteration; and I have encountered a few other passages which seem, at first sight, to contradict each other. But, in every instance of apparent contradiction, I have discovered that what I have said on the one side and the other is equally true, according to the point of view. I have decided, therefore, not to strive for that foolish consistency which is the hobgoblin of little minds. What I have desired is, rather, to maintain the free play of an unprejudiced, receptive mind over the entire panorama of the contemporary stage.

C. H.

New York City: 1917.

CONTENTS

PROBLEMS OF THE PLAYWRIGHT

I

CONTRAST IN THE DRAMA

In this time of the tottering of definitions, it is desirable that the dramatic critic, in the interest of future playwrights, should seek some certain element of narrative that may be accepted as essential to success upon the stage. In view of the fact that several of the younger realistic writers of Great Britain have successfully evaded the famous assertion of the late Ferdinand Brunetière that the essential element of drama is a struggle between human wills, it appears to be necessary to agree with Mr. William Archer that the Brunetière formula can no longer be accepted as a definition of the drama.

The potency of this attack upon a theory which for twenty years has been regarded as an axiom must not be over-estimated. Not even the author of *The Great Adventure*—from which any positive assertion of the human will has been carefully excluded—would deny that the narrative pattern praised in unexceptionable terms by Brunetière is the one pattern which is most likely to interest an audience assembled in a theatre, or that at least nine-tenths of all the acknowledged masterpieces of the drama, both in the past and in the present, will be found upon examination to incorporate some conflict between human wills. Exceptions—according to the Latin proverb—*test* a rule; but they do not necessarily prove that, as a rule, it has lost its validity. In shifting our critical position, we are merely admitting that the element of conflict is not *essential* to the drama; it is far from our intention to suggest that, in the vast majority of cases, this element is not desirable.

But even to admit that an element which was formerly considered as essential can now be regarded only as advantageous is to feel ourselves somewhat in the position of mariners whose ship has sunk beneath them. This position is pertinently indicated by the familiar phrase "at sea." It is always disconcerting to renounce a seeming certainty; and the normal mind seeks ever to erect some other image to replace an idol that is overthrown. There is a world of meaning in the traditional announcement, "The king is dead; long live the king!" When definitions die, we must immediately seek new definitions to succeed them.

This necessity was felt by Mr. Archer when he dealt his gentle death-blow to the theory that conflict is essential to the drama. He proceeded at once to present a new pretender to the vacant throne. The following sentences, which are quoted from page 36 of Mr. Archer's *Play-Making*, define his new position:—
"What, then, is the essence of drama, if conflict be not it? What is the common quality of themes, scenes, and incidents, which we recognize as specifically dramatic? Perhaps we shall scarcely come nearer to a helpful definition than if we say that the essence of

drama is *crisis*. A play is a more or less rapidly-developing crisis in destiny or circumstance, and a dramatic scene is a crisis within a crisis, clearly furthering the ultimate event. The drama may be called the art of crises, as fiction is the art of gradual developments."

This theory of Mr. Archer's affords us at least a floating spar to cling to, in the midst of the sea of uncertainty into which we have disturbingly been dropped. It is undeniable that the drama tends to treat life more crisply and succinctly than the novel, both because of the physical limitations of the theatre and because of the psychological demands of the actors and the audience. One way of attaining this crispness and succinctness is to <u>catch</u> <u>life</u> <u>at</u> <u>a</u> <u>crisis</u> and to exhibit the culminating points—or, as Mr. Archer says in a later passage, "the interesting culminations"—of the destinies of the characters concerned. But is this the only way? No one would venture to deny that Mr. Archer's formula applies to at least nine-tenths of all the acknowledged masterpieces of the drama; but so did the formula of Brunetière. It is obviously advantageous for the drama to catch life at a crisis; but is it absolutely necessary? If we can find as many exceptions to Mr. Archer's rule as Mr. Archer found to Brunetière's, we shall be compelled to decide that the element of crisis is no more *essential* to the drama than the element of conflict.

Let us now ask Mr. Archer if he can find any crisis in Lady Gregory's one-act comedy entitled *The Workhouse Ward?* This dialogue between two beggars lying in adjacent beds attains that crispness and succinctness which is advocated by the critic, without exhibiting a crisis in either of their lives. The whole point of the play is that we leave the beggars precisely in the same position in which we found them. Yet this comedy is undeniably dramatic. It has been acted successfully in Ireland and England and America, and has proved itself, in all three countries, one of the most popular pieces in the repertory of the Abbey Theatre Players. Would Mr. Archer maintain that *The Great Adventure* exhibits " a more or less rapidly-developing crisis in destiny or circumstance," or that any of the eight scenes of this comedy, except the very first, can be regarded as " a crisis within a crisis, clearly furthering the ultimate event? " Is there any crisis in *The Madras House* or in *The Pigeon?* Or, to go back to Shakespeare, would Mr. Archer attempt to define as " a crisis within a crisis " such a passage as Act V, Scene 1 of *The Merchant of Venice*, in which Lorenzo and Jessica discourse most eloquent music underneath the moon? Is there any crisis in the scenes between Orlando and Rosalind in the Forest of Arden?

To defend the element of crisis as essential in such instances as these would necessitate the same sort of verbal jugglery that would be required to establish the element of conflict. It would seem, therefore, that Mr. Archer has not led us any nearer to a certainty than we were before. The friendly spar is floated from our desperate grasp and we find ourselves once more floundering in the sea.

Is there, after all, such a thing as an *essential* element

Why not — Adjustment? A progressive process of adjustment to himself, to others, and to environment.

CONTRAST IN THE DRAMA 5

of drama? Is there a single narrative element without
which a dramatic scene cannot succeed? I think that
there is; but I am willing to revoke this decision so
soon as any writer shall show me an exception to the
rule. It seems to me at present that the one indispensable element to success upon the stage is the element
of *contrast*, and that a play becomes more and more
dramatic in proportion to the multiplicity of contrasts
that it contains within itself.

The sole reason why *The Workhouse Ward* produces
a dramatic effect is that the two beggars are emphatically different from each other. The moonlight scene
in *The Merchant of Venice* is interesting on the stage
because of the contrast between the contributions of
the two lovers to their lyrical duet. Both *The Pigeon*
and *The Madras House* derive their value from the fact
that they exhibit a series of contrasts between characters. *The Great Adventure* is dramatic because the
drifting hero is wonderfully contrasted with the practical and sensible heroine and every scene of the play
reveals some minor contrast between antithetic minds.
What is the dramatic element in the soliloquies of
Hamlet? Do they not derive their theatrical effectiveness from the fact that they present a constant contrast between very different human qualities which, in
this case, happen to have been incorporated in a single
person? Such a play as *Every Man in His Humour*
stands outside the formula of Brunetière, because it
exhibits no struggle of contending wills; it also stands
outside the formula of Mr. Archer, because it exhibits
neither a crisis nor a series of crises; but it is a great

Or — an attempted adjustment — being the adjustment of man to environment, mental and spiritual laws — and to other men.

comedy, because it exhibits an unintermitted series of contrasts between mutually foiling personalities.

One of the most amusing comedies of recent years affords us an emphatic illustration of the principle of contrast. This is *General John Regan*, the first dramatic composition by Canon Hannay, of St. Patrick's, Dublin,—a genial Irish gentleman who had previously published several novels signed with the utterly English and very solemn pen-name of " George A. Birmingham." *General John Regan* is merely an amplified anecdote. It exhibits no conflict of contending wills; neither does it disclose a crisis in the life of any of the characters; but it is dramatically interesting because it sets forth a series of delightful contrasts between a dozen very different people.

A rich American tourist who is motoring through Ireland is halted in the sleepy little town of Ballymoy. In order to give the inhabitants something to think about, he casually remarks that he has come to look up the early records of the life of General John Regan, the Liberator of Bolivia,—the most renowned of all the native sons of Ballymoy. Nobody has ever heard of this mythical hero; but the dispensary doctor, a lively-minded man named Lucius O'Grady, plays up to the suggestion that has been offered by the stranger. Dr. O'Grady selects a ruined cottage as the birthplace of the famous general, points out the town jail as the residence of his boyhood, and confers upon the tongue-tied maid-servant of the village inn the honorable designation of Only Surviving Relative. He persuades the adventurous American to start a subscription to erect

a statue to the Great Liberator in the market-square
of Ballymoy, and compels all the leading citizens to
contribute to the fund.

The entire second act is taken up with Dr. O'Grady's
preparations for the civic event which is to mark the
unveiling of the monument. This act exhibits no contention of wills, but merely a general contagion of
enthusiasm which overwhelms the wills of all the characters. It would merely be a jugglery of words to
insist that this act exhibits a crisis in the history of
Ballymoy; and even Mr. Archer must admit that it
does not show a crisis in the individual career of any
of the characters. The most amusing scene of all is a
lengthy dialogue between five representative citizens of
Ballymoy who are gathered round a table in the village
inn to discuss the details of the civic project. What is
the source of interest in this scene? What is that
specific quality by virtue of which it must be termed
dramatic? Apparently—since all other explanations
fail—it must be the delightful contrast between the
five very different characters that take part in the conversation.

It is decided in the second act to purchase, at a
reduced price, a second-hand mortuary monument that
has been rejected in Dublin by the relatives of the
deceased; and in the last act this monument is unveiled
by the taciturn maid-servant, dressed fantastically as a
fairy. Dr. O'Grady has had the audacity to invite the
Lord Lieutenant of Ireland to preside at the ceremony.
This dignitary has sent down his aide-de-camp to protest against the hoax; but Dr. O'Grady coerces this

very English and utterly helpless underling into making an address, which is regarded by the populace as an official acceptance of the monument.

This composition is very rich in characterization and unusually humorous in dialogue. Canon Hannay thoroughly knows his Ireland, and he writes with that imaginative glibness which is always evident in Irish humor. His play successfully defies those definitions of the drama which till very recently were held as axioms, and it seems to prove that the sole essential to success in comedy is a sufficiently interesting contrast between characters.

II

BUILDING A PLAY BACKWARD

AUTHOR'S NOTE.—The first section of the present chapter was originally published in THE BOOKMAN for February, 1914. It was this article which suggested to Mr. Elmer L. Reizenstein the pattern for his celebrated play, *On Trial*,— a fact which Mr. Reizenstein graciously acknowledged in the public press at the time when his play was produced. The second section of the present chapter was written immediately after the popular triumph of *On Trial*.

I

MR. JOHN GALSWORTHY'S recent novel, *The Dark Flower*—which is a great work of art—tells three distinct love-stories, that happen to the same hero at different periods of his career. In order to avoid monotony, the author has employed a different chronological pattern for each of the three sections of his novel. In telling the first story, he begins at the beginning; in telling the second story, he begins approximately at the middle; and in telling the third story, he begins at the very end.

It is obvious that, so long as the novelist exhibits his events in a pattern that reveals their logical relation, it is not at all necessary that he should present them in chronological succession. In the first chapter of *Pendennis*, the hero is seventeen years old; the second

chapter narrates the marriage of his parents, and his
own birth and boyhood; and at the outset of the third
chapter, he is only sixteen years of age. Stories may
be told backward through time as well as forward.
Thackeray often begins a chapter with an event that
happened one day and ends it with an event that happened several days before,—working his way backward from effects to causes, instead of forward from
causes to effects.

In reviewing any passage of our own experience, we
are more likely to think backward from the last event
than forward from the first. Retrogression in time is,
therefore, a natural device of narrative; and it is not
at all surprising to find it thoroughly established as a
convention of the novel. What *is* surprising, on the
other hand, is the fact that it has not yet been established as a convention of the drama.

I know of no play in which events have been exhibited
in a pattern of reverted time. Of course, a present
event is frequently employed as the exciting cause of a
conversation which expounds some previous event; and,
in such instances, the discovery of what has happened in
the past is often more important to the audience than
the observation of what is happening in the present.
But, in these expository passages, the past events are
merely talked about and never actually acted on the
stage. In *Romance*, by Mr. Edward Sheldon, a prologue
in the present is followed by a three-act play which narrates events that happened over forty years before;
but, in the structure of the play itself, there is no
retrogression in time. More interesting, from our pres-

ent point of view, is the device of Sir Arthur Pinero in turning back the clock at the outset of the third act of *The Thunderbolt*. At the end of the second act, in the house of Thaddeus Mortimore, a servant arrives with a message from his brother James. The third act, in the house of James Mortimore, overlaps the second act in time; and an entire scene is acted out before the servant is instructed to set out with the message for Thaddeus. This simple expedient, which is used in nearly every novel, seemed exceedingly surprising in the drama; but there can be no question that, in *The Thunderbolt*, its employment was both useful and successful.

Might it not be interesting to go a step further and build an entire drama backward,—to construct a three-act play, for instance, in which the first act should happen in the autumn, the second act in the preceding summer, and the third act in the previous spring? Let us imagine a tragedy, for instance, in which, with no preliminary exposition, a murder or a suicide is acted out in the initial act. This would naturally awaken in the audience a desire to understand the motives which had culminated in the crime. Then, in the second act, we could exhibit the crucial event which had made the murder or the suicide inevitable. Again, the audience would be stimulated to think backward from effects to causes and to wonder what had brought this crucial event about. Lastly, in the third act, several previous events could be displayed, which would finally clear up the mystery by expounding the initiation of the narrative.

Or, to invent an example in the mood of comedy, let us imagine a first act which should exhibit the hopelessly unhappy home life of a kindly and reasonable man who is married to a peevish and unreasonable woman. The heroine is pretty, let us say, and there are some seeds of poetry in her nature that flower every now and then to momentary loveliness. But, like many people who are not incapable of poetry, she abandons herself utterly to the emotion of the moment; and whenever this emotion is not pleasant, she makes life miserable for anybody who is near her. Because she is pretty, she has always been spoiled. She is selfish, she is jealous, she is vain; and whenever these ignoble motives are in any slight degree assailed, she breaks out into a violent fit of temper. Just now, in response to an insistent question, her husband has told her that she looks better in pink than in blue. The heroine, whose instinct is antagonistic, at once prefers blue; she does not see why her husband, if he loves her—he *said* he loved her—should not admit that she would look well in anything; and she proceeds to kick the furniture. The husband seeks refuge in reading *The Wind in the Willows*—whereupon she knocks the book out of his hand. Very gently he remarks: "You didn't seem like this, dear, before we were married." And on that backward-looking line the curtain falls.

The second act shows them in their courtship, two years before. The romance of falling in love has brought out all the lyric loveliness that is latent in the complex nature of the heroine. Her prospective husband sees her at her best, and only at her best. Her family could tell him that she is hard to live with; but—glad enough to get her married—they refrain from doing so. Besides, her brother is a gentleman. The hero is his friend: but what can a decent fellow do in such a dilemma? The heroine seems lovable indeed, when she graciously accepts a large bouquet of orchids, and reads aloud by golden lamp-light the forlorn and lovely little lyrics of Christina Rossetti. The hero proposes marriage: is accepted: and the curtain falls.—Would not this little comedy gain greatly in ironic emphasis by being acted backward in time instead of forward? The question, "What happened before?", is fully as suspensive as the question, "What happens next?": and, in this instance, it is by far the more important question of the two.

Though novels are frequently narrated in a pattern of reverted time, this proposal to build a play backward may seem so revolutionary that most technicians would dismiss it as impossible. But, why? The answer, of course, is obvious; but I am not at all sure that it is final. To follow a narrative forward, from cause to effect, requires a synthetic exercise of mind; and to follow it backward, from effect to cause, requires an analytic exercise. Of these two activities of mind, the analytic demands a greater alertness of intelligence, and a greater fixity of attention, than the synthetic. The collective mind of a helter-skelter theatre audience is less alert and less attentive than the individual mind of a cultivated reader. Furthermore, the reader of a novel, if his mind becomes muddled by the juggling of chronology, may always suspend his reading to turn back a dozen or a hundred pages and reread some finger-pointing passage whose significance he has forgotten; whereas the auditors of a play can never halt the performance to reinform themselves of some point that they have missed. Also, the theatre-going public abhors novelty, and never reads the program. These arguments—and many more—are so familiar that they need not be repeated in detail. Yet something may now be said upon the other side.

To students of the history of the drama, one of the most important phenomena of the last hundred years has been the very rapid development that has taken place, from decade to decade, in the intelligence of the theatre-going public. The average audience is at present more alert and more attentive than ever before in the history of the theatre. This point is evidenced by the fact that, throughout the last century, the technique of the prevailing type of drama has grown progressively less synthetic and more analytic. The prevailing pattern of the drama sixty or seventy years ago was the pattern that was worked out by Eugène Scribe for the so-called "well made play." Scribe devoted his first act to a very thorough exposition, and only at the curtain-fall introduced an element of forward-looking action. Then, at the outset of the second act, he started his narrative in motion; and thereafter he followed it forward in time, to the climax and the close. He never asked his audience to think backward. He worked entirely from causes to effects, and centered his suspense in the obvious question, " What will happen next? "

Contrast this utterly synthetic pattern—a formula for putting two and two together, instead of a formula for taking four apart—with the intricately analytic pattern that was developed, forty years later, by Henrik Ibsen. Ibsen caught his story very late in its career, and revealed the antecedent incidents in little gleams of backward-looking dialogue. His method has often been compared with that of Sophocles; but there is this essential difference,—that, whereas the Athenian audience always knew the story in advance and therefore did not need an exposition, Ibsen was required to expound a series of antecedent circumstances at the same time that he was developing his catastrophe. For, instead of compacting his exposition into the first act—according to the formula of Scribe—he revealed it, little by little, throughout the progress of the play. In the first act, he expounded only so much as the audience needed to know in order to understand the second; in this, in turn, he expounded such further antecedent incidents as were necessary to an appreciation of the third act; and so on, to the end of the play. In *Rosmersholm*, for instance, he was still expounding in the very last moments of the final act.

This method requires the auditor to think backward, and therefore presupposes a more intelligent audience than the straightforward formula of Scribe. But, very recently, that masterly technician, M. Henry Bernstein, has gone a step further in forcing the audience to observe a story in retrospectory review. Instead of scattering his expository passages throughout the play, as Ibsen did, M. Bernstein now compacts them into a single act; but, with a startling overturning of the formula of Scribe, he exhibits this act last instead of first,—setting it forth as an epilogue, instead of as a prologue, to the action.

This new formula was first exemplified by M. Bernstein in *L'Assaut*, which was acted in America under the title of *The Attack*. A noted politician who is running for office is accused of having committed a crime many years before. Either he is innocent or he is guilty: and this dilemma is set before us in the first act. The second act develops the presumption that he is innocent, until his innocence is publicly established by process of law. This is the climax of the play. Then, his innocence being now beyond question, the hero confesses to the heroine that he was actually guilty. This is the end of the second act. What remains to be done? We naturally demand an explanation of the circumstances which, so many years before, had led this admirable hero to commit that reprehensible crime. In his third and last act, M. Bernstein expounds the facts at length and in detail. Now we know: and the play is over. This same formula is employed much more artfully in *The Secret*, a later and greater work, which is worthy of examination in detail.

Considered as a technical achievement, *The Secret* is perhaps the most wonderful of all the plays of M. Henry Bernstein. The work of this author is already so well known in America that it is scarcely necessary to state that his plays are nothing more than *tours de force*. His plots are marvelously constructed, his characters are true to life, his dialogue is pithy and compact; and yet we always feel by instinct that he is not a great dramatist. The reason for this feeling is that he never heightens our interest in life or adds to our understanding of it. He lacks the God-given ability to make us care about his characters. We see them suffer, but we do not take them to our hearts and feel their sufferings as our own. His work is too objective, too abstract, to appeal to us as human. But, considered solely as a craftsman, he is the most ingenious artist in the drama at the present time.

In *The Secret*, M. Bernstein, for a full half of his play, makes us think [or, rather *allows* us to think] that his heroine is one sort of person; and then turns about, in the second half of the second act, and proves to us that she is a totally different sort of person. Amazed at the contradiction of the two opinions of her character which we have held successively, we find ourselves still groping for an explanation of this personal enigma. This explanation is afforded in the third and final act. Here again, as in *The Attack*, M. Bernstein has deferred his exposition till the end of the play, instead of giving it at the beginning. Thereby he has created what may be called an analytical suspense,—a suspense of asking not, "What happens next?", but, "Why did these things happen?" This is perhaps the nearest approach to building a play backward which has ever yet been made in the theatre of the world.

It will be noted also that M. Bernstein has brushed aside one of the most commonly accepted dogmas of the theatre,—the dogma that a dramatist must never keep a secret from his audience. The entire purpose of his pattern is to deceive his auditors for half the play, and then to use the other half to undeceive them. A considerable section of his second act runs parallel to the third act of *Othello*, with the heroine playing the part of Iago; but as yet we have seen no reason to suspect that she is not a generous and honest woman. It is as if Shakespeare, up to the middle of his third act, had allowed us to see Iago only as he appeared to the eyes of his general—" This fellow's of exceeding honesty,"— and had not allowed us to perceive the error until it became evident to Othello himself.

If this pattern had been proposed in advance to any jury of dramatic critics [including the present writer], it would have been rejected as unfeasible, because of the traditional belief that no audience will submit to the necessity of altering its entire conception of a character in the middle of a play. Yet M. Bernstein deliberately chose this pattern, in defiance of tradition; and his play has pleased the public, in both Paris and New York. Here, again, we encounter a practical evidence of the vanity of dogma, and an indication that no principle can ever be considered final in dramatic criticism.

But, at present, the most important point for us to notice is that M. Bernstein has turned the formula of Scribe completely upside down, and has chosen to end his drama at the point where Scribe would have begun it.

Shall the development of backward-looking narrative stop with M. Bernstein? If not, the only possible next step will be to act out events upon the stage in an order that reverses that in which they are presumed to have occurred. The actual action of *The Attack* and *The*

Secret is straightforward in chronology; and it is only in his psychological effect upon the audience that M. Bernstein appears to build his plays backward. Regarding that next step, which now seems so revolutionary, the critic can only wonder if some very clever playwright will attempt it in the future.

There are certain stories which are seen most naturally if we follow them forward from causes to effects; but there are certain other stories which can be understood most truly only if we follow them backward from effects to causes. As a matter of experiment, it would be extremely interesting if some playwright should soon set before us a story of this type in the perspective of reverted time.

II

At the very outset of the autumn season of 1914, a great success was achieved by a youth of twenty-one whose name had never before been heard of in the theatre. Like Lord Byron, this new playwright awoke one morning to discover that he had grown famous overnight. His name—which is familiar now—is Elmer L. Reizenstein; and the title of his play—which crowded the Candler Theatre every night for many months—is *On Trial*.

The most remarkable feature of the success of *On Trial* is that it is emphatically a success of art for art's sake. The piece has been accurately described by the youthful author as " an experiment in dramatic technique "; and its instantaneous and huge success affords a hitherto unprecedented indication that our public has grown sufficiently interested in the technique of the drama to welcome plays whose strongest bid for favor is their technical efficiency.

Until this indication of a turning of the tide in favor of stagecraft for the sake of stagecraft, it had been generally agreed among observers of our current drama that popular success depended more on subject-matter than on technical dexterity. Nearly all the plays that have run, in recent seasons, more than six months in New York have succeeded because of something in the theme or in the story that caught the fancy of the public. While technical masterpieces like *The Thunderbolt* have failed, inferior fabrics like *Within the Law* have played to crowded houses for a year because of a certain timeliness of interest in their subject-matter. *Peg o' My Heart* succeeded because it told a pretty, sentimental story, while *Hindle Wakes* failed because it told a story that was neither pretty nor sentimental. By inference from examples such as these, it had appeared that the material of a play was the only thing our public cared about, and that technique—even the technique of a Pinero or a Stanley Houghton—would afford no royal road to popular favor unless it were expended on a story that was novel or timely or pretty or sentimental.

But the subject-matter of *On Trial* is scarcely interesting in itself. The play has no theme; and the story that it tells is not sentimental or pretty or timely or even novel. A profligate induces an inexperienced young girl to spend a night with him at a road-house by promising to wed her on the morrow. The next morning the girl's father appears at the road-house, accompanied by a woman who is already married to the profligate. The villain runs away, and the girl is taken home by her father. Shortly afterward, her father dies; and some years later the girl meets and marries an honorable man. A daughter is born to them, and they develop a very happy home. It appears that the heroine was justified in concealing from her husband the misfortune that had befallen her before she met him. But the husband meets the profligate in the business world, is befriended by him, and even borrows money from him. This money he repays in cash; but the profligate takes advantage of the accidental renewal of acquaintance with the heroine to force her to yield to him again, under threat of allowing the past iniquity to be exposed. The husband, discovering the recent intrigue, seeks out the profligate and shoots him dead. A few moments before the shooting, the private secretary of the profligate has stolen from the latter's safe the cash that had just been paid him by the murderer; and it therefore appears to the police that robbery was the motive for the murder. The husband seizes on this circumstantial evidence to shield his wife and child from scandal. He confesses himself guilty of murder for the sake of robbery, and asks only to be sent to the electric chair. But the court insists on assigning counsel to defend him; and the defendant's lawyer, by calling the wronged wife to the stand, makes clear the real motive for the shooting. The private secretary of the dead man is also called as a witness; and when the defendant's counsel succeeds in forcing

him to confess that it was he who had rifled the
safe and that this robbery had had no connection with
the murder, the jury agree at once in acquitting the
defendant.

It will be noticed that this story is entirely traditional. At no moment does it exhibit any note of novelty. It is sound enough, indeed, to seem worthy of
retelling; but no one can deny that it is trite. The
characters concerned in the story are also true enough
to life to warrant their revisiting the glimpses of the
footlights; but they are neither original nor likable
nor particularly interesting. Why should the public
flock to the theatre to meet a man who leads a girl
astray, or another man who shoots him dead? Why
should the public still shed tears over a wronged wife,
and a child who remains pathetically unaware of a scandal that has destroyed the happiness of her parents?

From questions such as these, it should become apparent that Mr. Reizenstein was dealing with a story that
by no means contained, within itself, the elements of
sure success. Did he succeed, then, because of any trick
of writing in his dialogue? The answer is, emphatically, no. The best that can be said of the writing of
On Trial is that it is direct and simple and concise; but
the dialogue is utterly devoid of literary charm and of
that human richness which is akin to humor. Hundreds
of plays which have been obviously better written have
failed at once, in recent years, upon our stage. Why,
then, did *On Trial* capture the public by assault?

The reason is that Mr. Reizenstein utilized the novel
device of building his story backward. This device was

interesting in itself, because it had never been employed
before on the American stage; and Mr. Reizenstein's
employment of it was made doubly interesting by the
fact that he revealed, in this experiment, a technical
efficiency that is truly astonishing in the first work of
an author with no previous experience of the stage. Instead of inventing a story and then deciding how to
tell it, this adventurous young playwright started out
with an idea of how to tell a story in a novel way and
then invented a story that would lend itself to this pre-
determined technical experiment.

We have observed already that the story of *On Trial*
is rather commonplace; but Mr. Reizenstein has made it
seem, in Browning's phrase, both " strange and new "
by revealing it from the end to the beginning, instead
of from the beginning to the end. Instead of starting
out with motives and developing them to their ultimate
expression in facts, he has started out with the accomplished facts and then delved backward to reveal the
motives which had instigated them.

In the first act of *On Trial* we see the murder committed on the stage. In the second act we see enacted
an incident two hours before the murder which makes
us aware of the exciting cause of the subsequent event
that we have previously witnessed. But it is not until
the third act, which reveals in action an event that
happened thirteen years before, that we are permitted
to discover and to comprehend the motives which ultimately culminated in the shooting that we saw in the
initial act. By telling his story backward, from effect
to cause, the author has added an element of theatrical

suspense to a narrative which otherwise might have been dismissed by the public as an oft-repeated tale.

It must not be inferred from the success of Mr. Reizenstein's experiment that there is, inherently, any greater virtue in building a play backward than in following the chronological sequence which has always heretofore been traditional in the drama. The choice of method must depend on the type of story that the playwright has to tell. It remains as true to-day as ever that the great majority of dramatic stories may be set forth most effectively if they are built up, synthetically, from causes to effects. It is only a particular type of narrative—and stories of this type will always remain in the minority—that can be set forth most effectively if they are analyzed from effects to causes. This statement must be emphasized, lest the public should be threatened with a rush of plays whose only claim to interest should be that they aim to illustrate the Biblical maxim that "the last shall be first and the first shall be last." The famous experiment of Columbus with the egg was bad for the egg: there are many objects in the universe that are not meant to stand on end.

III

THE POINT OF VIEW

THE present period of the drama is one that lends itself peculiarly to technical adventure. The rapid development in the physical efficiency of the theatre that has taken place in the last half century, and the simultaneous increase in the alertness and intelligence of the theatre-going public, have made it possible for playwrights to inaugurate a series of innovations that have broadened the boundaries of the technique of the drama. Traditional ideas, which formerly had stood for centuries, of what can be done in the theatre and (more particularly) what cannot be done, are now being altered every season, as adventurous playwrights press forward to the accomplishment of technical tasks which have never been attempted before.

In the previous chapter we had occasion to celebrate the successful transference to the service of the drama of a technical expedient which has long been customary in the novel—the expedient, namely, of constructing a story from effects to causes and revealing it in a pattern of reverted time. There are many other narrative devices which have long been used in the short-story and the novel, that might be transferred, with equal advantage, to the strategy of the contemporary drama. In past years, the critic has often been required to insist that the art of the novel is one thing and the art of the drama is another; but, under present-day conditions, he is also required to admit that the difference between the two crafts is by no means so decided as it used to be. For one thing, the gap between the novel and the drama has been bridged over by the moving-picture play—an artistic product which is equally novelistic and dramatic; and, for another thing, the recent improvements in stage machinery, which have made it possible to shift a set in less than thirty seconds of absolute darkness and absolute quiet, have also made it possible for the playwright to adopt a freer form of narrative than was imposed upon him twenty years ago. We may confidently expect that, in the next few years, the drama will avail itself more and more of narrative devices which, though thoroughly established in the novel, have hitherto been regarded as beyond the reach of stagecraft.

Students of the technique of the novel are aware that, ever since the outset of the eighteenth century, the novelist has been permitted to project his narrative from either of two totally different points of view, which may be called, for convenience, the internal and the external. He may reveal his story internally, as it appears to the mind of one or another of the actors who take part in it; or he may reveal it externally, as it would appear to a disinterested mind sitting aloof from all the characters and regarding them with what Mr. Alfred Noyes has greatly called " the splendor of the indifference of God." Heretofore, only the second of these points of view has been permitted to the dramatist. He has been obliged to set his characters equidistant from "the god-like spectator" (to quote Mr. Archer's phrase), and has been required to reveal them through an atmosphere of inviolable objectivity.

Novelists like George Eliot have been accustomed to avail themselves of the privilege of vivisecting the brains of their characters and analyzing those most intimate thoughts and emotions that never translate themselves into speech or express themselves in action; but, since the renunciation (both for better and for worse) of the technical expedients of the soliloquy and the aside, the dramatist has been denied this great advantage of entering the mind of any of his characters and forcing the audience, for the moment, to look at the entire play from this individual and personal point of view.

Recently, however, a few adventurous playwrights have discovered a more effective means than any series of soliloquies and asides for shifting the audience, at any moment, from an external and objective point of view to a point of view that is internal and subjective. The second act of that beautiful and well-remembered play, *The Poor Little Rich Girl*, was exhibited from the point of view of a child whose mind is drifting under the influence of an opiate; and in a more recent play entitled *The Phantom Rival*, an entire act is devoted to the exhibition of events that happen only in the fancy of one of the leading characters.

The success of such experiments as these sets the dramatist on an equal footing with the novelist in the very important matter of being permitted to shift the point of view from which his story is to be observed. The full advantage of this technical innovation has not yet been reaped in the theatre; but a whole new field has been opened up to future playwrights. Would it not be interesting, for instance, to show a certain scene as it appeared from the point of view of one of the characters concerned, and subsequently to reënact the entire scene as it appeared from the very different point of view of another of the characters? This ironical device has already been employed in the novel, by such technical experimentalists as Mr. Arnold Bennett. Before long we may expect to see it successfully employed upon the stage.

The Phantom Rival was written by Ferenc Molnar, a Hungarian dramatist who has nearly always shown an adventurous originality in his technical attack. The American version was made by Mr. Leo Ditrichstein.

In the labor-saving first act of this play, the theme is outlined in a conversation between a writer and an actor, which takes place in a restaurant. The writer expounds a theory that most women treasure throughout their entire lives an idealized image of the man who has first awakened them to a consciousness of love, and that, even though they subsequently marry some one else, they continue, in the secret recesses of their minds, to compare their husband, to his disadvantage, with this phantom rival.

This explicit conversation is a sort of prologue to the play, in which neither the writer nor the actor is involved. The leading figure in the comedy is a woman married to a husband who is jealous not only of her present but also of her past. He discovers that before her marriage she had been interested in a certain Russian; and, though this Russian had returned to his native country seven years before, the husband now insists that his wife shall read to him the treasured letter which the lover of her youth had sent to her at parting. In this letter, the eager foreigner had told her that he would come back to her some day—as a great general, or a great statesman, or a great artist, or even, if the worst befell him, as a humble tramp who would lay the wreckage of his life beneath her feet. The husband sneers at this highfaluting letter, and thereby stimulates the imagination of his wife to rush to the rescue of his phantom rival.

She drifts into a day-dream, in which her mind, hovering between sleep and waking, bodies forth an image of her former lover in the successive guises of a great general, a great statesman, a great artist, and a humble tramp. These scenes are exhibited entirely from the heroine's point of view. She knows nothing of the actual conditions of any of the careers about which she is dreaming; and, naturally enough, her phantom lover appears to her as an utterly impossible sort of person, acting out heroical absurdities and talking all the while the stilted language of a Laura Jean Libbey novel.

In the third act we are recalled to actuality. The former lover of the heroine, returned from Russia, makes a business call upon her husband, and reveals himself to her as an utterly undistinguished and small-minded character.   Comparing this trivial little person with the huge dreams she has had of him, the wife is forced to admit that her husband is the better man and to expel the phantom rival from the regions of her fancy.

IV

SURPRISE IN THE DRAMA

In recent years our native playwrights have devoted a great deal of attention to technical experiment. It might be argued that they would have fared better if they had thought more about life and less about the theatre; but, though they have discovered comparatively little to say, they have at least devised many means of saying things ingeniously. This is, perhaps, the necessary mark of a drama that is still so young as ours. Youth cares more for cleverness than it cares for the more sedentary quality of insight. When Mr. George M. Cohan is ninety years of age—and our theatre has grown hoary in the interval—he will have more to tell us about life, but he will no longer make a pattern so astonishingly dexterous as that of *Seven Keys to Baldpate*.

Mr. Reizenstein's *On Trial* is typical of the current aspect of our growing drama. In subject-matter, it is "weary, stale, flat, and unprofitable"; for it tells us nothing about life that has not been told—and often told more wisely—in innumerable antecedent melodramas. But in method, it is novel and exceedingly ingenious.

Not all of the adventurous experiments of our American playwrights have been so signally successful; but all of them are worthy of theoretical consideration. In the present chapter, it may be profitable to examine the concerted assault which has recently been made against the time-honored tradition of the theatre that a dramatist must never keep a secret from his audience.

Concerning this tradition, Mr. William Archer said in 1912, "So far as I can see, the strongest reason against keeping a secret is that, try as you may, you cannot do it. . . . From only one audience can a secret be really hidden, a considerable percentage of any subsequent audience being certain to know all about it in advance. The more striking and successful is the first-night effect of surprise, the more certainly and rapidly will the report of it circulate through all strata of the theatrical public." This statement, which seems sound enough in theory, has failed to prove itself in practice; and the fact of the matter seems to be that the "theatrical public" is far less cohesive than Mr. Archer has assumed. News does not travel, either rapidly or readily, through all its very different strata. This fact was indicated by the career of Mr. Roi Cooper Megrue's surprise-play, *Under Cover*. Although the piece had previously run a year in Boston, the vast majority of those who saw it on the first night in New York were completely taken in by the dramatist's deception; and, even after the play had run for many months in the metropolis, and had been analyzed repeatedly in the press, it was still observable that the majority of those who came to see it were still ignorant of the precise nature of the trick that was to be played upon them. They came to the theatre with a vague notion that the plot would be surprising, but they did not know the story in advance.

Mr. Max Marcin, the author of a clever surprise-play, *Cheating Cheaters*, complained, after the first night, that it was unfair for the newspapers to print summaries of his plot, thereby revealing in advance to future audiences the nature of the trap the dramatist had set for them. This protest, perhaps, was justified in theory; but, in fact, the author had no reason for complaint. Even that minority of the theatre-going public who habitually read the first-night notices in the newspapers do not long recall specifically what is said in them. All that they carry away from the reading is a vague impression that the play was praised or damned: it is only the few people who do not pay for tickets to the theatre who read these notices more deeply and remember the details.

The reports of current plays that circulate by word of mouth among the ticket-buying public are nearly always very vague. A man will tell his friends that a certain piece is " a good show "; but rarely, if ever, would he be able to pass on in conversation a coherent statement of the plot. Though *Cheating Cheaters* was played to large audiences for many months, the big surprise of the plot remained a mystery to three-fourths of all the people who attended it. Those of us who go professionally to the theatre do not always realize how little the general public knows in advance about current plays with which we ourselves are thoroughly familiar.

Despite, then, what Mr. Archer said in 1912, it has

been subsequently proved by several experiments that
it is entirely possible to keep a secret in the theatre.
But the question still remains whether it is worth while
to do so. The success of a surprise-play proves nothing; for it does not prove that the same play would not
have been equally successful if the surprise had been
eliminated from the plot.

Consider *Under Cover*, for example. The hero was
introduced to the audience as a smuggler, engaged in
the perilous enterprise of sneaking a valuable neck-
lace through the customs. For two acts he was pursued
by customs-house officials; and, when ultimately cap-
tured, he bought them off with a bribe. Then, in the
last moments of the play, the dramatist revealed the
hidden fact that the hero was not a smuggler after all,
but an official of the United States secret service engaged in tracking down corruption in the customs-
house.

It cannot be denied that the suspense of the melodrama was increased by the retention of this secret till
the final moment; but, on the other hand, several other
elements of interest were sacrificed. For instance, the
love-story was imperiled by the fact that the audience
had to watch the heroine fall in love with a man who,
by every evidence, appeared to be a criminal. Furthermore, the author had to tell lies to his audience in those
passages in which the hero was left alone on the stage
with his confederate; and telling lies, even in a melodrama, is a hazardous proceeding. The play was a
great success; but what evidence is there to prove that
it might not have been equally successful if the author

had taken the audience into his confidence from the start and permitted the public to watch, from the standpoint of superior knowledge, the corrupt customs-house officials walking ignorantly into the trap which had been set for them? I do not state that this is so; but I do state that the only way to prove that it is not so would be to build the plot the other way and try it on the public.

Of course, the strongest argument against keeping a secret from the audience is that this procedure, in the admirable phrase of Mr. Archer, " deprives the audience of that superior knowledge in which lies the irony of drama." The audience likes to know more about the people in a play than they know about themselves; for this superior knowledge places the spectators in the comfortable attitude of gods upon Olympus, looking down upon the destinies of men. It is not nearly so amusing to be fooled as it is to watch other people being fooled; and this would seem to be a fundamental fact of psychology. Against this fundamental fact, the success of a dozen or a hundred surprise-plays can scarcely be regarded as weighing down the balance. The audience, for instance, would feel much more sympathetic toward the heroine in *Under Cover* if, all the while that she was falling in love with a person who appeared to be a criminal, the audience knew that he was really an honest man.

But another argument against keeping a secret from the audience is that, in order to do so, it is nearly always necessary to tell deliberate lies to lead the audience astray. There is an instance of this in an interesting play by Mr. Jules Eckert Goodman, entitled *The Man Who Came Back*. This play leads us around the world and back again, following the fortunes of a prodigal son who has been cast adrift by his father. On the way, we meet another person drifting without anchor,—a certain Captain Trevelan. This British idler marries a girl whom he has run across in a cabaret in San Francisco; and, encountering the couple later on in Honolulu, we are shown at considerable length that their marriage has turned out unhappily. In the last act, we are told suddenly that Trevelan is not a British captain at all, but merely a New York detective who has been employed by the hero's father to travel round the world and keep watch upon the movements of his prodigal son. This statement comes, indeed, as a surprise; but nothing is ever said to explain away the wife that Trevelan has left behind in Honolulu. Was she also a detective, or did Trevelan really marry and desert her, for the purpose of preventing the audience from guessing his identity? The play as a whole is not imperiled by this jugglery, since the mysterious detective is merely an incidental figure in the plot; but we feel that the author has severely compromised himself for the sake of a single effect of sharp surprise in the course of his concluding act.

Another important point to be considered is that, when the appeal of a play is dependent mainly on surprise, the author is impeded from drawing characters consistently. It is impossible to draw the sort of person that the hero really is, and at the same time to persuade the audience, until the final revelation of the secret, that the hero is another sort of person altogether. Deception of this kind can, therefore, never be accomplished in a play that is sufficiently serious in subject-matter to demand reality in characterization. The pattern of surprise is available only for farces and for melodramas, in which the incidents are all that count and the characters are secondary. To deceive the audience successfully in high comedy or in tragedy would require a falsification that would consign the play to ruin. The public consciously will swallow lies only in regard to stories that do not seriously matter.

To sum the matter up, the sort of surprise which must be regarded absolutely as inacceptable in any play is the sort which depends for its success upon a clear negation of what has gone before. Nothing can be gained by the procedure of telling the public one thing for two hours and a half and then telling the public in two minutes that it has merely been deceived. Such jugglery is easy to encompass, and is sometimes entertaining in effect; but it leads away from that interpretation of the underlying truth of life which is the end of art.

V

THE TROUBLESOME LAST ACT

THERE is an old saying in the theatre that hell is paved with good first acts; for many a play has started out with promise and failed to fulfil that promise in the end. It must not be supposed, however, that first acts are easy to construct. In fact, the very contrary is true; for the technical problem of laying out a well-ordered exposition is one of the most difficult for the playwright to attack. But, even if he falters in his handling of this problem, he may be carried safely by his subject-matter. If the project of his play is at all interesting, and particularly if it shows the trait of novelty, a barely adequate exposition of this project will attract the attention of the audience and hold it until time is called by the first curtain-fall.

In the subsequent acts, however, the attention of the audience is shifted from a consideration of the material itself to a consideration of what the playwright does with this material; and this is the reason why a faltering technique is more disastrous to a play in those acts which come subsequent to the exposition. A certain expectation has already been aroused; and the audience will be disappointed if this expectation

38

is not satisfied with proper emphasis. To climb the
ladder to a climax without ever missing footing on an
upward step is a technical task that calls for nice dis-
crimination. The climax itself is usually easy to
achieve. It is the first thing that the author has
imagined; it is, indeed, the *raison d'être* of his play;
and the " big scene " so much admired by the public
has seldom cost the playwright any trouble. But this
climax is customarily succeeded by a last act that is
troublesome indeed; and it is precisely at this point that
the majority of plays are dashed upon the rocks of
failure. It is harder to write a satisfactory last act
than to write twenty good " big scenes " or ten adequately interesting acts of exposition. These figures
have been gathered from observing many plays. The
fact, then, is empirical: but wherein lies the explanation
of the fact?

The main difficulty in laying out a satisfactory last
act arises from the fact that it comes by custom after
the climax of the play and is consequently doomed to
deal with material inherently less dramatic than what
has gone before. To state the matter in the simplest
terms, it is more difficult for the playwright to conduct
a falling than a rising action. Whatever follows a
climax must appear an anti-climax; and the playwright, like the mountain-climber, is inclined to stumble
on the downward trail.

Why not, then, obliterate this downward trail?,—
why not build the action to its climax and then suddenly cut off any further consideration of the story?
The negative answer to this question is based upon tra-

dition; and it is therefore necessary that the origins of this tradition should briefly be examined.

In Greek tragedy the climax of the play was always followed by a period of falling action, in which the tragic tensity was lessened and the mood was softened to serenity. Nearly all the literary critics have assumed that the Greeks adopted this pattern in obedience to some esthetic theory; but to a critic of the drama it seems more sensible to suppose that this pattern was imposed upon them by the necessity of providing for an exodus of the chorus from the orchestra. The chorus could not march out while the three actors on the stage were still in the throes of the climax; and it could not remain in the orchestra after the play was over. Hence a period of falling action had to be provided as a sort of recessional for the supernumeraries.

The anti-climax at the close of Elizabethan tragedy may be similarly explained by reference to the physical peculiarities of the Elizabethan theatre. After Shakespeare had strewed the stage with bodies in the last act of *Hamlet*, he had to provide a period of diminished tensity during which the accumulated dead could be carried off the stage. The simple reason for this fact is that he had no curtain to ring down. Hence, in the original text, the long continuance of unimportant talk after the entrance of Fortinbras. Hence, also, in the original text of *Romeo and Juliet*, the interminable speech of Friar Laurence at the conclusion of the tragedy. This, obviously, was provided to afford sufficient time to carry off the bodies of Romeo and Juliet and Paris.

We are so accustomed to the proscenium curtain in the modern theatre that we are likely to forget that this revolutionary innovation was not introduced until the latter half of the seventeenth century. For more than two centuries it has been possible to drop the curtain and suddenly exclude from observation all the actors on the stage; but this fact has not as yet succeeded utterly in overturning a tradition of the drama which had been necessitated by the physical requirements of the preceding twenty centuries.

But, granted our proscenium curtain, is there any real reason why we should continue longer to follow the Greeks and the Elizabethans in their custom of carrying a play beyond its climax to an anti-climax? It is evident that Ibsen did not think so. Both in *A Doll's House* and in *Ghosts* he rang the final curtain down at the highest point of tensity, and left the most momentous question of the play still undecided.

The great example of Ibsen should make us bold to try to do away entirely with the period of falling action that characterized the close of Greek and Elizabethan tragedy. The best way to deal with the troublesome last act is not to write it at all. The insistence of this motive accounts, historically, for the fact that, late in the nineteenth century, the traditional five-act pattern was discarded for a four-act form, and that, early in the twentieth century, this four-act pattern has, in turn, been superseded in favor of a three-act form. These two progressive changes in the standard structure of the drama have been occasioned by a growing desire to do away with the troublesome last act.

The extreme of this treatment is exhibited in the famous close of *The Madras House*, by Mr. Granville Barker. The final curtain cuts off a conversation in mid-career; and the stage-direction reads, " She doesn't finish, for really there is no end to the subject." This piece was designed by Mr. Barker to illustrate the thesis that a play should have no end, since, in life itself, nothing is terminal and nothing is conclusive. The play, however, was an utter failure; and the disaster that attended its production seemed to prove that the public preferred the traditional pattern to Mr. Barker's unprecedented attempt to approximate the inconclusiveness of nature.

But this attempt to obliterate the troublesome last act might have been more hospitably welcomed if Mr. Barker had chosen to cut off his play at the moment of greatest interest and highest tensity. There seems to be no theoretic reason why the periodic structure developed for the short-story by Guy de Maupassant should not be successfully transferred to the service of the serious drama. It ought to be possible, by the exercise of sufficient ingenuity, to hold back the solution of a serious plot until the very last line of the last act. This feat was successfully accomplished by Mr. Augustus Thomas in one of the most skilful of his lighter plays, *Mrs. Leffingwell's Boots*.

In farce, however, the problem of the playwright is more difficult. A farce is customarily developed to its climax through a series of misunderstandings between the various characters. On the one hand, it appears impossible to close the play without clearing up these foregone misunderstandings by explaining them to all the characters involved; but, on the other hand, these eleventh-hour passages of explanation must deal necessarily with materials of which the audience has all the time been cognizant, and must, therefore, result in the falling-off of interest that attends the hearing of a twice-told tale. If some master could invent a method to do away entirely with the troublesome last act of farce, he would indeed confer a boon on future playwrights.

Nothing has been said thus far concerning that falsification in the last act of a play which is commonly assumed to be demanded by the public. In an absolute sense, any ending to a play is false to nature, since in life itself there can never be an utter termination to a series of events; and it has, therefore, frequently been argued that, to end a play, the dramatist is justified in cogging the dice of circumstance in favor of those characters with whom the audience has come to sympathize. This argument, apparently, holds good for comedy, since it is supported by the constant practice of such great dramatists as Molière and Shakespeare. But in proportion as a play becomes more serious, the audience will tend more and more to be disappointed by any ending that does not follow as a logical result from all the incidents that have preceded it. Shakespeare is allowed to falsify the end of *As You Like It;* but the audience would be deeply disappointed if Hamlet were permitted to live happily forever after the conclusion of the play.

There are certain plays, and not all of these by any means are tragedies, that—to use a phrase of Steven-

son's—" begin to end badly "; and to give them arbitrarily a happy ending results merely in preventing the
audience from enjoying the exercise of that contribu-
tory faculty which the late William James described as
" the will to believe." Those managers, therefore, are
misguided who persist in assuming that the public will
prefer an illogical happy ending to an unhappy ending
that has clearly been foreshadowed. Yet the recent
history of the drama shows many instances of plays
with two last acts—the one preferred for its logic by
the author, and the other preferred for its optimism
by the manager. Thus, *The Profligate* of Sir Arthur
Pinero has two last acts. In the first version, the
profligate takes poison; and in the second version he
lives happily forever after. In a recent farce by the
same author, *Preserving Mr. Panmure*, one last act
was provided for the production in London and a different last act was provided for the production in New
York; and it appears that the same astonishing procedure is destined to be followed in the exhibition of Sir
Arthur's latest play, *The Big Drum*. When Henry
Bernstein's *Israël* was produced in Paris, the hero committed suicide at the close of the play; but when the
piece was subsequently produced in New York he merely
married a girl in a picture hat. This change, suggested by the late Charles Frohman,—although it reduced the entire play to nonsense,—was accomplished
with the consent and connivance of the author. Both
The Legend of Leonora, by Sir James Barrie, and *The
New Sin*, by Mr. B. Macdonald Hastings, were produced in New York with troublesome last acts which

did not exist at all when the two plays were first produced in London. It will be seen, therefore, that even authors of acknowledged eminence are not entirely immune from falsifying the concluding moments of their plays when pressure is brought to bear upon them by friendly and persuasive managers. To rescue comparatively unestablished playwrights from this insidious insistence, the only certain remedy will be the general adoption of a new dramatic pattern in which the troublesome last act will, by common consent, remain unwritten.

VI

STRATEGY AND TACTICS

In his very valuable lecture on *Robert Louis Stevenson: The Dramatist*, Sir Arthur Pinero has drawn a distinction between what he calls the " strategy " and the " tactics " of play-making. He defines *strategy* as " the general laying out of a play " and *tactics* as " the art of getting the characters on and off the stage, of conveying information to the audience, and so forth." Though this definition is by no means complete, it is sufficiently suggestive to afford a convenient addition to the terminology of dramatic criticism. The distinction between strategy and tactics is a distinction between large and little, between the general and the particular; and while to strategy it seems appropriate to apply the adjective " dramatic," it appears more logical to link the adjective " theatrical " with tactics.

It is easily evident that a genius for strategy and a talent for tactics do not necessarily go hand in hand. Every great dramatist must be a great strategist,—a master, as Sir Arthur says, of " the general laying out of a play "; but the utmost cleverness in tactics is usually attained by dramatists who hover, at their best, a little lower than the greatest. A mind that is capable of imagining the large is often neglectful of the little.

46

Thus, the general laying out of the later acts of *Romeo and Juliet* is masterly and massive; but the particular turn in tactics because of which Romeo fails to receive the message from Friar Laurence is merely accidental, and must be regarded, therefore, as a fault in art. A secondary playwright, less obsessed with the grandeur of the general conception, would probably have been more careful of this dangerous detail; for minor men, who deal with minor themes, have more attention left to be devoted to theatrical perfections.

Ibsen also, though supreme in strategy, is often faulty in his tactics. Consider, for example, the last act of *Hedda Gabler*. The general laying out of this act is unexceptionable; for all that is exhibited would, sooner or later, inevitably happen. But the tactics are defective; for, yielding to the irretardable impulsion that seemed hurrying the play to its catastrophe, the author has permitted Mrs. Elvsted and Professor Tesman to begin their calm work of collaboration in piecing together Eilert Lövborg's posthumous book while the body of their ironically martyred friend is still lying unburied in a hospital. This is a mistake in tactics that a lesser playwright would have caught at once and remedied; for a lesser playwright would have known himself unable to afford the risk of lying about life at the culminating moment of a drama.

We admire Alexandre Dumas, *fils*, for his mastery of strategy,—particularly in the laying out of first acts and in the command of memorable curtain-falls; but, in the minor point of tactics, even so great an artist was excelled by so clever a craftsman as Victorien Sardou.

Sardou was seldom a great strategist, for he loved the theatre more than life and preferred invention to imagination; but, precisely because of this restriction of his talent, he attained an eminence as a theatrical tactician which, thus far, has never been surpassed.

If we turn to a consideration of our own American drama in the light of this distinction, we shall see at once that the majority of our native playwrights are weak in strategy but strong in tactics. The life-work of the late Clyde Fitch is clearly illustrative of this assumption. Fitch was almost inordinately clever in his tactics. He could always expound a play with ease and interest by the aid of some original and dexterous invention. He seemed supremely clever in delineating minor characters, and in inventing means by which these minor characters should seem to have a finger in determining the destiny he had to deal with. But, at the same time, he nearly always failed in the general laying out of his play. He could not draw a leading character consistently throughout a logical succession of four acts. Even in his highest efforts, like *The Truth*, he permitted his tactics to override his strategy and allowed a big dramatic scheme to shatter itself into a myriad of minor clevernesses.

The same merits in tactics and defects in strategy remain apparent in the most typical products of the American drama of to-day. It would, I think, be futile to deny that our most representative playwright at the present time is Mr. George M. Cohan. Mr. Cohan and the growing host of those who imitate him have mastered the tactics of the theatre; they are cleverer than Hauptmann, more inventive than Brieux; but none of them has yet laid out a play with the serene supremacy of strategy apparent in the planning of *The Weavers* or *The Red Robe.*

So long as we continue to fix our eyes upon the theatre instead of allowing them to wander over the unlimited domain of life, so long as we continue to value invention more dearly than imagination, so long as we continue to worship immediate expediency in preference to untimely and eternal truth, we shall continue to advance in tactics and to retrograde in strategy; we shall continue to improve the technique of the theatre, but we shall contribute nothing to the technique of the drama.

On the other hand, such a piece as *The Unchastened Woman,* by Mr. Louis K. Anspacher, appears at the first glance more like a European drama than an American play; for it is strong in strategy and weak in tactics. The author has imagined one of the most vital characters that have appeared in the American drama for a long, long time: his heroine steps living from the limits of his play and continues her existence in the vast domain of life at large: but the play itself in which she figures is far less clever in its tactics than the average composition of the average American craftsman.

Caroline Knolys—as this memorable heroine is called —reveals a family resemblance to Hedda Gabler; but she is projected, not in the mood of tragedy, but in the mood of sardonic comedy. Like Hedda, she is a woman of talent, who, finding no productive exercise for her abilities, uses them to thwart the productivity of all the people with whom she comes in contact. Like Hedda, also, she is morally a coward, and impedes herself from the commission of any tangible crime because of a fear of the consequences. She is incapable of love; but she takes delight in alluring men to love her, for the sake of having a finger in their destinies and distressing their sweethearts or their wives. She has ceased all marital relations with her husband; but, valuing the protection of his name, she carefully avoids the commission of any act which might make it possible for him to divorce her. Meanwhile, her husband—a much more normal and honorable being—has established a relation with a mistress; but Caroline, knowing this, refuses to divorce her husband, but merely holds her knowledge as a sword to threaten him.

The character of this despicable and fascinating heroine is studied very thoroughly; and the impression of reality conveyed affords sufficient proof of the efficiency of the author's strategy. But neither of the two stories which he has invented as frameworks for this central figure is interesting in itself; and the tactics of the play are crude and blundering.

As an example of the author's crudity in tactics, the first entrance of the heroine may be cited. She is returning to her husband's house after a long trip abroad. We are told that she has become involved in trouble at the dock because she has tried to smuggle through the customs many purchases without declaring them and has attempted to bribe a Government inspector. The whole incident is hashed over in a dialogue between Caroline, her husband, and a woman friend of hers.

The incident itself is sufficiently indicative of the heroine's character; but to begin the exposition of so prominent a person with a retrospective narrative of an incident that has already happened off the stage is clearly a mistake in tactics. It would have been far better to allow the heroine to *do* something, in the sight of the audience, which was equally indicative of the iniquity of her nature.

This initial launching of the heroine is followed by a passage in which the author permits her to sit still while her husband, at considerable length, informs her— and incidentally informs the audience—of his intimate opinion of her character. Here, again, we note a fault in tactics; for surely it would have been more clever to avoid this expository passage by exhibiting the heroine in the self-explanatory terms of action.

In conducting both the second act and the third, Mr. Anspacher has removed from the stage his only really interesting character several minutes before the fall of the conclusive curtain and has allowed the dialogue to straggle on to an annoying anti-climax. This is a mistake in tactics which a mere apprentice to the craft of making plays might presumably be trusted to avoid; but the disconcerting fact remains that, though Mr. Anspacher is comparatively ineffective in his tactics, he is surprisingly efficient in the larger points of strategy.

Especially praiseworthy, for example, is his procedure in leaving his unchastened woman still unchastened at the end. She has been forced, in the last act, to submit to an unavoidable humiliation; but, at her final exit, she manages, by her sheer genius for creating mischief, to annihilate the victory of those who momentarily have triumphed over her. To conceive and to create an unpleasant person and to avoid the usual temptation to reform this person before the final curtain-fall is an achievement in sheer strategy which has seldom been accomplished in our native drama. The merits of this play are large, and its defects are little. Half a dozen of our American playwrights might have worked the pattern out more cleverly; but the important and preponderant fact remains that few, if any, of these other tacticians of our theatre have imagined and created so true a character as Caroline Knolys.

VII

PROPORTION IN THE DRAMA

EVERY play is a dramatization of a story that covers a larger canvas than the play itself. The dramatist must be familiar not only with the comparatively few events that he exhibits on the stage, but also with the many other events that happen off-stage during the course of the action, others still that happen between the acts, and innumerable others that are assumed to have happened before the play began. Considering his story as a whole, the playwright must select his particular material by deciding what to put into his play and what to leave out of it; and any number of different plays may be made from the same story by different selections from the material at hand.

Considering the entire story of *Hamlet*, for instance, it would be possible to make an interesting play in which the climax should be the seduction of Queen Gertrude by her handsome and unscrupulous brother-in-law, and the murder of the king by Claudius should constitute the catastrophe. In this play, the young prince Hamlet, remaining ignorant of what was going on about him, would play but a minor part and would be dramatically interesting only as a potential menace to the machinations of his plausible but wicked uncle. Many

other plays might be selected from the entire drift of
narrative from which Shakespeare derived the specific
dramatization that we know so well; and it is by no
means illogical to assume that the same great dramatist might have made as great a tragedy of one of these
innumerable other hypothetic plays.

But after the dramatist has made a definite selection
of events to be exhibited, the nature of his play will
still depend on the sense of proportion with which he
develops the materials selected. What characters,
what motives, what incidents shall he emphasize, and
what others shall he merely shadow forth in the dim
limbo of his background? Suppose the dramatist of
Hamlet to have decided to begin his play after the
murder of the king and to end it with the retributive
execution of the murderer. It would still be possible to
project Claudius as the central and most interesting
figure in the tragedy. He might be exhibited as a man
self-tortured by the gnawing of remorse, harrowed by
an ever-growing doubt of the security of his assumed
position, wounded to the quick by the defection of his
queen, and ultimately welcoming the stroke that cut the
knot intrinsicate of all his tortures. In a dramatization
so conceived, the young prince Hamlet would once more
be relegated to a minor rôle. A shift in the proportions
of the narrative would alter the entire aspect of the
tragedy.

Whenever we go to a play, we witness only one of a
myriad possible dramatizations of the entire story that
the playwright has imagined. If we are dissatisfied
with the drama, this dissatisfaction may frequently be

traced to a disagreement with the playwright concerning his selection of material. Often we wish that the author had begun his play either earlier or later in the general procession of events from which he chose his incidents; often we feel that much that we have seen might better have been assumed to happen off the stage, and that certain other incidents that happened off the stage would have thrilled us more if we had seen them. But even more frequently, we may trace our dissatisfaction to a disagreement with the playwright concerning the proportions of his narrative. We wished to see more of certain characters and less of others; we were keenly interested in certain motives which he only half developed, and bored by certain other motives which he insisted on developing in full. We cared more about Laertes than Polonius—let us say—and were disappointed because the garrulous old man was given much to say and do and his gallant son was given comparatively little.

When a play with an obviously interesting theme fails to hold the attention and to satisfy the interest, the fault may nearly always be ascribed to some error of proportion. Too much time has been devoted to secondary material, too little to material that at the moment seemed more worthy of attention. The serious plot of *Much Ado About Nothing*, for example, tends to bore the audience, because they have grown to care so much for Beatrice and Benedick that they can no longer take any personal interest in what happens to Hero. When M. Rostand began the composition of *L'Aiglon*, he conceived Flambeau as the central figure of the drama. Later in the course of composition, the young Duc de Reichstadt ran away with the play; and *L'Aiglon* became, in consequence, a vehicle for Sarah Bernhardt instead of a vehicle for Constant Coquelin. M. Rostand was right in his ultimate perception that the weak son of a strong father would be more interesting to the public that a *vieux grognard à grandes moustaches;* and an obstinate effort to keep Flambeau in the center of the stage would have diminished the popularity of the play.

In handling any story, the dramatist is fairly free to select the incidents to be exhibited and to determine the proportions of the composition he has chosen; but there are always two exigencies that he cannot safely disregard. The first of these is covered by Sarcey's theory of the *scène à faire,*—or the " obligatory scene," as the phrase has been translated by Mr. Archer. An obligatory scene is a scene that the public has been permitted to foresee and to desire from the progress of the action; and such a scene can never be omitted without a consequent dissatisfaction. The second exigency is that the dramatist must proportion his play in agreement with the instinctive desire of the audience. He must summarize what the public wishes to be summarized, and must detail what the public wishes to be detailed; and he must not, either deliberately or inadvertently, antagonize the instinctive desire that he has awakened. If the author has caused the public to care more about Shylock than about any other person in his play, it becomes, for example, a dramaturgic error to leave Shylock out of the last act. If the audi-

ence [as may be doubted, in this instance] really wants
Charles Surface to make love to Maria, it becomes a
dramaturgic error to omit any love-scene between the
two. When *Ruy Blas* was first produced, the public was
delighted with a minor character, the shiftless and
rollicking Don César de Bazan. Thereupon, Dennery,
with the permission of Hugo, made this character the
central figure of a second melodrama, in which the
public was permitted to see more of him.

There are certain characters that afflict the audience
with disappointment whenever they leave the stage, and
there are certain other characters that afflict the audience more deeply by remaining on the stage and con-
tinuing to talk; and the distinction between the two
types can seldom be determined before a play has been
" tried out," with the assistance of some sort of audience. To fight against the popular desire in the matter
of proportion is to fight in vain.

VIII

HARMONY IN PRESENTATION

It is seldom that we receive from a theatrical performance an impression that satisfies our sense of harmony. The elements that go into the making of an acted play are so many and so diverse that it is very difficult to blend them all into a composition that shall be free from any discord. The function of the stage-director has often been compared with that of the leader of an orchestra; but this comparison makes no record of the fact that it is immeasurably more difficult to produce a play than to conduct a symphony. What would the public think of the performance of a symphony if twenty of the instruments were out of tune, if half a dozen of the violinists played in different keys at once, and if a dozen of the other musicians paid no attention to the tempo of the leader? Harsh words would undoubtedly be spoken; and the conductor would be permitted to resign. Yet an impression that is precisely analogous to this is produced by more than half of the performances in the leading theatres of New York. Why is it that the public tolerates this arrant lack of harmony? One reason is that the majority of theatre-goers never notice it; and another, and a better, reason is that the more sensitive minority of theatre-goers may probably suspect how very, very difficult—in the present state of the theatre in America—is the task with which the stage-director is confronted.

Suppose, for the sake of illustration, that a certain play be perfectly constructed and perfectly written. In that case, the final work of art has, at the most, been only half completed. Next, the piece must be perfectly cast: that is to say, a group of actors must be tactfully selected, each of whom is not only capable of playing his own part in conformity with the author's intention but is also able to assist all the other actors to achieve the best possible effect with the parts that are allotted to them. The members of the company must not only act well, as individuals, but they must also act together, as contributors to a collaborative work of art. A single performance that is out of key may disrupt the harmony of the entire composition. But, supposing that this perfect play be perfectly cast and perfectly acted, it may still fail of its effect unless it be perfectly staged. A red curtain hanging behind a pink evening gown, a misdirected spot-light that casts emphasis upon an insignificant detail, some minor incongruity of furniture, or any of a myriad other trivial details may introduce a note of discord that will utterly disrupt the illusion of the play.

It would be impossible to deny that the average performance in New York is less harmonious than the average performance in London or Paris or Berlin. The main reason, of course, is that the American theatre is conducted with a less sincere regard for art than the theatres of the foremost European nations. But another reason should be mentioned also, in justice to the half-dozen American stage-directors who really care for art and try their best to call it into being. This reason is that our stage is more cosmopolitan than that of any European country. Nine-tenths of all the plays produced in France are set in France, are written by French authors, and are acted by French actors; but only a bare majority of the plays produced in America are written and acted by Americans. Our stage is very hospitable to plays from other lands. Those imported from Great Britain are usually performed for us by British companies; but all other European plays must be translated and must be played by native actors who find it very difficult to transform themselves into Frenchmen or Germans or Norwegians. But not only are our plays selected from a dozen different countries, but our actors, also, are recruited from many different climes. We have upon our stage many American actors who always talk American and many British actors who always talk British; we have a few actors, trained either in America or in Great Britain, who talk the standard language which betrays no locality of origin,—that rarely heard language which is known as English; and we have several foreign actors who speak British or American with a French or German or Russian intonation. From such heterogeneous elements as these it is very difficult to coördinate a harmonious performance.

An emphatic contrast to our own discordant efforts was afforded by the perfectly harmonious performance of *Change*, a Welsh play that was acted in this country in 1914 by an imported company of Welsh players. The acting of this company was so simple and sincere, so real and true, that many of the newspaper reviewers thought that it was not acting at all and described it as " amateurish." It is rather sad to remark that, in the vocabulary of newspaper reviewers, this charming adjective has lost its original meaning of " loverly."

Change was the first work of a new dramatist of decided promise, Mr. J. O. Francis. To this piece was awarded the prize offered by Lord Howard de Walden for the best Welsh play by a Welsh author; and it was well received when it was produced by the Stage Society at the Haymarket Theatre in London. It was not well received in New York. Many of the reviewers complained because the characters, being Welsh, did not seem to be American. " Why should we take any interest in Welsh working-people? ", was their remark. Even so, many Americans have wondered why the late J. Pierpont Morgan should have taken any interest in Raphael and Rembrandt,—neither of whom ever painted a tired business man.

Another complaint that was registered against this play was—to state it in the clearest terms—that the plot was less important than the characters and the action was less interesting than the dialogue. One might as well complain of Keats, because poetry meant more to him than medicine. Doubtless many an apothecary would look upon the *Ode on a Grecian Urn* as a truant waste of time; but it is not necessary to consider art from the point of view of the apothecary. It is the first principle of criticism that a work of art

should be judged in accordance with the intention of
the artist.   In *Change*, this new writer, Mr. J. O.
Francis, allied himself deliberately with that already
well-established school of British realists who set character above plot and dialogue above action.   A man is
not to be sneered at because he chooses to set to work
in accordance with the principles of Stanley Houghton,
John Galsworthy, Githa Sowerby, and St. John Ervine,
all of whom have written great plays; nor is he to be
condemned for his evident unwillingness to insert a
scene from Sardou into the fabric of his drama.

What Mr. Francis gave us was a sincere and sympathetic study of a dozen people, each of whom had a
mind of his own, and all of whom were worth knowing.
Their interrelations with each other resulted inevitably
in a crisis which, though not objectively theatrical, was
deeply and poignantly dramatic.   The dialogue was a
luxury to listen to,—it was so absolutely real, so simply
yet so eloquently human.

The theme of this play is the tragedy that results
from the distressing fact that the elder and the younger
generations can never understand each other.   This
theme has frequently been discussed in the theatre in
the last few years; but it is none the less new on that
account, because there can be nothing either new or old
about a theme which is eternal.   The special poignancy
of *Change* arises from the fact that, though the author
stands apparently on the side of the younger generation, he has been scrupulously fair to the older people
of the play and has presented their case with a sympathetic insight which is utterly unprejudiced.

It is always a concession to surrender to the mood of impatience; but it is difficult not to be impatient with that apparently incurable provincialism of our reviewers and our public which resulted in the failure of this play. *Change* was a beautiful composition, and it was beautifully acted; for Beauty *is* Truth, Truth Beauty —whatever the apothecaries say.

IX

HIGH COMEDY IN AMERICA

No other type of drama is so rarely written in
America as that intelligently entertaining type which
is variously known as High Comedy, or Comedy of
Manners, or Artificial Comedy. The purpose of High
Comedy is to satirize the social customs of the upper
classes, to arraign with wit the foibles of the aristocracy. It must conform to the requirement of comedy
that the plot shall never stiffen into melodrama nor
slacken into farce, and it must attain the end of entertainment less by emphasis of incident than by the nice
analysis of character. The medium of Artificial Comedy is conversation; it dallies with the smart sayings
of smart people; and the dialogue need not be strictly
natural, provided that it be continuously witty. The
world of High Comedy is a world in which what people
say is immeasurably more important than what they
do, or even what they are. It is an airy and a careless
world, more brilliant, more graceful, more gay, more
irresponsible than the world of actuality. The people
of High Comedy awaken thoughtful laughter; but they
do not touch the heart nor stir the soul. By that token
they are only partly real. They have merely heads,
not hearts,—intelligence and not emotion. They stimu-

64

late an intellect at play, without stirring up the deeper sympathies. For this reason High Comedy is more difficult to write than the sterner types of drama. It cannot strike below the belt, like melodrama, nor, like tragedy, attack the vital organs of compassion; it can only deliver light blows upon the forehead; it must always hit above the eyes. *[handwritten marginal note: Clever putting!]*

In the genealogy of English drama, High Comedy can boast an ancient and an honorable lineage. It was introduced in England in 1664 by Sir George Etheredge, who imported it from France; for, during that exile of all gentlemen to Paris which is known in history as the Protectorate of Cromwell, Etheredge had studied manners at the French court and the Comedy of Manners at the theatre of Molière. He was soon followed by that great quartet of gentlemanly wits, composed of Wycherley, Congreve, Vanburgh, and Farquhar, who carried English comedy to unexampled heights of brilliancy and irresponsibility. Unfortunately for their fame, the work of these masters was tinged with an utter recklessness of all morality, at which later generations have grown to look askance. Of this tendency— as Charles Lamb has defined it—"to take an airing beyond the diocese of the strict conscience," High Comedy was purged by Colley Cibber and Sir Richard Steele, who introduced, however, the infra-intellectual alloy of sentiment. Then came the richer period of the genial Goldsmith and the incomparable Sheridan, which gave us the greatest of all Comedies of Manners, *The School for Scandal*. Charles Lamb, who had seen this masterpiece performed by many of the members of the original company, lived long enough to pen the solemn sentence,—" The Artificial Comedy, or Comedy of Manners, is quite extinct on our stage." But even while this requiem was being written, the type was being kept alive in occasional comedies like the *London Assurance* of Dion Boucicault; and, late in the nineteenth century, it was brilliantly revivified by the clever and witty Oscar Wilde and the more humorous and human Mr. Henry Arthur Jones.

It is the privilege of American writers to share with their British cousins the common heritage of English literature, and most offshoots of the ancient stock have been successfully transplanted overseas; but there are certain of these offshoots which thus far have failed to flourish in America because we have had so little time, comparatively, to till our literary soil. Our native drama is already thoroughly alive in respect to melodrama and to farce; but it is not yet thoroughly alive in respect to High Comedy.

This fact, however, is not at all surprising; for High Comedy is the last of all dramatic types to be established in the art of any nation. It has frequently been said that it takes three generations to make a gentleman; but it takes more than three to develop a Comedy of Manners. Manners do not become a theme for satire until they have been crystallized into a code; and, to laugh politely, a playwright must have an aristocracy to laugh at. To all intents and purposes, the United States is still a country without an upper class; and the chaos of our social system precludes the possibility of social satire.

Before we can develop a Comedy of Manners in America, we must first develop an aristocracy to satirize. At present our few aristocrats are cosmopolitans; and, if they should be mirrored on the stage, our audience would think them un-American. For not only do we lack the subject-matter for High Comedy, but we also lack an audience that is educated to appreciate it. Compare the *clientèle* of the Criterion Theatre in London with the *clientèle* of any of our theatres on Broadway. Our American audience is more heterogeneous, more democratic, and possibly more human; but it is certainly less cultivated, less refined. It is composed for the most part of the sort of people who are embarrassed by good breeding and who consider it an affectation to pronounce the English language properly. It is not surprising, therefore, that—as Mr. Walter Prichard Eaton has pithily remarked—most of our American comedies must be classed as <u>Comedies of Bad Manners</u>. We laugh uproariously at impoliteness on our stage, because we have not yet learned to laugh delicately at politeness. We are amused at the eccentricities of bad behavior, because we have not yet learned to be amused at the eccentricities of good behavior. We are still in the stage of learning how to laugh, because we are still in the stage of learning how to live.

There are very few ladies and gentlemen in the American drama,—there are none, for instance, in the very popular and thoroughly representative plays of Mr. George M. Cohan; but the primary reason is that there are very few ladies and gentlemen in the American audience, and the secondary reason is that there are very few ladies and gentlemen in American life. It would not be fair to blame our native dramatists for the dearth of High Comedy in America. Bronson Howard, in the first generation, and Clyde Fitch, in the second, strove earnestly to give us a native Comedy of Manners; but their successors in the present generation have, for the most part, given up the difficult endeavor. It is a thankless task to write about aristocrats for an audience that is unprepared to recognize them, and to search for subject-matter for a Comedy of Manners in a country that is still a little proud of the misfortune that it has no upper class.

For these reasons, the achievement of a genuine American High Comedy should be celebrated with especial praise. *The New York Idea*, by Mr. Langdon Mitchell, is perhaps the only play of American authorship which conforms to all the requirements and exhibits all the characteristics of the traditional Comedy of Manners. There is only enough action to keep the characters conversing; and this action is never serious enough to stir the deeper sympathies. The characters are airily intelligent; and while their levity precludes them from ever lifting the play to any mood more serious than that of comedy, their intelligence prevents them from allowing it to lapse to farce. All the characters are deftly drawn; and every one of them is witty. The dialogue is, from first to last, unfalteringly brilliant; and, while it never calls forth the loud guffaw that speaks the vacant-minded audience, it is continuously accompanied by a ripple of delighted laughter.

The New York Idea is a satire of the tendency of a certain section of American society to indulge unduly in the inspiriting adventure of divorce. Cynthia Karslake really loves her husband; but she has divorced him in a moment of pique and has become engaged to the stolid Phillip Phillimore. Thereupon Karslake proceeds to make himself good-naturedly annoying by openly making love to the divorced wife of Phillimore. Cynthia is stimulated by the sting of jealousy to realize her love for the husband she has lightly tossed away; and, at the very moment when her marriage to Phillimore is about to be pronounced, she balks at the ceremony, and flees from Phillimore to become reconciled with Karslake. The former Mrs. Phillimore ultimately marries Sir Wilfred Gates-Darby, a witty Englishman who, throughout the play, has made love to both the women and announced to each of them that the other is his second choice.

The New York Idea was first produced in 1906 by Mrs. Fiske, and was revived nine years later by Miss Grace George. Its brilliancy has not been dimmed by the decade that has passed since the time when it was written; and in that decade no other High Comedy of American authorship has been brought forth to rival it in excellence. It is not only a good play for the theatre, but a good play for the library as well; for it attains that tone of literary distinction which is very rarely reached in our plays of native authorship.

X

THE GEORGE M. COHAN SCHOOL OF PLAYWRIGHTS

ANYBODY who is seriously interested in the development of a native drama in America must devote particular attention to the work of George M. Cohan, not merely because of the merit of his plays, but even more because of his extremely potent influence over a constantly growing group of younger writers. We have had American playwrights in the past who were superior to Mr. Cohan—Clyde Fitch, for instance, and Augustus Thomas at his best—but none of these has founded what might be called a school, nor developed a formula for making plays that can be used successfully by many men less gifted than himself.

In the last half-dozen years, a clear majority of all the plays of native authorship that have been most popular upon our stage have shown a family resemblance to each other; and the formula of Mr. Cohan is undeniably the father of the family. This fact has been particularly evident in the case of those plays which have been sufficiently successful to be exported from New York to London; so that, in the British capital, the two adjectives " American " and " Cohanesque " have lately come to seem synonymous. To our cousins overseas, the label " Made in America " conjures up no image of *The Great Divide* or *Kindling* or *The Scarecrow* or *The Witching Hour* or *The Truth;* it suggests, instead, a play by Mr. Cohan or by any of the growing group who follow in his footsteps.

In any ultimate history of the American drama, the chapter devoted to these current years must bear the name of Mr. Cohan in its caption. Whatever verdict may be reached in a final summing up of the merits and demerits of his work, our hypothetical historian will not be able to deny that Mr. Cohan is the most representative American dramatist of the present period. He is known to be a very modest man, and it may be doubted that he has ever thought of himself as the founder and the leader of a school; but his influence is evident in nearly all the plays which at present are enjoyed by the public and are praised by the critics because of certain qualities which have come to be regarded as " typically American."

It is necessary for the critic, therefore, to inquire what is meant by a play that is " typically American," or, to use the other label, " Cohanesque." What is Mr. Cohan's formula for making plays—that magic formula which many other authors have accepted as an " open sesame " to fame and fortune? The recipe is really very simple. The hero is a young man who, in the first act, is exhibited as down and out, or at least at a low ebb of his fortunes, because luck has been against him, or because he has made a mess of his own life by indulging certain weaknesses or vices. Toward the end of this first act, he conceives a daring and hazardous scheme for making an incalculable fortune at the expense of a public which is assumed to be easily gullible; or else this scheme is suggested to him by a friend, or imposed upon him by the drift of circumstances. In the second act, the hero starts out to win his way in the world by the impetus of this adventurous scheme. In intention he is at first dishonest, or at least not entirely decided in his ideas of right and wrong; but, as his scheme begins to work, he finds it more profitable to play the game straight than to play it crooked, and is converted to probity by the unforeseen success of a project which he had expected to be a little dangerous. By the time the last act is reached, the hero has made a fortune not only for himself but also for many minor characters whom he had considered as little more than fools when they gave their faith to his project at the time when it was launched. The boom which he has brought about results in unprecedented prosperity for an entire town; and the hero who began life as a failure lives happily forever after as a captain of success.

This summary—though a little abstract—might be employed by any critic of the drama in reviewing such plays by Mr. Cohan as *Get-Rich-Quick Wallingford*, *Broadway Jones*, and *Hit-the-Trail Holliday*, or such plays by other authors as *The Fortune Hunter*, *Ready Money*, *It Pays to Advertise*, and many others which might with equal pertinence be mentioned. The essential element in the formula is that the play must offer a farcical encomium upon the subject of success in life. The hero, who, in the first act, is regarded, and regards himself, as a hopeless failure, must ultimately make a fortune for himself, and for many other people who rather foolishly believe in him, by putting into practice some preposterously imaginative scheme. The " typically American " quality of the play arises from the fact that to imagine the preposterous is the particular achievement of American humor that is at once most humorous and most American. In this particular achievement Mr. Cohan has somehow managed to accept the mantle of such immortal American humorists as Benjamin Franklin and Mark Twain, although it is by no means inconceivable that he may be unfamiliar with their writings.

The success of the Cohan formula upon our stage is rather surprising, in view of certain theories which always heretofore have been accepted by commentators on the drama. It has been assumed, for instance, through uncounted centuries, that no play can ever be successful without a love-story; yet there is not a single love-scene in any of Mr. Cohan's plays. The hero may marry the heroine at the conclusion of the drama; but he has never made love to her at any moment while the action was in progress. It has also been assumed by recent critics that no modern drama can succeed unless it interests primarily the female section of the public, since the majority of the patrons of the contemporary theatre is made up of women and their escorts, and that the proper subject of successful modern drama is, therefore, an analysis of femininity; but Mr. Cohan's plays are written frankly for an audience of men, and deal almost entirely with matters in which only male characters are involved. He has created a hundred living men, but not a single living woman; and his success seems all the more remarkable when we remember that he has never made a conscious or deliberate appeal to the women in his audience.

A closer examination of the Cohan formula will lead us to evaluate the merits and the defects of the representative American drama of the present period. In respect to characterization, this drama is rich in quaint and curious minor parts, but is poor in leading parts with leading motives. Mr. Cohan and his followers have given us a galaxy of minor characters that may be remembered with delight for their truthful tallying with nature; but they have given us no single figure of a hero or a heroine who can be regarded as sufficiently alive and real to step easily and boldly from the framework of the play in which they figure into the immortal regions of imaginative memory.

In respect to plot, Mr. Cohan and his followers are exceedingly adept. They excel in bustle and in movement. Something seems always to be happening upon the stage; and the entrances and exits of the actors are deftly timed to attain the maximum of theatrical effect. At times the deeper possibilities of dramatic tension are sacrificed to sustain this superficial hurrying to and fro; but, on the other hand, there are no waste moments, or empty places, in the play.

In respect to dialogue, these plays are written in a curious vernacular,—the special slang of the theatregoers of Broadway. The scene is usually set, perforce, in some little city of New England or the Middle West;

and it is, in actuality, inconceivable that the sheltered inhabitants of these localities should be familiar with the latest turns of slang that are current in Times Square. Mr. Cohan's dialogue is just as artificial as the rigid rhetoric of Mr. Percy MacKaye; but it sounds colloquial to the public that he writes for, and it awakens easily the confidential laughter that arises from the quick response of recognition.

Of the technical merits of Mr. Cohan's plays it would be superfluous to speak in praise. Few recent entertainments, for example, have been more intelligently planned than *Seven Keys to Baldpate*. Mr. Cohan is gifted with a keen sense of theatrical effect, a remarkable appreciation of the efficiency of certain actors, and a positive genius for predicting in advance the predilections of the public. But is his "typically American" drama a great drama; and is it, after all, resumptive of America? . . . These questions must be asked by anybody who is seriously interested in the development of a native drama in this country.

In answer to these questions, it should be noted first of all that, in all the plays that have been written by Mr. Cohan and his emulators, there is no single character that may be called a lady or a gentleman, in the sense in which these words are understood in England. But are there, in America, no ladies and no gentlemen? . . . Furthermore, there is not a single character that may be called cultured, or even especially well educated. But are there no educated people in America? . . . No character can truthfully be said to talk the English language, since everybody talks the special language of Broadway. But is English a dead language in America? . . . We are taken to a world where there is no such thing as love, nor religion, nor idealism, nor self-sacrifice, but only the will to succeed and the impulse to get the better of one's neighbor. But are the higher motives actually absent from the American imagination? . . .

It appears that, in the current life of present-day America, there are many noble motives which have remained untouched and unexploited by Mr. Cohan and his school. The adjective "American" has not yet really shriveled to identity with the adjective "Cohanesque." Though Mr. Cohan rules our stage at present, some greater leader of our native drama must, in future years, arise. The enormous territory of our vast and dreaming life is still awaiting a profound and great explorer. How long, the critic wonders, must we wait until some huge Columbus of the theatre shall achieve, for the dramatic art, an ultimate discovery of America?

XI

YOUTH AND AGE IN THE DRAMA

One of the most pleasing plays of American authorship in recent years is *Old Lady 31*, by Rachel Crothers. Miss Crothers, who has long been noted for her mastery of the delicate art of dialogue, has written many plays of promise in the past; but this latest piece is easily the best of her productions. It is poignantly beautiful, for the simple reason that it is penetratingly true. Occasionally, in the past, Miss Crothers has shown a regrettable tendency to insist upon her own extremely feminine opinions about life,—as in *A Man's World* and *Ourselves*, to cite a couple of examples; but, in *Old Lady 31*, she shows us life itself, relieved from the intrusion of opinion—and we stand up and remove our hats, as is our custom in the shining presence of reality. It would be futile to deny the success of this remarkable production, either as a work of art or as a popular entertainment. The casual and careless theatregoer has gone to see it—has wept and laughed, in the wonder-working mood of happy pathos, or pathetic happiness—and has come away from the performance a sadder and a wiser [and, in consequence, of course, a better] man. Yet the interesting fact remains to be discussed that Miss Crothers has succeeded with a subject-matter that, for many years, has been tabooed as dangerous by nearly all of our theatrical purveyors whose habit is to feel the pulse of the public; for the *milieu* of the story is an old ladies' home, and the theme of the play is the psychology of several superannuated people whose active lives have long been past and done with. The appeal of youth to youth—which most of our commercial managers insist upon as a necessary requisite to popularity—is singularly absent. The popular success of *Old Lady 31* reopens the entire controversy that concerns the question whether or not the dramatist can ever please the public with an essay in appreciation of old age.

The project of *Old Lady 31* was suggested to Miss Crothers by a novel that was written by the late Louise Forsslund. The story follows the declining fortunes of a pair of aged lovers whose affection for each other has grown " durable from the daily dust of life." Abe and Angie are very old; and they have been constrained to spend the little money they had scraped together, through the savings of a life-time, against " the years that gently bend us to the ground." But, by selling their little cottage and their furniture and nearly all their pitiful and dear belongings, they have raised the hundred dollars that is requisite to secure admittance for Angie to the Old Ladies' Home. Abe, on his part, will have to subsist on charity at the Poor Farm, five miles away. These simple facts are set forth in a prologue, which shows the two old people saying a sad last farewell to the little cottage which has been their home for many years.

The first act discloses the veranda of the Old Ladies' Home, and introduces us to several superannuated women who are gossiping in rocking-chairs concerning the expected arrival of Angie. These women, who no longer have anything to do in life, have all the more to think and feel and say. But something unforeseen attacks and overwhelms them when Angie arrives, accompanied by Abe, who is trundling along her poor belongings on a hand-cart. Abe tries to say good-bye to Angie and to set forth smilingly afoot for the Poor Farm five miles away; but this attempted parting is more than the old women at the Home can bear to see. When Troy fell, the followers of Æneas emitted the immortal phrase, " We have been Trojans—Troy has been "; and of these faded wrecks in rocking-chairs it might be said, with equal pathos, " They have been women." In this moment, they remember; and—recalling the keen life they used to know—they insist that Abe shall not be parted from his Angie, but shall be received surreptitiously into the Home as Old Lady 31.

The unaccustomed presence of a man in the house stirs all the thirty women to a vivid recollection of those feelings which, in Wordsworth's phrase, may be described as " intimations of immortality." The memory of sex survives its function; and a woman is no less a woman though she may be seventy or eighty or ninety years of age. The immediate effect of the reception of Abe into the Old Ladies' Home is to accelerate the coursing of the blood in all the thirty inmates, so that they become again in spirit the mothers, sisters, wives, and sweethearts that they used to be. Like bees about a flower, they buzz and flutter round the old, old man who sits in an easy-chair among them; and, when he falls ill, they fight among themselves and scratch each other to win the privilege of nursing him. This unusual situation—for it is indeed amazingly uncustomary on the stage—is studied by Miss Crothers with a very subtle sense of characterization.

To Abe at last—who, despite the fact that he is very old, is still a man—there comes a sense that it is very irksome to be mothered by so many women. He is being killed with kindness; and—as men of any age will do at times—he grows extremely tired of the other sex. He desires to go forth and have his fling, afar from the sight of any women; and, to this end, he plans clandestinely to run away with an old crony to spend a glorious evening with the men—the real men—of the Life-Saving Station on the terrible and tingling coast that is besieged eternally by the insidious sea. This is his idea of a single, great, and last " good time,"—to drink a draught of fellowship with men of mighty sinews whose business it is to fight against the forces of the brutal gods, and not to lose the struggle. He leaves behind a letter for his Angie, to tell her that he is going to the Poor Farm and will never again return to be an inmate of the Old Ladies' Home.

Angie reads that letter. It would perhaps have broken her old heart, if Angie had not known what every woman knows,—that men are merely children and must come home to their mothers before the sun goes down. Abe comes home, of course. He has had his little fling; and he is glad enough to be received again as the adopted son—more dear, indeed, because of his momentary waywardness—of the thirty mother-hearts that have never missed a beat for him in the Old Ladies' Home.   Angie is there, among them, like a moon among the stars.   She chides him, and scolds him, and puts him to bed,—as in the years that were; and we do not need to be told that " they lived happily forever after."

Two young people—and only two—appear in the fabric of this play:—an ambitious young workman who is poor, and the rich daughter of one of the directors of the Old Ladies' Home.   They love each other ardently, and ultimately marry.   Their story is adequately plausible, and, moreover, it is prettily told: but, somehow, it does not seem to matter.   For once, the interest is focused so tremendously on people who are ending life that the audience has no attention to devote to people who are merely starting out to test it.   These two young lovers—though truthfully and sympathetically drawn—might be deleted from the story without detracting from its interest.

Here, then, we have a play that amuses and enchants the audience because it deals, in the ingratiating mood of sympathetic understanding, with the subject of old age.   Yet this is a subject which most of our commercial managers have always been afraid of.   It has been their theory that youth must be served in the theatre, and that the heroine, in particular, must always be a young and pretty girl.

A little while ago, when *The Boomerang* was settling down to its record-making run at the Belasco Theatre, the present writer happened to enjoy an interesting conversation with Mr. Belasco concerning the career of that very slight but delicately modulated comedy. In discussing the basic reasons for the quite extraordinary popularity of this play, which he admitted to be fragile, Mr. Belasco said that the public flocked to see *The Boomerang* because it dealt with the emotions of young people, in terms that young people could easily appreciate. He then advanced the interesting theory that the average age of the theatre-going public is only twenty-two or twenty-three, and that, to attract a great deal of money to the box-office, it is necessary first of all to please the girl of twenty-two and the young gentleman whom she allures to take her to the play. If the young folks are satisfied, said Mr. Belasco, the success of any undertaking in the theatre is assured.

Whether or not this diagnosis of the case is justified from the standpoint of commercial calculation [and commercial calculation is a potent factor in dramatic art], it must be stated that the efforts of the dramatist would be extremely stultified if he should feel himself condemned to write forever for girls of twenty-two. There are many interesting and important things in life that an author cannot talk about to young girls, for the simple reason that young girls are not sufficiently experienced to understand them. The reach of the drama should be coextensive with the range of life; and any aspect of the life of man that may be made to seem interesting on the stage should be regarded as available for projection in a play. If a dramatist has

created Romeo—whom any girl of twenty-two can understand—must he be forbidden, at some subsequent
period of his own development, to create King Lear?
Must the drama deal eternally with youth, and never at
all with age?

These questions recall to vivid recollection a conversation with Sir Arthur Pinero which took place in
London in the spring of 1910.   Two of the very greatest plays of this great master of the dramaturgic art—
The Thunderbolt and *Mid-Channel*—had recently received a rather scant appreciation from the London
public.   The present writer suggested that one reason
for their lack of popularity was the fact that neither
play contained a character that the average frequenters
of the theatre could easily and naturally love.   "You
make them hate the Blundells, you make them hate the
Mortimores; and they go away confirmed in the uncritical opinion that you have made them hate the play.
They hate the play all the harder because the characters are so real that they cannot get away from them or
get around them.   You make your auditors uncomfortable by telling them the truth about certain men and
women who are very like themselves.   They do not like
to listen to uncomfortable truths; they decide, therefore, that they do not like to hear you talk; and they
tell their friends to stay away."   By some such argument, the critic sought to draw an answer from the
dramatist.

Sir Arthur's answer may be recorded most clearly
in a paraphrase that is freely recomposed from materials that are registered in memory.   It ran, in the

main, as follows:—" It takes me a year to make a play,—six months to get acquainted with the characters, and six months to build the plot and write the dialogue. All that time, I have to seclude myself from the companionship of friends and live only with the imaginary people of my story. Why should I do this— at my age? I don't need money; I don't desire—if you will pardon me for saying so—to increase the reputation that I have. *Sweet Lavender* made my fortune; *The Second Mrs. Tanqueray* made my reputation: and for many years I have not needed to write plays. Why, then, should I go on? Only because the task is interesting. But it would not be interesting to me unless I were interested personally in the people of my plays. You say the public hate the Blundells and the Mortimores. I do not care. I love those twisted and exacerbated people, because—you see—they interest me. I think I must have what the critics call ' a perverted mind.' [It should be noted that the wise and brilliant playwright said this with a smile.] The only characters that seem to interest me nowadays are people whose lives have somehow gone awry. I like to wonder at the difference between the thing they are and the thing they might have been. That, to me, is the essence of the mystery of life,—the difference between a man as he is and the same man as God intended and desired him to be. But to see this, you must catch your man in the maturity of years. Young people—sweet young people in particular—no longer seem to interest me: I would rather spend my evenings at the Garrick Club than go down to the country and live six months with an imaginary company of people like Sweet Lavender. She was a nice girl; but, after the first hour, there was nothing more to know about her. I now prefer the Mortimores; for there is always something more to find out about people such as they are. You cannot exhaust them in an hour, or six months. Young people are pretty to look at, and theatre-goers like them, as they liked my little Lavender, so many years ago; but, now that I have lived a little longer, I prefer people with a past. A future—that is nothing but a dream: but a past—there you have a soil to delve in."

These words—as has been stated—are merely paraphrased from memory; but the sense is fairly representative of the attitude of mind of our greatest living playwright toward his art. Sir Arthur Pinero might not disagree with Mr. Belasco in the managerial opinion that the safest path toward making money in the theatre is to write about young people for the young; but he himself—having made sufficient money with *Sweet Lavender* [the *Boomerang* of thirty years ago] —prefers, for his own pleasure, to write plays about people who have reached a maturity of years.

On the score of art alone—without regard to commerce—a great deal might be said in support of heroes and of heroines that are no longer young. A story of adventure or of love demands an atmosphere of youth; but there are many things in life more interesting to the adult mind than adolescent love or extravagant adventure. The greatest plays are plays of character; and character is nothing more nor less than the sum-total of experience.   What a person is, at any moment, is merely a remembered record of all that he has been.   To be alive, a person must have lived; and very few people have lived at all at twenty-two.

The greatest artists who have dealt with character have always preferred to depict people in the maturity of years instead of in the heyday of that superficial beauty which is nothing but a passing bloom upon the face of youth.   Consider Rembrandt, for example—the most searching and most deeply penetrant of all the portrait-painters of the world.   A Rembrandt portrait is a record of all that life has written on the face of the sitter; and the portrait becomes meaningful almost precisely in proportion to the age of the person whom the artist looked at.   Like Velasquez, Rembrandt painted what he saw: but with this difference,—he had to have something to see.   The disinterested Spaniard could depict the vacant faces of the royal family with absolute fidelity to fact and yet achieve a triumph of the minor artistry of painting; but Rembrandt, to be interested, had to have a sitter who had lived.   If the all but perfect artist of the Netherlands can be regarded ever to have failed at all, he failed in the depiction of young girls.   There was nothing in their faces for such a man to see.   He was most successful in his portraits of old women and old men; for in these he was allowed to wonder—to quote once more the meaning of Pinero—at the difference between the thing they were and the thing they might have been.   He depicted character as the sum-total of a life-time of experience.

Must the playwright be denied this privilege because

the average theatre-goer is a girl of twenty-two? The
success of *Old Lady 31* is a salutary fact to bolster up
our wishes on the negative side of this contention. Abe
and Angie, in this play, are more interesting at seventy
or eighty than they ever could have been at twenty,
before time and the mellowness of ripe experience had
written genial wrinkles on their brows. Rembrandt
would have loved to paint a portrait of these two; and
Rembrandt, in the heaven of eternal artists, sits very
high in the Celestial Rose.

Another point to be considered is that young people,
when imagined by the dramatist, must be depicted by
young people on the stage. Hence a premium is set
on youth and beauty among our actors and, more especially, our actresses. A young girl endowed by nature
with a pretty face and fluffy hair is made a star, while
many older and less lovely women who know more—
much more—about the art of acting are relegated to
the ranks. The greatest interpretative artist in the
world, Madame Yvette Guilbert, said recently in a public address that no woman could act well before she had
attained the age of thirty-five. Twenty years of study
of such technical details as those of diction and of gesture, and a maturity of personal experience, were
absolutely necessary before an actress could be fitted to
stand forth before the public as an interpreter of human
nature. If this is true—and the solid fact must be
accepted that Madame Guilbert herself is now a finer
and a greater artist than she seemed even capable of
becoming twenty years ago—the premium that now is
set upon the youthful charm of youthful actresses is

seen to be a very shallow thing. What boots it, after all, to be a star at twenty-five, unless a woman can become, like Sarah Bernhardt, a central and essential sun at seventy?

Much, of course, might be said, conceivably, on either side. On the one hand, there is Keats, who died at twenty-five; and, on the other hand, there is Ibsen, who did not begin his greatest work till after he was fifty. Those whom the gods love die young or live long, as the chance may fall; and there is no mathematical solution of the mystery. But this much may be said with emphasis, in summing up:—that there is no valid reason why the dramatist should be denied the privilege of dealing with character at its maturity in terms that are intelligible to the adult mind. Youth may be served in the theatre; but old age is still of service, as a theme for the serener contemplation of a ripe intelligence. Despite the imperious and undeniable appeal of youth, there must always be a place upon the boards for the dramatist who says,—

Grow old along with me!
The best is yet to be,
The last of life, for which the first was made:
Our times are in His hand
Who saith, " A whole I planned,
Youth shows but half; trust God; see all nor be afraid!"

XII

YVETTE GUILBERT — PREMIÉRE DISEUSE

THE stage is very empty; it is almost pitifully lonely. The back-drop [borrowed from some scenic storehouse] displays a conventional picture of a conventional French garden. There is no carpeting upon the bare boards of the platform. Forward, in one corner, a grand piano looks incongruously out of place; and at the instrument is seated a totally uninteresting man. The lights have been turned up, and a momentary hush has quenched the buzzing in the auditorium.

A woman enters through the wings, walks downward to the center of the stage; and at once the house is filled and thrilled with the sensation that this is one of the great women of the world. She is wearing a medieval costume—a robe to set you dreaming of the little church at Castelfranco and the magic carpet hung behind the head of the Virgin of Giorgione: but it is not the costume, but the woman wearing it, that has enchanted your attention. " She walks in beauty, like the night of cloudless climes and starry skies."

She has reached the center of the stage; she pauses and stands still; she is about to speak. A thousand ears instinctively yearn toward her. In a few sentences of finely chiseled French, she announces that she is going to render an old ballad of the people—a ballad

of the fifteenth century—that tells the story of the birth
of Christ. That is all; but, somehow, you have experienced already a drift of very great adventures. First,
you have seen a woman walking greatly; and no other
woman can do that, since Modjeska passed away.
Next, you have seen a woman greatly standing still;
and no other woman can do that, except *la* Duse, whom
a nation calls divine. Then, you have heard a woman
speak; and you have been reminded of the goal of all
your striving, ever since you were a little child and felt
yourself first tortured by the imperious and yet elusive
eloquence of words.

From the inconspicuous piano a few notes have been
emitted; and the great woman has begun to enunciate
the words of the old ballad. The stage is not empty
any longer; it will never be lonely any more. The silly
old back-drop has faded quite away. The piano has
become invisible. You are looking forth, in a wonderful clear night of stars, over the hushed housetops of
the town of Bethlehem. From somewhere in the distance comes the high-pitched, thin, and drowsy call of
the night-watchman droning forth the hour. You are
back in the mysterious and dreaming East, where millions meditate upon the immanence of God—back in
that year of years from which our time is dated. You
see a heavy, weary woman toiling toward a tavern; you
see her rebuffed rudely by a fat-pursed hostess; you
share the timorous despair of her humble husband; you
are relegated to the stable, and breathe the breath of
cattle. There is a pause—a silence. Then, suddenly,
there comes a chant as of a host of angels, trumpet-

tongued, blaring forth the miracle of birth beneath the dancing of a million stars.

No play has ever made you conscious, with such keenness, of so much of human life; no music has ever given such wings to your imagination. You begin to wonder what has happened to you; you begin to realize that, in the drama of your own experience, the thrilling stage-direction has at last been written,—" Enter Art "! But, once again, the great woman pauses, and is silent, and stands still, and speaks. Next, she tells you, she will render an old-time ballad of the death of Christ. This ballad, in the sixteenth century, was chanted every Eastertide before the portals of all the great cathedrals of France. There is a silence, and a pause. " Including the Cathedral of Rheims," the artist adds: and you feel great tears welling up into your eyes.

Thence, forward through the centuries, she leads you through the history of France, projecting many ballads of the people, nearly all by nameless authors—some tragic, some poignantly pathetic, others charmingly alluring, others brightly gay. She changes her costume to suit the changes of the centuries; she alters her carriage, her gestures, the conduct of her voice, to suit the alterations of the moods that she imagines. But, every time, she seems to crowd the stage with many living people; and always she overwhelms the audience with the spirit of the piece that she is rendering.

You come away from her performance, swimming in a phosphorescent sea. For two hours you have worshiped in a temple where beauty is truth, truth beauty; and now you know that nothing else on earth is worth the knowing. You have been seeking, all your life, for Art; and at last you have met it face to face; and you are not afraid, but there is a terrible, sweet singing in your soul.

You have been reminded, in a single afternoon, of the great person that you meant to be when you were twenty-one; you have been enlisted, once again, in the little army of the good and faithful who labor evermore without discouragement to make the world more beautiful; you have been allured once more to such a love of the loveliness of language that you no longer hear the strident voices of the people in the street; you have been taught to imagine the possibilities of civilization; you have sold your soul to Art, and deemed the bargain generous.

There is no word in English for that medium of art of which Yvette Guilbert is the supreme and perfect master. It is not acting, it is not singing, it is not recitation; yet it combines the finest beauties of all three. It offers simultaneously an interpretation of literature and an interpretation of music; and it continually reminds you of what is loveliest in painting, in sculpture, and in dancing. The French call her a *diseuse*—that is to say, a woman who knows how to say things; and when we think how few people in the world this phrase could justly be applied to, we shall no longer wonder at the rarity of her performance.

The art of saying things, as exemplified by Madame Guilbert, has become, indeed, a synthesis of all the arts. Details have been selected from the methods of all the known media of expression and have been arranged in a perfectly concordant pattern. All the arts are merely so many different languages to give expression to the same essential entity; and this essential entity—which constitutes the soul of art—is rhythm. Painting, sculpture, and architecture make rhythmic patterns to the eye; music, poetry, and prose made rhythmic patterns to the ear. The art of Yvette Guilbert does both. By her bodily movements, her gestures, her facial expression, she makes patterns in space, to charm the eye; and by her enunciation of words and music, she makes patterns in time, to charm the ear. She has developed a universal language—a way of appealing simultaneously and with equal power to the deaf and to the blind.

The secret of her art is a mastery of rhythm—the quintessential element of all the arts that have ever been developed by mankind; and of this element her mastery is absolute. She is one of the great artists of the world—not only of our time but of all times. She belongs to that high company that is graced by Donatello, Gian Bellini at his best, Mozart, and Keats—the perfect masters of a finally perfected medium.

Her art, alas!, is not like theirs immortal, for the medium of her expression is the perishable temple of the human soul; but to us, who are privileged to see and hear her, the beauty that she bids to be appeals more poignantly because of the tragic sense that it is transient. It seems, indeed, an image of that " Joy, whose hand is ever at his lips, bidding adieu."

But Yvette Guilbert is not only a great artist, she is also a great woman; and this fact adds the final needed note to a performance that is necessarily so personal as hers. There are not so many really great people in the world that it can ever cease to be a privilege to come into their presence. She is a great woman, because—in Whitman's phrase—she "contains multitudes." She sits serene upon that height of civilization toward which uncounted generations have been toiling since the dawn of time; and, throned upon the summit, she "throws little glances down, smiling, and understands them with her eyes."

She is not only supreme in art; she is also supreme in personality. She seems to incorporate within herself the very essence of the nation that has engendered her. "Though fallen on evil days—on evil days though fallen, and evil tongues," a clear majority of living men still realize that there is such a thing as truth, and such a thing as beauty, and such a thing as right, and are ready to die for the idea that civilization is a better thing than barbarism. To all who are so minded, the most inspiring ideal that is tingling in the world today is the ideal of that beleaguered country that is holding firm the ramparts of the only world worth living in: that country of the neat and nimble speech, that country of sweet reason and unfathomable tenderness of heart, that country of liberty, equality, fraternity, that country which is the second home and foster-mother of all the artists of the world who meditate beneath the stars. All that this leader of the nations has to say seems summed up and expressed in the incomparable art of this incomparable woman. It is as if great France had blown a kiss to us across the seas.

XIII

THE LOVELINESS OF LITTLE THINGS

For those who seek adventure among beautiful achievements, there is a special pleasure in contemplating the loveliness of little things. The tiny temple at Nîmes is not so great an edifice as the Cathedral of Amiens, but it is much more perfect and more fine. The mind is overawed by the tremendous seraphim of Tintoretto, cutting through chaos with strong, level flight; but the heart goes out with keener fondness to the little angels of Fra Angelico, that demurely set one tiny foot before the other on the pansied fields of Paradise. The vastest work of Byron is *Don Juan*, with its enormous incongruity of moods; but his loveliest work is the simple-mooded little lyric that begins, " She walks in beauty." Could any colossus of sculpture be so dainty or so delicate as the little bronze Narcissus of Naples, whose uplifted finger is eternally accompanied by a melody of unheard flutes? What is Shakespeare's finest and most perfect work? It is not *Hamlet* nor *Macbeth*; it is not even *Othello*; it is, I think, the tiny song beginning, " Take, oh, take those lips away." It is conceivable that any of his great plays might be improved by a hundred alterations in the lines; but to change a single syllable of that forlorn and lovely lyric would be like scratching the face of a little child.

It is one of the paradoxes of art that its very finest works are nearly always minor works. The pursuit of perfectness is incompatible with the ambition for amplitude, and a vast creation can seldom be completely fine. A cameo is a more perfect thing than a cathedral; and lovers of all that is most delicate in versification must turn to minor poets, like Catullus. The major poet can afford to be careless, but the minor poet is constrained to write perfectly if he is to write at all. With the major poet, mere art is a secondary concern; he may, indeed, be a great artist like Milton, or he may be a reckless and shoddy artist like Walt Whitman. But the minor poet loves art for the sake of art; he pursues perfection, and can rest content with nothing less faultless and less fine. Amid the drums and tramplings of all the great Elizabethan tragedies, there is no passage quite so perfect in pathetic delicacy as Mr. Austin Dobson's little lyric in dialogue entitled, " *Good night, Babette.*"

Such exquisite minor works as this and all the others we have mentioned must be regarded as the little children of art. They awaken an affection that can never be inspired by those gigantic presences before which we bow our heads in awe. It is a great thing to strew roses in the triumphal path of Cæsar, but it is a sweeter thing to deck with daffodils the blown hair of some dancing little maid. In the autobiography of Benvenuto Cellini, we learn that the dearest heir of his invention was not the tall and agile Perseus that now

takes the rain in Florence, but the precious little salt-
cellar which now arrests the wanderer through many
rooms in the vast museum of Vienna. In this minor
work, the artist's medium was not bronze, but gold; he
was not making a monument for multitudes to gape at,
but was perfecting a tiny and a precious thing for the
eyes of the enlightened few. In this regard, a minor
work of art may be defined as a work of art designed
for the minority.

In many modern languages, like French and German
and Italian, the sweetest way of expressing endearment
is through the use of a diminutive. " Mütterchen," in
German, means not merely "little mother " but "dear
little mother " as well; and when the younger Lippi was
nicknamed Filipino, the name meant not so much " little
Philip " as " the well-belovèd Philip."   There is a
famous passage in Dante's *Purgatory*, at the outset of
the twenty-eighth canto, where the poet's keenness of
affection for the perfect world is expressed by his appreciation of the little birds that sing on little branches
in tree-tops swung lightly by a little breeze; and this
succession of diminutives is like a reaching out of tiny
fingers groping for the reader's hand.

Whoever has looked upon the sweetest painting in
the world must know the love of little things. When
you enter the tiny chapel of the Frari Church in Venice
where the masterwork of Gian Bellini sits enshrined,
you begin instinctively to walk in whispers. Your first
impression is that of an ineffable serenity—a quiet that
you must not interrupt. But this serenity arises partly
from the fact that the Madonna is such a little lady,

and that the winged musicians that stand listening beneath her throne are the youngest of the children of the angels. And her own child, despite his sturdiness of standing, seems such a little boy beside those dwarfed athletes that bulge their muscles in Raphael's cartoons. And the strips of landscape beyond the venerable saints open such enticing, tiny vistas of the earth. . . . Tintoretto may swoop roaring through immensity; but here is an artist whose heart was as a nest for all the sweet, winged wishes of the world. He reminds you of little children kneeling in the night and whispering "God bless . . ." to all the things that are.

Similarly, the devotees of the drama must always keep an open home within their hearts for the reception of the little children of this most adult of all the arts. There are certain plays that one would like to mention always with an Italian diminutive—with some such nickname as "Prunella," for example. There is no vastness and no grandeur in their structure—only an intimacy of little perfectnesses. One feels a bit afraid lest they might be seen by some one incapable of tenderness for tiny things. To this category must be assigned that exquisite dramatic poem of Alfred de Musset, *A Quoi Rêvent les Jeunes Filles;* and in this same context the reader must also be invited to consider such a fantasy as *Prunella*, by Mr. Laurence Housman and Mr. Granville Barker.

Prunella is a young maiden who lives immured in a little house and garden with three forbidding aunts, Prim, Privacy, and Prude. Along comes a company of strolling players, headed by Pierrot and Scaramel, who gain access to Prunella and awaken in her a longing to flee away into the mysterious and alluring world. Pierrot wins her love, and, aided by Scaramel and the others, abducts her from her prison-house at night. In the last act, after Pierrot has tired of her, she wanders home friendless and disenchanted. But Pierrot had learned [it is sweet to think he may have learned this little truth from Mr. Austin Dobson] that " love comes back to his vacant dwelling." His loneliness has taught him the value and the need of the old, old love that he knew of yore. Prunella once again becomes his Pierrette, and they look forward toward a life whose love is real.

This story is, in all essentials, the same story that was told in *Sister Beatrice;* but it lacks those overtones of eternity which Maeterlinck has imparted to his narrative. It was apparently the purpose of the authors of *Prunella* to emulate the pretty and witty art of such a piece as *Les Romanesques* of M. Edmond Rostand, but they lacked that brilliant exuberance of fancy which was demanded by their task. Every once in a while the authors permit us to regret that the piece could not have been written for them by Théodore de Banville or Mr. Austin Dobson. Several of Mr. Housman's lyric stanzas are delightful; but his handling of rhymed couplets is pedestrian, and the prose passages lack that illumination, as by a flock of fire-flies, that is desirable in a composition of this type.

XIV

THE MAGIC OF MR. CHESTERTON

It is not often that those of us who frequent the theatres in New York are permitted to quote with pertinence that noble phrase of Wordsworth's,—" Great men have been among us." Most of the plays that we are asked to see—however clever be their deft adjustment of a calculated means to a previously estimated end—have been written, all too undeniably, by men no greater than ourselves. While admitting, with due deference, our inability to manufacture so satisfactory an entertainment, we still remain uncomfortably conscious of our own ability to manufacture something else that shall be equally praiseworthy in its kind. Mr. George Broadhurst may know more about the business of making plays than we do; but there are many other matters concerning which we feel that we know more than Mr. Broadhurst. In this mood—which is, as has been said, uncomfortable—we miss that genuflection of the spirit, that graceful upward looking of the eyes of the intelligence, which we instinctively desire to pay out as a tribute to a mind that is unquestionably bigger than our own.

It has often been remarked that women like to be

mastered,—that they like to be bent and beaten by a physical and mental power that is strong enough to conquer them.   Even so, appreciators and adorers of the arts like to bow before the power of a mind that they perceive to be more mighty than their own.   Those of us who reverently enter any temple of the arts are evermore desirous of recognizing and trumpeting the miracle that " great men have been among us."   Our knees are always more than ready for a genuflection; but too often—all too often—we strain our ears in vain to catch the swishing of those garments whose edges we may seize with dignity and kiss with adoration.   We come into the holy place with prayers upon our lips, but we find it tragically empty of a god to listen to our chants of praise.

Aspiring young authors often ask advice as to how to go about the business of learning to write interesting plays.   Ought they, like Shakespeare, to begin their apprenticeship as actors?   Ought they, like Ibsen, to begin as stage-directors?   Should they study with Professor George Pierce Baker of Harvard University, or with Mr. George M. Cohan of Broadway?   They are usually told to crawl into the theatre as quickly as possible, in any capacity whatever, and to spend at least a decade in the theatre, picking up a practical knowledge of all the tricks of the dramatic trade.   If only for the sake of variety, the present writer would like to offer another kind of counsel.   It might not be a bad plan if the aspiring young author should devote the first thirty-five or forty years of his life to the task of growing up to be a great man, and should subsequently sit down in some comparatively idle moment and write a play to please himself. Whatever pleases a great man is likely to please at least the sort of people who recognize a great man when he speaks to them; and could any playwright desire a more honorable audience?

Magic is the first and only play by Mr. Gilbert K. Chesterton. Mr. Chesterton has had no training whatsoever in the technique of the theatre. Indeed, since he settled down in his big chair in Beaconsfield, he has rarely, if ever, gone to the theatre so many as half a dozen times in any season. Yet *Magic* goes to show how good a job may be accomplished by a very able mind that chooses, for a change, to undertake a task in an unfamiliar medium. Mr. Max Marcin or Mr. Roi Cooper Megrue might have built this play a little better; but, on the other hand, it may be doubted if either of them would ever have thought of building it at all. And, when it came to the writing of the dialogue,—well, G. K. C. knows how to write, and that also is a little matter that requires an apprenticeship of twenty years. . . .

Magic is beautifully written, in that peculiar mood of intermingled poetry and humor that seems to be exclusively the property of the English-speaking race. The French, like Edmond Rostand, can be at the same time witty and poetic; the Germans, like Goethe, can be at the same time poetic and satirical; the Italians, like Dante, can be at the same time sardonic and poetic; but only the English, from Chaucer to Chesterton, can command that paradoxical and almost mystic mood which is both laughable and lovable,—both lovely and laughing.

Magic is a very interesting play, for the simple reason that Mr. Chesterton is a very interesting man. The important thing about Mr. Chesterton is not what he thinks about anything in particular, but what he thinks about everything in general. It is the mark of a great man that his vision of the universe is so coördinated that what appeals to him in this or that detail is mainly the fact of their relation to each other. When a man, for instance, has encompassed the religion of Keats, the thing that interests him thereafter about beauty is the simple fact that it is true, and the thing that interests him about truth is the simple fact that it is beautiful. Pragmatical philosophers assert that any religion will serve, so long as it may prove to be of service; but, without a religion, a mind is at the mercy of every wind that blows, like a ship without an anchorage. The mark of a great man is that he has succeeded in discovering a religion that, at least, is suited to himself and serves adequately to coördinate the apprehensions of his intellect. (At this point, it may not be superfluous to remind the reader parenthetically that, if any of our American playwrights—with the possible exception of Mr. Augustus Thomas—have discovered a religion, they have succeeded in concealing the discovery from those of us who listen to their plays.)

Unless a man can tell us clearly what he thinks about the universe in general, his scattered thoughts concerning this or that detail must be regarded as of very small importance. Not until we know a man's opinion about

God are we ready to appreciate his opinions about ships and shoes and sealing-wax and cabbages and kings. In the great gigantic jig-saw picture-puzzle of the universe, the pattern is the only thing that really counts. The important thing about Mr. Chesterton is that his mental attitude toward anything is consistent with his mental attitude toward everything.

Mr. Chesterton's religion is exceedingly simple. Despite a general impression to the contrary, he is not a member of any established church,—neither of the Church of England nor of the Church of Rome; but, to his friends, he is accustomed to describe himself as an Early Christian. He believes in miracles. He believes, in other words, that the business of the universe is conducted on two planes—the natural and the supernatural. He believes that this world, for instance, is inhabited not only by those temporary tenants that are known as human beings (" more or less human," certain satirists would say), but also by such eternal tenants as ghosts and goblins, saints and fairies, devils, angels, and many other sorts of disembodied spirits.

In this belief (which, of course, is only a detail of a larger pattern of coördinated mysticism), Mr. Chesterton is utterly sincere. His mind would not be willing to accept a world that had no magic in it. That is the kind of person that he is; and, if we disagree with his religion, we have at least the privilege of recognizing that he is, at least, a person of that kind, and that he means what he says, and means it absolutely.

With Mr. Chesterton's belief in miracles, the present

commentator disagrees entirely. One of the most magnificent attributes of that abstraction which we call conveniently the Mind of God is the idea of Law. To assume what Stevenson has termed " some wilful illegality of Nature," would seem less wonderful than to assume an irrefragible continuance of the august decree. It is so great a thing to make and keep a law that it would be comparatively trivial to break it. The simple facts of birth and death are so amazing that our finite minds, to lose themselves in wonder, are not required to imagine any rising of the sloughed and rotted body from the tomb. When the Law itself is so majestic, why search for any more astounding majesty in some capricious and illogical remission of the Law? Why seek for any rising from the dead, in a world wherein it may be, on occasion, so magnificent a thing to die? Why accuse God of committing miracles, when miracles can only be regarded as indications of a momentary change of mind?

Mr. Chesterton, in *Magic*, has asserted that a man endowed with simple and enormous faith may—merely by taking thought, and without recourse in any way at all to scientific trickery—perform a miracle whose causes he himself is utterly incapable of fathoming. Mr. Chesterton believes what he says,—even as the authors of the early gospels believed that the Great Person whose religion they were trying to expound was capable of turning water into wine. To this assumption that the Mind of God descends, upon occasion, to indulge in the capricious exercise of " wilful illegalities," the present writer is required to oppose a contrary belief.   To put the matter rather poignantly—if God has time enough to waste on such trivial trickery as changing a red lamp into a blue lamp at the call of the conjurer in Mr. Chesterton's play, how does it happen that He was too busy, at the moment, to prevent the present war?   The trouble with any idea of Deity that is too intimate and personal is that we are tempted all too easily to inquire why a God that is so human should care so little about ordinary human justice.   A God like Mr. Chesterton's, who has time to drop in of an evening for a personal visit to the drawing-room of a Duke, ought assuredly to be able to attend immediately to such matters as the burning of Louvain or the shattering of Rheims Cathedral or the sinking of the *Lusitania*.

But, though the present writer disagrees with Mr. Chesterton's religion, he is ready at least to remove his hat in Mr. Chesterton's presence, because of the unusual and, in consequence, impressive fact that Mr. Chesterton has a religion, and knows what it is, and is eager to express it and to preach it with enthusiasm.

XV

MIDDLE CLASS OPINION

In their mental attitude toward any subject, all people may be divided into three classes, which may be called most conveniently by those terms so dear to sociologists and snobs,—a lower class, a middle class, and an upper class. The lower class is composed of those people who know nothing at all about the subject in question; the middle class is composed of those people who know a little about the subject, but not much; and the upper class is composed of those people who know a great deal about it. Any single individual may hold a lower class opinion on one subject, a middle class opinion on another, and an upper class opinion on a third. Thus, the same man might know nothing about poetry, a little about politics, and a great deal about plumbing. Again, a person with an upper class opinion about dogs may hold a lower class opinion about dogmas. Nearly everybody is an expert in his line and an ignoramus in certain other lines; but, toward a considerable number of intervening matters, nearly everybody holds a middle class opinion,—the opinion of one who knows a little, but not much.

Every work of art appeals for the approbation of all three classes of observers—those who know nothing about the art that is being exercised, those who know a little about it, and those who know a great deal about it. Every professional dancer, for example, must be judged by people who dance well, by people who dance a little, and by people who do not dance at all. If, like Mordkin or Nijinsky, he can capture the approbation of all three classes of observers, his reputation is assured; but such an absolute and undisputed triumph is very rare in the history of art.

In the history of art, it frequently happens that the opinion of the lower class is supported and affirmed by the opinion of the upper class. The adage about the meeting of extremes is curiously sustained by this phenomenon. But, in such cases, it nearly always happens that the middle class dissents sharply from the united and preponderant opinion of those who know less and those who know more. Indeed, the statement may be ventured that the mental middle class is nearly always a class of dissenters.

Let us consider how this formula works out when applied to concrete instances. People who know nothing about painting regard the efforts of the cubists as absurd; people who know a great deal about painting regard them, also, as absurd. These efforts are considered seriously only by people who know a little about painting, but not much. "A little knowledge"—as the most common-sensible of English poets stated—"is a dangerous thing." Here we have an instance of the sharp dissent of middle class opinion from the united opinion of the lower and the upper classes. The extremes meet; but the middle term refuses to conjoin.

Again, let us consider, in this regard, the reputation of Tennyson as a writer. Among the lower class—the class of people who know nothing whatsoever about the art of writing—Tennyson is the most popular of all British poets. Among the upper class—a class composed, in this instance, of the twenty people in England and the ten people in America who know how to write the English language—Tennyson is revered as the finest artist (with the certain exception of Milton and the possible exception of Keats) in the entire history of English verse. In this case, again, the few experts agree with the multitudinous proletariat. But among the middle class—the class of people who know a little about writing, but not much—the perfect art of Tennyson is sneered at and spoken of with scorn. Representatives of middle class opinion always prefer the artistry of Browning—or say that they do. In saying so, and thus dissenting from the opinion of the lower class, they think they are asserting their superiority. Little do they realize that, at the same time, they are emphasizing their inferiority to those who know much more than they do about the art of writing.

Browning is a great poet—a greater poet, it is possible, that Tennyson—but the point to be noted in the present context is that he has been taken up by the middle class of readers not because of his merits as a poet, but because of his defects as a writer. Browning is praised by the middle class not because he is admired by the upper class but because he is not admired by the lower class. The cult of Browning is essentially a snobbish cult,—a cult just as snobbish as that undervaluation of the art of Tennyson which has arisen merely from an ineradicable spirit of dissent.

Unfortunate is any artist—even though he be so great a man as Browning—if he endures the danger of being praised by middle class opinion. Such a man is always praised for his defects,—the faults that make him different and queer. The mind of the middle class is incapable of criticism. The lower class—to quote a common formula of words—may not know anything about art, but it knows what it likes and what it doesn't like; and this knowledge is basically human and essentially sincere. The upper class is capable of criticism on a higher plane. Any man who has ever written a good sentence [such men are very rare] knows that Tennyson can write, because he knows that Tennyson can beat him at a difficult endeavor that, in Dante's phrase, has kept him lean for twenty years. But people of the middle class pride themselves mainly on liking things that other people do not like. Their favorite adjective is " different." They flatter themselves by propagating fads.

This analysis will help us to define the position of Mr. Bernard Shaw in the contemporary English-speaking theatre. Both lower class and upper class opinion set him lower than Sir Arthur Pinero and Mr. Henry Arthur Jones; but he is set much higher than either of these rivals in the opinion of the middle class. [It should, perhaps, be noted in parenthesis that Sir James Barrie is exempted from this comparison because it has been his fortune to secure the equal approbation of all three classes of opinion.] People who know nothing about the drama prefer Pinero and Jones to Shaw; people who know a great deal about the drama prefer Pinero and Jones to Shaw; but people who know a little about the drama, but not much, always prefer— or say that they prefer—Shaw to Pinero and Jones. The sort of people who organize Browning Circles never read *The Second Mrs. Tanqueray* or *The Liars*; they always read *Getting Married*, and pride themselves on " being different."

The preference of lower class opinion for Pinero and Jones is indicated by statistics. For every hundred performances of the plays of Mr. Shaw throughout the English-speaking world, a thousand performances of the plays of Pinero and Jones have been demanded. This popular verdict would not be so impressive were it not supported and affirmed by the verdict of the upper class. Suppose we should select the very best play of each of these three dramatists: in the case of Mr. Shaw, the selection would be *Candida*; in the case of Mr. Jones, it would be *Michael and His Lost Angel*; and, in the case of Sir Arthur Pinero, it would be either *The Second Mrs. Tanqueray*, *Iris*, *Mid-Channel*, or *The Thunderbolt*: and suppose that these plays should be submitted to a jury of experts composed of the twenty foremost dramatists and dramatic critics in England and the ten foremost dramatists and dramatic critics in America. There can be no question that, in the verdict of this jury, Mr. Shaw would come out third,— just as he has come out third in the vote that has been recorded by the lower class.

The man who knows a great deal is never made bash-

ful by agreeing with the man who knows nothing at all.
It is only the man who knows a little, but not much, who
feels uncomfortable in conformity. Mr. Shaw is lauded
as the foremost English playwright of the day only by
people who are conscious that they are disagreeing
with the lower class but are utterly unconscious that
they are also disagreeing with the upper class.

It has been the misfortune of Mr. Shaw to assemble
and to concentrate the admiration of a special public,—
a public that is composed almost entirely of people of
the mental middle class. This fact is a misfortune, because—to repeat a previous statement—the mind of
the middle class is incapable of criticism. When Pinero
and Jones write bad plays, like *A Wife Without a
Smile* or *Lydia Gilmore*, these plays are rejected by
the lower class and condemned by the upper class; but
when Shaw writes a bad play, like *Misalliance*, it is
praised by his special public in precisely the same terms
that have been applied to his good plays, like *Man and
Superman*. No middle class person would dare to say
that a bad play by Mr. Shaw was a bad play; because,
by doing so, he would relinquish his assumption of
superiority over the lower class.

The thing called " fashion " is always a function of
the middle class. A workman wears a flannel shirt when
he wants to; an aristocrat wears a flannel shirt when he
wants to; but a middle class person does not dare appear in public without a linen collar. To assert his
social superiority to the workman he is obliged to confess his social inferiority to the aristocrat. It is the
same in matters of opinion regarding art. A middle

class person prides himself on disagreeing with the lower class when he asserts that *Candida* is more " intellectual," more " literary," more " paradoxical," more heaven-knows-what, than *The Second Mrs. Tanqueray*. Meanwhile, the greater play is valued more highly, not only by the many whom this middle class dissenter prides himself on looking down upon, but also by the few who, without pride and without protest, look down upon him with an unobserved, indulgent smile.

To say that it is fashionable to praise Mr. Shaw is, therefore, only another way of saying that his plays are commonly regarded as exempt from criticism. The middle class assumes that, like a king, Mr. Shaw can do no wrong. The lower class, knowing nothing of kings, still knows that they are not infallible ; the upper class, knowing kings particularly well, also knows that they are not infallible ; no king is a hero to his valet— or his queen : but the middle class plumps itself upon its knees and tries to persuade itself that a king must always be immune from criticism. Mr. Shaw has made himself a king in the imagination of the middle class of theatre-goers. It is the danger of kings that they may come to look upon themselves through the eyes of their admirers,—that they may come to regard themselves with a middle class opinion. It is evident from the prefaces of Mr. Shaw that he has latterly assumed a middle class opinion of himself. This has been bad for his art. In his estimation of his own work, a man should be influenced by the opinion of people who know nothing ; he should also be influenced by the opinion of people who know a great deal : but when he accepts the opinion of people who know a little, but not much, his work must suffer. In such a case, there is a loss to him; but, alas!, there is a greater loss to humanity at large.

Mr. Shaw's *Pygmalion*, for instance, is one of the most delightful entertainments of recent seasons; but it is not a great play. If one were to judge it only by comparison with the majority of comedies that somehow get themselves presented in the theatres of New York, one would have to rank it very high indeed; but it does not rank so very high when it is judged by comparison with Mr. Shaw's best work, or with the best work of his rivals.

What it lacks, primarily, is structure. Each of the five acts presents an incident in dialogue; but, though these incidents succeed each other like the chapters of a novel, they are not bound together tightly like the incidents in *Candida*. A spectator might step in for any single act, and go away again with a sense that he had seen a one-act play.

One of the most amusing characters—the father of the heroine—performs no necessary purpose in the pattern. If he were left out of the cast some evening, the audience would never know the difference; and, on the other hand, he might be introduced with equal pertinence into any other play of Mr. Shaw's.

But Mr. Shaw most disappoints the critical observer when, finding himself face to face with a great dramatic situation, he shrugs his shoulders and refuses to wrestle with it like an artist and a man. His Pygmalion is a professor of phonetics; and his Galatea is a gutter-girl whom the professor has transformed into an acceptable imitation of a Duchess by devoting six months to the task of teaching her the vocal intonations of the aristocracy. But the transformation has struck deeper than Pygmalion had anticipated; and Galatea has developed the glimmerings of a human soul. It happens that whoever calls a human soul into existence, whether inadvertently or by intention, must assume responsibility for that soul's continuance and sustenance. " What are you going to do with me now?," Mr. Shaw's Galatea asks, in effect, of his Pygmalion. The professor of phonetics does not know. Neither does Mr. Shaw. The playwright shuffles, and evades the issue, and rings the curtain down.

In other words, Mr. Shaw ran away from a dramatic opportunity which, if it had fallen to Pinero, would have imposed an extra year of meditation, out of which a great play would probably have emerged. But Mr. Shaw, having been amusing for two hours, was contented to let the matter go at that. He is an entertaining artist, surely; but a great artist?—not at all.

XVI

CRITICISM AND CREATION IN THE DRAMA

BRANDER MATTHEWS, not many years ago, in reviewing a book on *Types of Tragic Drama* by the Professor of English Literature in the University of Leeds, defined it as an essay in " undramatic criticism." The author of that academic volume had persistently regarded the drama as something written to be read, instead of regarding it as something devised to be presented by actors on a stage before an audience. His criticism, therefore, took no account of the conditions precedent to any valid exercise of the art that he was criticising.

The contemporary drama suffers more than that of any other period from the comments of " undramatic critics " who know nothing of the exigencies of the theatre. In the first place, the contemporary drama is more visual in its appeal than the drama of the past, and what it says emphatically to the eye can hardly be recorded adequately on the printed page. In the second place, the rapid evolution of the modern art of stage-direction has made the drama more and more, in recent years, unprintable. And, in the third place, the contemporary drama, with its full and free discussion of

116

topics that are current in the public mind, requires—more than that of any other period—the immediate collaboration of a gathered audience. Such a drama can be judged with fairness only in the theatre, for which it was devised.

The fallacy of " undramatic criticism " of contemporary drama is a fallacy to which professors in our universities are particularly prone. The reason is not far to seek. The prison-house of their profession confines them, for the most part, to little towns and little cities where no actual theatre, that is worthy of the name, exists. Condemned to see nothing of the current theatre, they are driven back to the library, to cull their knowledge of the modern drama from the dubious records of the printed page. Thus, in the enforced and tragic solitude of Leeds or Oklahoma, they are doomed to arrive at the opinion that Bernard Shaw, whose plays are published, must be a greater dramatist than J. M. Barrie, whose best plays have not yet been yanked and carted from the living theatre to find a sort of graveyard in the printed page.

In an interesting and well-written book about *The Modern Drama*, by Professor Ludwig Lewisohn of the Ohio State University, there is a chapter of fifty-three pages devoted to " The Renaissance of the English Drama." In this chapter, the author expresses the opinion that the work of Pinero and Jones is of no account whatever, because, writing drama, they choose to be dramatic, and, writing for the theatre, they choose to be theatrical. He prefers the plays of Galsworthy, Barker, and Shaw, because these plays are less theatrical and less dramatic. With this argument—despite its paradox—it is not at all impossible to sympathize. It is possible, for instance, to remember a sudden entry into the vestibule of the Laurentian Library in Florence, which induced an unexpected singing of the soul in praise of Michelangelo because, although an architect, he had dared for once to do a thing that was not architectural at all. But the reader loses faith in the leading of Professor Lewisohn when the discovery is ultimately made that, in this entire chapter of fifty-three pages, the name of J. M. Barrie has never once been mentioned.

In an equally interesting and still more monumental book on *Aspects of Modern Drama,* by Frank Wadleigh Chandler, Dean of the University of Cincinnati, no less than two hundred and eighty contemporary plays have been minutely analyzed. This book is supplemented by an exhaustive bibliography of the modern drama which covers fifty-six closely printed pages of small type. Yet nowhere, in the text or in the bibliography, is J. M. Barrie mentioned as a modern dramatist. In this scholarly and weighty treatise, the man who imagined *Peter Pan* is utterly ignored.

In another recent volume, called *The Changing Drama,* by Professor Archibald Henderson, of the University of North Carolina, an attempt has been made—according to the preface—" to deal with the contemporary drama, not as a kingdom subdivided between a dozen leading playwrights, but as a great movement, exhibiting the evolutional growth of the human spirit and the enlargement of the domain of esthetics." Yet, in this volume of three hundred and eleven pages, the name of J. M. Barrie never once appears.

Can it be that three scholars so well informed as Professor Lewisohn, Professor Chandler, and Professor Henderson have never heard of J. M. Barrie? It may be that such a masterpiece as *Alice Sit-By-The-Fire*— which has not been published—has never been performed in Columbus, Ohio, Cincinnati, Ohio, or Chapel Hill, North Carolina: but is that any reason why a scholarly professor, condemned to live in the prison-house of one of these localities, should presume to write a comprehensive book about the current drama without so much as mentioning the name of the best-beloved of modern dramatists,—a man, moreover, who is famous in the world of letters and has been made a baronet because of his services, through art, to humankind? These academic commentators should remember that their books may possibly be read by certain people who live in London and New York, and who have never missed a play of Barrie's, because his excellence has long been recognized by all dramatic critics, because every woman knows that he is the wisest of contemporary dramatists, and because every child perceives that he is easily the most enjoyable.

In those books about the modern drama in which the name of Barrie is astoundingly ignored, the name of Bernard Shaw is invariably mentioned with ecstatic praise. Of all contemporary dramatists, Shaw is easily the favorite among the professors of " undramatic criticism." Before we read their books, we may always count upon them to consider *Candida* a greater play than *Iris*, and *You Never Can Tell* a better comedy than *The Liars*, and *Fanny's First Play* a subtler satire than *Alice Sit-By-The-Fire*. What can be the reason for this curious reaction of the " undramatic critics "?

Two answers to this interesting question suggest themselves to an investigating mind. The first answer is comparatively trivial; but it is not, by any means, too silly to demand consideration.

In all these academic books about the modern drama, the ranking of the living British dramatists is proportioned directly in accordance to the pompousness with which their plays have been printed and bound and published to the reading world. This " undramatic criticism " of the current drama appears, upon investigation, to be based on nothing more than the setting-up of type.

When the early plays of Bernard Shaw were unsuccessful in the theatre [at a time when Pinero and Jones were being rewarded by their greatest triumphs] the disappointed dramatist decided to make an untraditional attack upon the reading public. He equipped his plays with elaborately literary stage-directions [the sort of stage-directions which, though interesting to the reader, are of no avail whatever to the actor]; he furnished them with lengthy prefaces, in many instances more interesting than the plays themselves; and he gathered them into volumes that were printed and bound up to look like books. These volumes, impressive in appearance and enlivening in content, were undeniably worth reading. They earned at once the right to be accepted as " literature "; and, among non-theatre-goers, they soon came to be regarded as the best contemporary contributions to " dramatic literature."

Meanwhile—among non-theatre-goers—the bigger and better plays of Jones and of Pinero were not accepted as " dramatic literature," because they happened only to be published in a form that made them look like plays instead of in a form that made them look like books. *The Second Mrs. Tanqueray* and *Mrs. Dane's Defence* were bound in paper covers and sold for twenty-five or fifty cents. The stage-directions were written technically for the actor, instead of being written more elaborately for the reader; and there were no prefaces whatever, to celebrate the greatness of the plays. No wonder, therefore, that the " undramatic critics " of the drama decided that the plays of Pinero and Jones were less important than the plays of Shaw! It was all a matter of the make-up of the printed page!

John Galsworthy and Granville Barker have followed the fashion set by Bernard Shaw, in publishing their plays. Barker's printed stage-directions are little novels in themselves. In consequence, Professor Ludwig Lewisohn considers Barker a greater dramatist than Pinero or Jones. No play of Granville Barker's has ever held the stage, in any city, for three successive weeks; yet Professor Lewisohn decides that *The Madras House* must be a greater play than *The Second Mrs. Tanqueray* [which has held the stage, throughout the English-speaking world, for more than twenty years], because the published text of *The Madras House* looks like a book and the published text of *The Second Mrs. Tanqueray* does not.

Barrie, of course, receives no consideration whatso-ever from the " undramatic critics," because his best plays have never yet been printed. *Peter Pan*, which is acted every Christmas-tide in London before thousands and thousands of delighted spectators, must be dismissed as negligible, for the accidental reason that a printed record of the lines has not been bound between cloth covers and offered to the reading public as a work of literature.

But we must turn attention now to a deeper, and a less facetious, explanation of the reason why the " undramatic critics " prefer the plays of Bernard Shaw to the plays of J. M. Barrie. They prefer the plays of Shaw because, to the academic and the non-theatric mind, these plays are much more easy to appreciate.

Shaw began life as a critic; and, ever since he took to writing plays, he has remained a critic. But Barrie began life as a creative artist; and, ever since he took to writing plays, he has remained a creative artist. Among minds, the ancient maxim holds irrevocably—like to like. It may be safely said that no academic scholar is endowed with a creative mind; for any person so endowed would not permit himself to be an academic scholar. As Bernard Shaw himself has stated, " He who can, does: he who cannot, teaches." From academic scholars, therefore, we cannot logically look for a spontaneous appreciation of creative art: all we can expect is a critical appreciation of criticism.

The basic aims of criticism and creation are, of course, identical. The purpose of all art, whether critical or creative, is to reveal the reality that underlies the jumbled and inconsequential facts of actual experience. Art makes life more intelligible, by refusing to be interested in the accidental and fortuitous, and by focusing attention on the permanent and true. But this common aim of art is approached from two directions, diametrically different, by men whose minds are critical and by men whose minds are creative.

The critic makes life more intelligible by taking the elements of actuality apart; and the creator makes life more intelligible by putting the elements of reality together. In a precisely scientific sense, the work of the creator is constructive and the work of the critic is destructive. The critic analyzes life; the creator synthetizes it.

The difference between these diametric processes may perhaps be made more clear by a concrete scientific illustration. Suppose the truth to be investigated were the composition of the substance known as water. The critic would determine this truth by taking some water and dividing it up into two parts of hydrogen and one of oxygen; but the creator would establish the same truth by taking two parts of hydrogen and one of oxygen and manufacturing some water by putting them together.

That Bernard Shaw is the keenest-minded critic who is writing for the stage to-day, no commentator could be tempted to deny; but he is not a creative artist, in the sense that Barrie—for example—is a creative artist. Shaw takes the elements of life apart; but Barrie puts the elements of life together.

This proposition has been admirably stated by Professor Ludwig Lewisohn, who is one of Shaw's most ardent celebrators. In a notably clear-minded passage, Professor Lewisohn has said:—" This remarkable writer is not, in the stricter sense, a creative artist at all. The sharp contemporaneousness and vividness of his best settings deceives us. His plays are the theatre of the analytic intellect, not the drama of man. They are a criticism of life, not in the sense of Arnold, but in the plain and literal one. His place is with Lucian rather than with Molière."

The same commentator has clearly pointed out that Shaw is incapable of creating characters that may be imagined to live their own lives outside the limits of the plays in which they figure. Instead of launching a living person into the immortal world of the imagination, Shaw writes an analytic essay on his character and sends him forth upon the stage to speak it. In *Pygmalion*, for instance, when the cockney father of the heroine remarks that he is " one of the undeserving poor," we know at once that he is not; for no member of that human confraternity could possibly be capable of such a masterly self-criticism. When the greengrocer in *Getting Married* says, in describing his own wife, " She's a born wife and mother, ma'am: that's why my children ran away from home," we accept the witticism for all that it is worth; but we know, from that moment, that the greengrocer is not a greengrocer, but merely a mouthpiece for an essayist whose initials are G.B.S.

The method of J. M. Barrie is diametrically different, because it is utterly creative. In *What Every Woman*

Knows, the humble but sagacious heroine has reconciled herself to the prospect of permitting her husband
to elope with the more attractive Lady Sybil Lazenby;
but suddenly she says to them, " You had better not
go away till Saturday, for that's the day when the
laundry comes home." In *A Kiss for Cinderella*, the
Policeman sits down to write a love-letter for the first
time in his life; and this is what he writes,—" There
are thirty-four policemen sitting in this room, but I
would rather have you, my dear." These people are
alive. They do not have to tell us anything about
themselves; and the author does not have to tell us
anything about them.

No dramatist who lacks the primal gift of spontaneous and absolute creation—however brilliant be his
talents as a critic—can finally be ranked among the
greatest. For this reason, the plays of Bernard Shaw
will ultimately be regarded as inferior to the plays of
J. M. Barrie, and the best plays of Pinero and of Jones,
and the few good plays of Galsworthy. All these other
dramatists have brought us face to face with many
characters whom we know to be alive; and Bernard
Shaw has not.

In New York, throughout the early months of 1917,
it was possible to see one night an excellent performance of *Getting Married* and to see the next night an
excellent performance of *A Kiss for Cinderella*. Any
open-minded person who afforded himself the luxury of
this experience must have felt inclined to rush home to
his library and throw the learned books of Professor
Lewisohn, Professor Chandler, and Professor Hender-

son out of the window into the star-lit and unrestricted street. It must, in all fairness, be admitted that *Getting Married* shows Shaw very nearly at his worst and that *A Kiss for Cinderella* shows Barrie very nearly at his best; but the contrast, after all, is less a contrast of quality than a contrast of method. Barrie creates life, and Shaw discusses it; and the difference is just as keen as the difference between a woman who gives birth to a child and a woman who merely appears upon the platform and delivers a lecture on the subject of birth-control.

Externally—in what Hamlet would have called " their trappings and their suits "—*Getting Married* is a realistic play that apes the actual, and *A Kiss for Cinderella* is a romantic play that flies with freedom through the realm of fancy. But—considered in their ultimate significance—it is the realistic play that is the more fantastic, and it is the play of fancy that is finally more real than its competitor. We believe *A Kiss for Cinderella*, because we know, as Barrie knows, that nothing in life is true but what has been imagined; and we do not believe the text of *Getting Married*, because we know that people, in a crisis of their lives, are not accustomed to sit down calmly and discuss their motives in a mood of critical intelligence.

Shaw attacks life with his intellect; Barrie caresses life with his emotions. Shaw will always be admired most by scholars and professors and " undramatic critics," who make their living by their intellects and, in consequence, are prejudiced in favor of intelligence. But Barrie will always be admired most by women and children and poets, who feel that the emotions are wiser than the intellect, and who know—without discussion—that the greatest reason for the greatest things is incorporated always in the single, mystic word,—" because . . . "

XVII

A KISS FOR CINDERELLA

I<small>F</small> millions and millions of lilies-of-the-valley were
miraculously turned to silver and simultaneously
shaken, there would arise a light and laughing music in
the world,—a music so delicate that it would be inaudi-
ble to ears that cannot hear. Whole nations [which are
nameless] would not hear it, because their ears are
thunderous with cannon and their mouths are noisy
with a blasphemous appeal for peace. But elsewhere,
where the world is quiet, many lovely things would
happen; and some of them are these:—

First of all, the infant children, too soft as yet to sit
up and take notice of anything but light and sound,
would turn their tiny heads upon their necks and smile
as if in memory of a noble thought, heard somewhere
long ago. Next, the Little People, whose other name
is Fairies, and who live forever in the minds of those
who cannot quite forget, would troop out under leaves
and petals, and join their hands and dance around in
rings. And high, high up beyond the tree-tops, the
ever-circling stars would sing as once they sang upon
the primal morning, ere yet the universe grew old. And
everywhere beneath the circling and the singing of the

stars, the Tall People, whose other name is Poets, would listen and would softly smile and exquisitely weep.

Whenever a Great Work is accomplished by a Great Man, it is as if a million lilies-of-the-valley were shaken to a silver singing; and then it is that tears are called into the eyes of the Tall People, whose other name you know.

"If you have tears," by all means go and shed them as a sort of exquisite libation to the latest masterpiece of Sir James Matthew Barrie, Baronet [for services to humankind]; but, if you have not tears, by all means stay away and make room for the rest of us who want to blow a kiss to Cinderella. It would seem, in solemn justice, that no man should really have a right to make so beautiful a play. The undeniably accomplished fact is too discouraging to all the rest of us, who would like to make good plays, if only our reach did not exceed our grasp. The perfect fact, no less, is discouraging to criticism; for, after seeing *A Kiss for Cinderella*, it seems so very silly to sit down and try to write about it without first borrowing or stealing the little Scotsman's magic pen. It is only an ordinary fountain-pen,—or so it seems; but the little Scotsman has been canny, and has fixed a lock upon it which prohibits it from flowing for anybody else. And that is very much too bad; for it is very difficult, with any other pen, to try to tell the story of *A Kiss for Cinderella.*—

Her name was Miss Thing, and she was a little slavey in a London lodging-house, and her face did not amount to much, but she had very small and very pretty feet. It must have been upon her feet that God had kissed

her, that day when she had come new-born into the
world; and doubtless that was one of God's very busy
days, when He had to hurry on. [Some days, God
grows a little absent-minded, because so many Emperors
and Kings are calling all-too-loudly on His name, and
the Celestial Telephone is kept jangling all day long by
people who have got the wrong number.] That is the
only reason I can think of why Miss Thing wasn't much
to look upon above her ankles. But don't forget her
very small and very pretty feet; for otherwise the story
might not happen.

The room she liked to sweep out more than any other
was a queer place called a studio, which sat high up
beneath the skylight of the London lodging-house; for
here lived Mr. Bodie. Bodie is a rather funny name;
and Mr. Bodie was a rather funny man, for he painted
pictures and told stories, and preferred to live, instead
of working for his living. He lived with a life-sized
plaster cast of the Venus of Melos, which he introduced
to visitors as Mrs. Bodie, in token of the mystic fact
that he was wedded to his art. The fun of sweeping
out his place was this,—that all around the room were
tacked up pictures that had been made, in playful
moments, by other artists [Mr. Bodie would have called
them his *confrères*],—Leonardo, and Gainsborough,
and Reynolds, and the tender-hearted Greuze. Also, in
odd moments, the little slavey could fish forth a tape-
measure from a pocket in her skirt and compare the
compass of her own waist with that of Mrs. Bodie's;
and, if the dimensions seemed discouragingly different,
she could always remember her own feet,—the little feet

that God had kissed. Mrs. Bodie had no feet, to brag about.

It must have been because of her feet that Mr. Bodie first called her Cinderella and told her a very ancient story, of which she seemed to be predestined as the heroine. The little slavey listened, and believed; because a story that is told [by any man who is wedded to his art] is much more real than that other, rather tedious, story which is drifted to us, day by day, on the casual tide of actual experience. Art is more than life; for life is short, but art is long. It was to prove this to all unbelievers that story-telling was invented, long ago, before the world grew old.

Mr. Bodie never knew where the little slavey lived. She had told him merely that the words, " Céleste et Cie.," were printed in large letters on her door. One day he happened to look up this legend. It belonged to a famous shop in Bond Street. Was Miss Thing, in the leisure moments of the night, a glorified dressmaker to the upper classes? He did not know. What were the upper classes to a man who was married to Mrs. Bodie? All he actually knew about the little slavey was that she had a passion for collecting boards.

It was this passion that caused Miss Thing to be observed by an astute policeman. Collecting anything, in war time, is suspicious; and boards—what did she do with the boards? Clearly, she must be a German spy.

And that is why the policeman, one night, trailed the little slavey to a tiny hovel in a dark street, far away from the center of things, and found the words, " Céleste et Cie.," painted on the door. He donned a false beard, of fearsome and wonderful dimensions [for this policeman was a master of disguise], and entered the sorry hovel where the little slavey lived. He found her plying an active business, as tailor, as laundress, as lady-barber, and ever so many other things; for " Céleste " was nothing but a *nom de guerre* for a useful little woman, with a face of no account, who wanted to be serviceable and would do anything for anybody for a penny.

She did not want the pennies for herself. She needed them for something else. And that brings us to the mystery of the collected boards. All round the walls of the little place of business of " Céleste et Cie." were hung great boxes made of boards. What did they contain? The astute policeman desired very much to know, for the sake of the safety of the Empire. Forthwith, there popped up from each box a tiny curly head. These little girls, hung up in boxes on the wall, were orphans of the war. There was Gladys, whose father was serving in the British fleet, and Marie Thérèse, whose father had been killed in France, and Delphine, whose father had been massacred in Belgium; and there was yet another. " What is she?," inquired the astute policeman; and the foster-mother answered, " Swiss." But, when the policeman stuck his hand into the box, his hand was bitten. " Swiss, did you say?," inquired the policeman, for indeed he was very astute. " She was one of those left over," said Miss Thing, " and I had to take her in." This fourth child was, in very truth, only one of those left over. Her name was Gretchen. She had a habit of popping up her head and asking that God *strafe* this or that. But that was only her way. She couldn't help the blood that coursed throughout her tiny veins,—now, could she? Her foster-mother was one of those who understood.

The exceedingly astute policeman went away; for the mysterious collector of boards was evidently not a spy. And then the miracle began. If it were not for the miracle, this narrative would not amount to much; but there is always a miracle in every life, however humble, and that is the reason why stories are told. For a story is nothing more nor less than the testimony of a Tall Person who has seen a miracle to the shorter people who have seen it not.

Miss Thing had said so often to Gladys and Marie Thérèse and Delphine and Gretchen that she herself was Cinderella that she had to promise them at last that the greatest of all balls would take place on a certain evening. The children expected it; and when children expect a miracle . . . oh well, you know. So, after the astute policeman had gone away, Miss Thing went out into the street, and sat upon a little stone beside the door inscribed " Céleste et Cie.," and waited for the Fairy Godmother to come. She waited a long time; and then the miracle occurred, for the Fairy Godmother suddenly appeared to her.

What actually happened—if you care to know—was merely this:—the little slavey sat upon the stone until she was frozen and enfevered, and the policeman found her in the gutter and picked her up, and took her to a public hospital, where she lay in a delirium for days;

and the policeman came to see her, and then, when she
was getting well . . .

But all that really happened was what went on in a
little chamber of Miss Thing's imagination, while her
frozen and enfevered body was lying in the gutter.
Nothing, in anybody's life, is real but what has been
imagined. We are not what we actually are, but what
we dream ourselves to be. " Men who look upon my
outside," said Sir Thomas Browne, " perusing only my
condition and fortunes, do err in my altitude "; and
" he that understands not thus much hath not his introduction or first lesson, and is yet to begin the alphabet
of man."

So the Fairy Godmother really appeared, and the
famous ball took place, even as Miss Thing had promised to the children that it would. It was indeed a
gorgeous ball; and the four little children, in their
nighties, looked down upon it from a box [only, now,
it should be printed Box] above the royal throne.
First there came the King and Queen; and the King
looked like a common laborer who used to collect boards
for the little slavey, and the Queen looked like Mrs.
Maloney (a patron of " Céleste et Cie."), and they both
talked an 'orrid cockney, but they sat in patent rocking-chairs and resembled certain drawings in a book
about a little girl called Alice. Then came a black
person with a mighty axe, who was deferentially referred
to as The Censor, and the Lord Mayor of London, and
a mysterious and very influential person called Lord
Times. And then there came the Prince himself, who
was very handsome and exceedingly astute and easily

inclined to boredom; and his features were those of the policeman, and he spoke as one having authority.

The time arrived to choose a consort for the Prince; and many famous beauties were brought in, to be inspected by him. For this supreme occasion, the walls of Mr. Bodie's diggings were denuded. In they marched,—the Mona Lisa, and the Duchess of Devonshire, and the Lady with the Muff, and the Girl with the Broken Pitcher, and a Spanish dancer by the name of Carmencita. The Prince looked them over, and was bored. It is a princely habit to be bored. But then the pearly curtains parted, and down a wonderful great stairway Cinderella came. Her face was not so much to look upon, for it was only the face of Miss Thing, a slavey in a London lodging-house, and nobody had ever praised her face; but then there were her feet,—the little feet that God had kissed, that day when He was busy and had hurried on.

It was her feet that caught the eye of the Prince and rescued him from boredom; for his face was that of the policeman, and the policeman was exceedingly astute. One little fleeting look at her fabled and incomparable feet, and she was chosen; and then the fun began. A street-organ, mysteriously near though far away, began to play the old, old songs that are heard along the Old Kent Road, which lies [as many people say] on the wrong side of the river; and the children clapped their hands; and the whole court broke into a dance. Then somebody rolled in a push-cart, painted gold; and everybody snatched an ice-cream cone without being asked to pay a penny; and everything happened as it really ought to happen, until a Bishop appeared, looking marvelously like a stuffed bird on Mr. Bodie's mantelpiece, and married Cinderella to the Prince, and then . . . a great bell boomed forth, tolling twelve.

And that was the end of Cinderella's dream,—which was not all a dream, for what we really know is only what we have imagined. That is the message of this play; and if you do not understand it, by all means stay away and make room for the rest of us.

Several weeks elapse; and then we see the little slavey sitting up in bed in a hospital for convalescents. The policeman comes to call upon her every day. He thinks that he is only a policeman; but she knows—she really knows—that he is a Fairy Prince. She has made up her mind that he will make up his mind to ask her to marry him; and she wishes both to hinder him and help him in his laborious proposal. But, when at last he starts in to propose, she cuts him short. She would like to look back upon the luxury of having refused him before finally accepting him; and she makes him promise to ask her a second time if she should happen to refuse him now. He asks; and she refuses,—with that little hint of sniffiness for which a woman's nose was made. There is a pause. Then suddenly, from underneath the sheets, a tiny hand is shot out to grasp a hand more mighty than her own. " Ask me again," she says. . . .

And then we become aware of The Romantical Mind of a Policeman. She has thought of an engagement ring; but he has thought of something else, less usual and more romantical. He produces, from a mass of wrapping-paper, two little things of glass; and he fits them on her feet, and lo! they are slippers, and that is why her name is Cinderella for all time. " It is a kiss," remarks the romantical policeman [who is, in truth, a Fairy Prince]. And that is why the play is called *A Kiss for Cinderella*. Now, this story, when recorded by a pen that has no magic in it, may sound as if it were a little mad; but, in reality it is not mad at all, but very, very real. Such things as this do happen every day, within the minds of the poor and the rejected of this world; and that is why the poor are not so poor, nor the rejected so despised, as we may think them; and that is, perhaps, the meaning of the saying that " the last shall be first,"—because they really are.

Whenever a million lilies-of-the-valley are shaken to a silver singing, there is nothing left to say for the un-silvered voice of criticism. . . . " If you have tears, prepare to shed them now." . . . " And if thou dost not weep at this, at what art thou wont to weep? " . . . " The rest is silence." . . .

XVIII

DRAMATIC TALENT AND THEATRICAL TALENT

I

SIR ARTHUR PINERO, in his lecture on *Robert Louis Stevenson: the Dramatist*, has drawn an interesting distinction between dramatic talent and theatrical talent. "What is dramatic talent?," he inquires. "Is it not the power to project characters, and to cause them to tell an interesting story through the medium of dialogue? This is *dramatic* talent; and dramatic talent, if I may so express it, is the raw material of *theatrical* talent. Dramatic, like poetic, talent is born, not made; if it is to achieve success on the stage it must be developed into theatrical talent by hard study, and generally by long practice. For theatrical talent consists in the power of making your characters, not only tell a story by means of dialogue, but tell it in such skilfully-devised form and order as shall, within the limits of an ordinary theatrical representation, give rise to the greatest possible amount of that peculiar kind of emotional effect, the production of which is the one great function of the theatre."

It is evidently the opinion of Pinero that dramatic talent is of little service in the theatre until it has been transmuted into theatrical talent; and, indeed, the history of the drama records the wreck of many noble reputations on the solid basis of this principle. There is, of course, the case of Stevenson himself. Concerning this, Pinero says, " No one can doubt that he had in him the ingredients of a dramatist," and again, " Dramatic talent Stevenson undoubtedly possessed in abundance "; but then he adds significantly, " And I am convinced that theatrical talent was well within his reach, *if only he had put himself to the pains of evolving it.*" But a greater instance is the case of Robert Browning. Browning was not merely, like so many of his eminent contemporaries, a reminiscent author writing beautiful anachronisms in imitation of the great Elizabethan dramatists. He was born with a really great dramatic talent,—one of the very greatest in the history of English literature. But theatrical talent remained beyond his reach. He tried to write plays for Macready, but these plays were ineffective on the stage; and, after many futile efforts, he retreated from the theatre to the library.

Many men whose native endowment of dramatic talent was less remarkable than Browning's have succeeded in the theatre by the developed efficiency of sheer theatrical talent. There is, of course, the case of Scribe, who was—at least, from the commercial point of view—the most successful dramatist who ever lived. Scribe knew little, and cared less, about life; but he knew much, and cared more, about the theatre: and, in the matter of making an effective play, he could give both cards and spades to Browning.

On the other hand, there are a few instances—a very few—of men who have succeeded in the theatre by the sheer power of innate dramatic talent, without the assistance of hard study and long practice of the traffic of the stage. There is, of course, the case of Gerhart Hauptmann. When Hauptmann wrote *The Weavers*, at the age of thirty, he had not yet progressed beyond the mere possession of the raw material of theatrical talent. This composition—the fourth in the chronological record of his works—was by no means skilfully-devised in form and order; but it is now acknowledged as his masterpiece, because of the overwhelming power of the artless and unimproved dramatic talent which it easily revealed.

It is, perhaps, a greater thing for an architect to dream a noble building than it is for a contractor to erect it. Pinero contends that it is only the finished edifice that counts, and that the architect is as impotent without the contractor as the contractor is impotent without the architect. Dramatic talent—which is born, not made—may be a greater thing than theatrical talent—which is made, not born. Pinero asserts that a great dramatist must be equipped with both. The great dramatist must have, like Hauptmann, " the power to project characters and to cause them to tell an interesting story through the medium of dialogue "; but he must also have, according to Pinero, the practiced power to " give rise to the greatest possible amount of that peculiar kind of emotional effect, the production of which is the one great function of the theatre." The best illustration, in the present period, of the second half of this requirement is, of course, afforded by the finest plays of Pinero himself. Endowed with a dramatic talent of a high order, he has evolved a theatrical talent which—in the opinion of the present writer—is unsurpassed and, thus far, insurpassable.

Looking at them in the light of this distinction, it is still a little difficult to place the plays of Mr. John Galsworthy. There can be no doubt whatever that he possesses dramatic talent in abundance. He is certainly a great writer and probably a great man; and, in turning his attention to the drama, he is not merely— like Robert Louis Stevenson—a man of letters toying with the theatre. He sees many things in life that are dramatic—profoundly and tremendously dramatic— and these things he strives to render in the technical terms that are current in the theatre of to-day. For this task he is endowed with many gifts. For instance, he has a careful sense of form, both in respect to structure and in respect to style; he has a keen sense of characterization; and, best of all, he comes into the theatre, as many less considerable men come into a cathedral,—to watch and—in a lofty sense—to pray.

Mr. Galsworthy, then, is not merely a man of letters playing a new game, of which he does not know, and scorns to learn, the rules. But two questions yet remain to be decided:—first, whether he has yet evolved a theatrical talent which is worthily concomitant with his innate dramatic talent, and, second, whether he will ever do so. The second question, of course, would be superfluous unless the first were answered in the negative. But has Mr. Galsworthy succeeded, thus far, in producing " the greatest possible amount of that peculiar kind of emotional effect, the production of which is the one great function of the theatre "? This is a question which is certain to call forth a divided vote. The present writer—*e pluribus unum*—must still be numbered on the negative side.

No play of Mr. Galsworthy's has ever, until very recently, made money in the theatre. This consideration might seem merely sordid, were it not for the fact that the drama is a democratic art and that it is undeniably the duty of the dramatist to appeal to the many, not the few. On the other hand, Mr. Galsworthy has never written a play which was unworthy of serious attention. His best plays are not so good as *The Second Mrs. Tanqueray*; but his worst plays are not so bad as *A Wife Without a Smile*. Always, in dramatic compositions, Mr. Galsworthy has had something to say; always, he has created living characters; always, he has told an interesting story through the medium of very interesting dialogue.

Why, then, has he failed to capture the great army of the theatre-going public? It is because he is not innately interested in the stage. Mr. Galsworthy is a great man of letters; he is probably a great man; but he is not—thus far, at least—a great man of the theatre. Some of his plays are very effective,—for instance, *The Silver Box*, *Strife*, *Justice*, and *The Pigeon*. Some of them are ineffective,—for instance, *Joy*, *The Eldest Son*, and *The Mob*. Others, like *The Fugitive*, hover tantalizingly between the two extremes. Yet all these plays, in workmanship, are equally painstaking. An ineffective play, like *Joy*, is just as well written, and nearly as well constructed, as an effective play, like *The Silver Box*. The difference, then, is not a difference in craftsmanship, but merely a difference in subject-matter. Pinero, the master-craftsman, can make a great play out of next to nothing, as he did in the instance of *The Thunderbolt*; but Galsworthy can make a great play only when he has happened—as in the case of *Justice*—to hit upon a subject that is so inherently dramatic that it will carry itself without the aid of any notable exercise of theatrical talent.

No one can deny that the best plays of Mr. Galsworthy are very good indeed; but the fact remains that, fine artist as he is, he cares much more about life than he cares about the theatre. This is the very thing that, in the vision of the leading literary critics, is said in praise of him; but, in the vision of the present writer, it is said a little—though only a little—in dispraise. Mr. Galsworthy seems never to have smelt the footlights. He has never been an actor, like Shakespeare and Molière; he has never been a stage-director, like Ibsen; he seems never to have " counted the house," like Lope de Vega and the two great dramatists who bore successively the name of Alexandre Dumas. To actors, to stage-directors, to managers who " count the house," and to dramatic critics, Mr. Galsworthy still appears as a lofty man of letters who has not yet utterly become a fellow-laborer in the greatest of all the democratic institutions of the world.

Nobody denies the innate dramatic talent of Mr. Galsworthy. Some few—including the present commentator—still deny that he has yet developed a theatrical talent that is worthy of his native gift. Two or three reasons for this failing—if it be a failing—are evident, and even obvious. In the first place, Mr. Galsworthy considers life as God would look at it, instead of considering life as the average man would look at it. In this respect, he fulfils the natural function of the novelist—to tell the individual what the public does not know—instead of fulfiling the natural function of the dramatist—to remind the public of what the public has unfalteringly known but seemed to have forgotten. Mr. Galsworthy never appears to sit with his spectators in the theatre. He does not really understand and love his audience. Otherwise, he would feel himself impelled to renounce the Olympian impartiality displayed in such a work as *Strife*, and would descend to the arena, to fight and bleed for the humanly and naturally partisan. But Mr. Galsworthy disdains to care about his public; and, only in a slightly less degree, he disdains to care about his actors. He asks them, every now and then, to refrain from doing things which would be exceedingly effective on the stage; and his only reason is that such things are seldom actually done in life itself. In other words, he rebels against an evolvement of theatrical talent from a native and indubitable dramatic talent. He seems, not infrequently, to smile a god-like smile and say, " This passage may not be theatrical; but, after all, it *is* dramatic. Life is bigger than the theatre; and, as the greatest of all novelists remarked, ' Life, some think, is worthy of the Muse.' "

It is quite evident that Mr. Galsworthy disagrees with the opinion of Pinero that " the one great function of the theatre " is " to produce the greatest possible amount of a certain peculiar kind of emotional effect." Given the subject-matter of *Justice,* for example, a theatrical craftsman like Pinero could easily increase the amount of this emotional effect that is produced. When Mr. Galsworthy wrote this play, he was interested solely in his subject-matter and not at all in the technique of the theatre.   The subject is inherently dramatic, and that is why the play is powerful; but the treatment of the subject is deliberately untheatrical.

Consider, for example, the unprecedented circumstance that the entire story of the play is told in the first act and the fourth, and that the narrative would still remain complete if the second and third acts were utterly omitted.   In the first act we are shown all the motives and told all the circumstances of Falder's crime; he confesses his guilt; and, when he is arrested, his conviction is a foregone conclusion.   The detailed report of his trial which is set before us in the second act is, in consequence, not technically necessary.   Nothing whatsoever is told us in this trial which we did not know before; and the act is therefore empty of surprise.   Furthermore, since the conviction of Falder has been certain from the first, the act is also empty of suspense.

When a self-confessed criminal has been convicted, he is naturally sent to jail; and consequently—from the point of view of craftsmanship alone—Mr. Galsworthy's third act adds nothing to the story. The narrative does not begin to move again until the fourth act, when Falder, having served his sentence, comes back to make his futile and pitiful attempt to begin life over again. For two entire acts—the second and the third—there has been no forward movement of the narrative. Here we have a pattern which Pinero would unquestionably have dismissed as offering an invitation to disaster; yet, curiously enough, these two acts, as Mr. Galsworthy has written them, are the most interesting of the four acts of the play.

The reason is that what we care about in *Justice* is not the story but the theme. The purpose of the author is not so much to interest us in what is done by Falder, nor even in what is done to Falder, as to interest us in a certain social fact. His sole desire is to force us to observe, with due consideration, the way in which that great machine without a soul, called Justice, habitually does its work. He makes us attend the trial because he wants to show us what an ordinary trial is like; and he makes us go to jail with Falder because he wants to show us what an ordinary jail is like.

As a further instance of Mr. Galsworthy's deliberate avoidance of " the greatest possible amount of emotional effect," consider the omission from his last act of what a craftsman like Pinero would certainly have seized upon as a *scène à faire*. Early in this act, before Falder reappears, we are told that the woman whom he loves, and for whom he stole the money, has been driven, by the economic necessity of supporting her children, to

sell herself to her employer during the period of Falder's incarceration. As soon as we receive this information, we foresee a big scene between Ruth and Falder
when Falder shall find out the tragic fact which we
already know. Not only do we expect this scene, but we
desire ardently to see it. Yet, when the moment comes
in which the hero receives this revelation, Mr. Galsworthy at once removes both Ruth and Falder from
the stage and shuts them up together in an adjoining
room; and the big scene which we wished to see takes
place on the other side of a closed door, while matters
much less interesting are discussed before us on the
stage. It is evident that Mr. Galsworthy deliberately
made this choice, in order that we might remain more
attentive to his theme than to the personal reactions of
his hero and his heroine.

It has been said above that Mr. Galsworthy disdains
to care about his actors; and this point may be illustrated from the text of *Justice.* Consider Cokeson, for
example, as an acting part. This character is naturally quaint and humorous; and he says many funny
things, although he does not realize that they are funny.
It is evident that the actor entrusted with this part
could easily call forth many big laughs from the audience if he should play for comedy; yet all these big
laughs would be what Mr. George M. Cohan calls " the
wrong kind of laughs." They would disrupt the mood
of the scene, and would distract attention from Falder
or from Ruth. Hence, for the sake of the general
effect, the actor playing Cokeson is required to sup-
press and kill the laughs which might easily be awakened

by his lines. He is given funny things to say and is obliged to say them as if they were not funny. In consequence, this character, although extremely life-like, is extremely difficult to play. No such task, for instance, is imposed upon the actor by Pinero when he projects a humorous character, like Cayley Drummle, in the very midst of a tragic complication.

The few points which have already been adduced are sufficient to indicate that *Justice* can by no means be accepted as a consummate example of theatrical talent; but it should always be remembered that theatrical efficiency is the one thing that Mr. Galsworthy has made up his mind to get along without. It must be admitted, also, that he gets along without it most surprisingly. So great is his dramatic talent that he seems to achieve more by leaving life alone than he could possibly achieve by arranging life in accordance with a technical pattern, however dexterous theatrically.

It would have been easy, for example, to make the trial-scene in *Justice* more theatrical, by any of a multitude of means. For instance, Falder might have been innocent, and might have been convicted falsely by the piling up of apparently incriminating evidence. Or, if guilty, still the motive of his crime might easily have been made more sympathetic. He might, for instance, have stolen the money to save a dying mother from starvation, instead of to elope with a married woman. Or he might have been persecuted by his employer, or treated unfairly by the prosecuting attorney, or judged unjustly by the judge. One, at least, of these obvious aids to the production of " the greatest possible amount of emotional effect " would have been snatched at by almost any other playwright. Any other playwright, also, would have increased the suspense and the surprise of the trial-scene by cleverly deleting from the antecedent act the complete exposure of the case against the hero.

Again, in the third act, any other playwright would have augmented the " emotional effect " by making the warden a tyrant instead of a man who is obviously trying to be kind. The very purpose of the play is to attack the prison-system; yet Mr. Galsworthy is, if anything, more fair to the warden and the prison doctor than he is to Falder and the other convicts.

The author's theory, of course, is that life itself is so dramatic that it needs no artificial heightening to make it interesting in the theatre. Whether or not this theory shall work in practice depends, as has been said above, upon the subject-matter of the play. In *The Eldest Son*, for instance, the omission of the *scène à faire* from the last act sent the play to failure at a time when Stanley Houghton's discussion of the same theme in *Hindle Wakes* was carried to a great success by a thorough development of the very passage which Mr. Galsworthy had chosen to evade.

But *Justice*, in which the subject-matter is inherently dramatic, is undeniably a great play,—despite the fact, or possibly because of the fact, that the treatment of the subject is deliberately untheatrical. The piece appeals profoundly to the sentiment of social pity; and, since it is absolutely true and overwhelmingly sincere, it seems all the more dramatic because it is meticulously untheatrical.

II

In the epilogue to *Fanny's First Play*, the popular dramatic critic, Mr. Flawner Bannal [whose name shows a significant resemblance to the French phrase, *flâneur banal*] is asked for his opinion of the piece that he has witnessed; and he dodges this direct question in the following bit of dialogue:—

THE COUNT.   What is your opinion of the play?

BANNAL.   Well, who's it by?

THE COUNT.   That is a secret for the present.

BANNAL.   You don't expect me to know what to say about a play when I don't know who the author is, do you?

THE COUNT.   Why not?

BANNAL.   Why not! Why not! Suppose you had to write about a play by Pinero and one by Jones! Would you say exactly the same thing about them?

THE COUNT.   I presume not.

BANNAL.   Then how could you write about them until you knew which was Pinero and which was Jones? . . .

THE COUNT.   But is it a good play, Mr. Bannal? That's a simple question.

BANNAL.   Simple enough when you know. If it's by a good author, it's a good play, naturally. That stands to reason. Who *is* the author? Tell me that; and I'll place the play for you to a hair's breadth.

THE COUNT.   I'm sorry I'm not at liberty to divulge the author's name. The author desires that the play should be judged on its merits.

BANNAL.   But what merits can it have except the author's merits?

This satiric conversation affords the only reasonable explanation of the fact that the plays of Mr. John Galsworthy have been persistently overpraised, both by popular dramatic critics like Mr. Flawner Bannal and by academic annotators who prefer to study the current drama in the library instead of in the theatre. Mr. Galsworthy is a great man: in his own familiar field of literary composition, he is a great artist: *therefore* [according to the syllogism of these commentators], any play by Mr. Galsworthy must be a great play.

In *The Modern Drama*, by Professor Ludwig Lewisohn of the Ohio State University, we encounter the assertion that Mr. Galsworthy, " above all other men now in view, seems called and chosen as the great modern dramatist of the English tongue." Thus—in a single *ex cathedra* statement—a literary artist who has merely turned to the theatre as a secondary medium of expression is regarded as a more important dramaturgic craftsman than the authors of *The Second Mrs. Tanqueray*, and *Michael and His Lost Angel*, and *Alice Sit-By-The-Fire*, and *Candida*, and *The Voysey Inheritance*, and *The Mollusc*, and *Hindle Wakes*, and *Don*. Any play by Mr. Galsworthy must be " a good play," for the overwhelming reason that it has been written by " a good author "; but no such overwhelming preëstablishment of a necessity for praise exists, apparently, in favor of any play by Pinero, Jones, Barrie, Shaw, Barker, Davies, Stanley Houghton, or Rudolf Besier.

The reaction of the scholarly and academic mind of

Professor Ludwig Lewisohn is supplemented, in this instance, by the reactions of most of our popular dramatic critics. Any play by Mr. Galsworthy that is produced within the region of Times Square is called a great play, as a matter of course, for the simple reason that it was written by an author who [like Cæsar's wife] is commonly regarded as superior to criticism. The Flawner Bannals of our daily press, who seldom hesitate to sneer at the lifelong-practised technical accomplishment of Pinero and Jones, and to smile indulgently at the tender and quite irresistible appeal of Barrie, are accustomed to remove their hats and stand in reverence when any play by Mr. Galsworthy is produced. This emotion, of course, must be recorded to their credit, for it is always a laudatory gesture to remove the hat; and the poorest play by Mr. Galsworthy is so much nobler in intention than nine-tenths of all the efforts of our local playwrights that the mood of reverence is unavoidable; but is it, therefore, reasonable to assume, without discussion, that *The Eldest Son* is a bigger play than *Hindle Wakes* or that *The Fugitive* is a greater play than *Iris?* Must an honest recognition of the fact that Mr. Galsworthy is a superior person force us also to assert that he is an impeccable playwright? If this argument should be accepted, the critic would be required to assume that Raphael [by virtue of that fabled " century of sonnets "] must have been a great poet because of his unquestionable talent as a painter.

That Mr. Galsworthy has earned a right to be regarded as one of the dozen leading playwrights now writing in the English language, no commentator would deny. His plays exhibit a distinction which sets them easily apart from the ordinary sort of trash that is produced within the region of Times Square. But it is one thing to elevate an artist to the peerage, and it is quite another thing to exalt him higher than his peers. Before admitting any playwright to the narrow upper circle of superiority, the critic is required to demand,— first, that the dramatist shall always have something to say; second, that he shall always be able to express his theme intelligibly through the medium of the contemporary theatre; third, that his characters shall be true to life without exception; and fourth, that his dialogue shall be written with simplicity and dignity. These requirements are always easily fulfilled by Mr. Galsworthy; but they have also been fulfilled, with equal ease, by Pinero, Jones, Barrie, Shaw, Barker, Davies, Houghton, Besier, and several other living writers of our English-speaking drama.

The quarrel of the present commentator is directed not against the popular opinion which regards the plays of Mr. Galsworthy as compositions to be considered reverently, but against a quite illogical exaggeration of this popular opinion which leads to the assumption that Mr. Galsworthy is a better playwright than any of his peers. In particular, the ire of the present critic is aroused when he encounters the frequently expressed opinion that Mr. Galsworthy is a greater playwright than Pinero,—or, to state the matter more specifically, that the author of *The Fugitive* is an abler dramatist than the author of *Iris*.

Mr. Galsworthy is not a great playwright. He may be a great man, he may be a great novelist, he may be a great writer; but he is not, on these accounts, to be regarded as a great dramatist,—any more than Rossetti, by virtue of his noble poetry, can be regarded as a noble painter. Mr. Galsworthy lacks essentially a feeling for the theatre,—a natural enjoyment of that spontaneous response which may be called forth from a gathered audience. He entered the theatre at a period comparatively late in his career; and he will never learn to love it [and, in consequence, to understand it] so deeply and so intimately as men who were brought up behind the footlights, like Sir Arthur Pinero and Mr. Henry Arthur Jones.

That Olympian impartiality of mind in considering a social thesis,—that God-like lack of special sympathy in regard to any of his characters,—that air of casually saying, " This is true, and it is no concern of mine; but what do you intend to do about it?,"—these traits, which appeal to the philosophic commentator, are repugnant to the ordinary theatre-goer. The average spectator prefers to see a struggle between people whom he is expected to like and people whom he is expected to dislike: he prefers to attend a play, as he attends a ball-game, with a pre-determined spirit to " root " for one team against the other. This elemental human impulse, Mr. Galsworthy has chosen to ignore. His plays are destitute of heroes and of villains. He has a disconcerting way of asking questions which he subsequently says that he himself is quite incapable of answering. Thus, in *The Pigeon*, he has posed a social problem which he asserts to be beyond the scope of resolution. The casual and accidental theatre-goer—for whom our plays are made—is not attracted by these difficulties: he prefers to take sides in a struggle that has sharply been defined and to applaud a protagonist who either wins his fight or " goes down scornful before many spears."

Mr. Galsworthy bears "without abuse the grand old name of gentleman." Among all contemporary writers of the English language, he is easily the most patrician. But the drama is a democratic art, and Mr. Galsworthy—in the theatre—often sacrifices the appeal of one who knows the people and enjoys what they enjoy. Always, there seems to hover over and about his plays an atmosphere that pre-assumes a lack of sympathy between the author and the audience. Mr. Galsworthy does not write for the theatre-going multitude; he writes only for himself and for his tutelary deity; and the multitude—the toiling, tired, laughing, weeping, sweating, sighing crowd—may take his plays or leave them, as they choose. The born playwrights— like Pinero, Jones, or Barrie—are sedulously careful always to avoid any assumption of superiority above the public. Their attitude toward life is not Olympian: they adopt, instead, as their device, the democratic motto,—" Out of many, one."

But the main deficiency of Mr. Galsworthy as a dramatist is his constitutional inability—or else disinclination—to make the most effective use of his materials. Mr. Galsworthy is singularly lacking in theatrical talent. It is conceivable, of course, that Mr.

Galsworthy would deny that "the one great function of the theatre" is "the production of a peculiar kind of emotional effect"; but a solidly-established fact cannot be overturned by a denial. Unless Sir Arthur Pinero is right in this assertion, we must be prepared to insist that there is no such thing as an art of making plays; and if the dramaturgic art does not exist, there can be no such thing as dramatic criticism. If Mr. Galsworthy—because of his non-technical intentions—must be regarded as immune from criticism on the score of craftsmanship, there is nothing to be said about his plays beyond a merely personal expression of a fondness or a lack of fondness for one composition or another.

As a matter of fact, Mr. Galsworthy tries always, in his plays, to "produce *a peculiar kind* of emotional effect"; but he has failed, in nearly every instance, to "give rise to the greatest possible amount" of this effect. He has never written a play—with the possible exception of *Strife*—that might not have been improved by the collaboration of a more accomplished craftsman, like Sir Arthur Pinero or Mr. Henry Arthur Jones. Mr. Galsworthy's besetting fault is a failure in construction. His plays, without exception, have been patterned carefully; but, with only one or two exceptions, they have been patterned ineffectively.

His main trouble is a failure to distinguish between those passages of a dramatic narrative that must necessarily be shown upon the stage and those other passages which may safely be assumed to happen off-stage between the acts. In other words—to quote a famous phrase of Sarcey's—he lacks an instinct for the *scène à faire*. This arraignment of his craftsmanship is aggravated—not alleviated—by the fact that, many times, he seems to dodge deliberately the " big scene " that stands waiting to his hand. The proper business of a playwright is to make a play; and it is not to be regarded as an indication of superiority for an artist to refrain deliberately from the most effective exercise of which his art is capable. Some years ago, a witty commentator said of Mrs. Fiske that she showed a tendency to " over-act her under-acting "; and it might be said of Mr. Galsworthy that he shows a tendency to under-dramatize his dramas.

Consider *The Fugitive*, for instance. This play has been called a masterpiece by many commentators. The story is interesting, the characters are true to life, the dialogue is written with that high regard for truth which is mystically indistinguishable from a high regard for beauty; and yet the play is ineffective, because it is faultily constructed. It is impossible to resist the impression that Mr. Galsworthy would have done far better with this story if he had used it as the basis of a novel instead of as the basis of a play; and the reason for this judgment is that the most significant and most dramatic passages of the entire narrative are those which are assumed to happen off the stage between the acts. The scenes which we are shown are less impressive than those other scenes which we are denied the privilege of witnessing.

If any evidence were needed to attest the immeasurable superiority of Sir Arthur Pinero over Mr.

Galsworthy as a dramaturgic craftsman, it would be sufficient merely to study side by side the text of *The Fugitive* and the text of *Iris*. The themes of these two dramas are very nearly similar. In each play, we are invited to review the gradual degradation of a woman of beautiful tastes and worthy impulses because she lacks sufficient strength to fight successfully against adversity. Clare Dedmond, like Iris Bellamy, is too fine to accept a regimen of life on terms that are unlovely; but neither heroine is fine enough to rise superior to the insidious assaults of poverty. To this extent, the fundamental stories of the two plays are identical; but there is a world of difference between the finished products.

Pinero, in the patterning of *Iris*, has not missed a single *scène à faire*. He seizes and develops all the high points of his story, and removes to the limbo of his off-stage narrative only such passages as are subsidiary to the conduct of his plot. But, in *The Fugitive*, we feel that several passages which are narrated retrospectively are more important than those other scenes in the course of which these off-stage happenings are expounded, so to speak, at second hand. Thus, we wish to see exemplified upon the stage the experience of Clare as a shop-girl in a department store, which is assumed to happen between the second act and the third; and, again, we are made uncomfortably conscious of a hiatus between the penultimate and the final act. We have seen Clare Dedmond drift, penniless and helpless, from the home of the lover who has sheltered her; and next we see her, six months later, at the point of accepting the career of a common prostitute: but we are never told by what means she has managed to keep herself alive throughout this rather lengthy interval.

Each successive crisis in the gradual disintegration of the character of Iris is shown and illustrated on the stage " in such skilfully devised form and order " as to " give rise to the greatest possible amount of . . . emotional effect."   Mr. Galsworthy's conduct of a similar story, in *The Fugitive*, is comparatively faltering and ineffective.   In this instance, Mr. Galsworthy has met a peer, in a fair fight on equal ground—just as he met a peer in Stanley Houghton when he wrote *The Eldest Son;* and, in both cases, he has been quite easily unhorsed by an antagonist who was more greatly gifted with an instinct for the exigencies of the theatre.

XIX

STEVENSON ON THE STAGE

I

THE recent great success of *Treasure Island* at the Punch and Judy Theatre has made many people wonder why so few of the buoyant and bracing tales of R.L.S. have been transferred to the service of the stage, and has attracted the immediate attention of literary students to the entire subject of Stevenson's relations with the theatre.

Stevenson was a man of many moods, and his attitude toward the question of composition for the theatre was subject to frequent oscillations; but the poles of his opinion may be pointed out by comparing two passages in his letters. At one time, he wrote to his father, " The theatre is a gold mine; and on that I must keep my eye! " Years later, he wrote from Vailima to Sir Sidney Colvin, " No, I will not write a play for Irving, nor for the devil. Can you not see that the work of *falsification* which a play demands is of all tasks the most ungrateful? And I have done it a long while—and nothing ever came of it." The first passage was penned in the high tide of his ambition as a playwright, and the second passage was written after this ambition had been quenched by disappointment.

Stevenson wrote four plays in collaboration with William Ernest Henley, and a fifth play in collaboration with Mrs. Stevenson. The last of these, *The Hanging Judge*, which was written at Bournemouth early in 1887, has never been acted, and was never printed, even privately, during the life-time of R.L.S. After her husband's death, Mrs. Stevenson printed a few copies and presented them to his intimate friends. I have seen a copy of this issue in the library of Mr. William Archer; but, in a very hasty reading, I failed to discover any noticeable merit in the play. In 1914, Mr. Edmund Gosse printed privately an edition of *The Hanging Judge* that was limited to thirty copies; but, so far as the general reader is concerned, the piece remains unpublished.

But the four plays which Stevenson produced in partnership with Henley are published in the works of R.L.S.; and all four of them, at one time or another, have been acted on the stage. *Deacon Brodie* was first produced at Pullan's Theatre of Varieties, Bradford, on December 28, 1882. In March, 1883, a performance of the play took place at Her Majesty's Theatre, Aberdeen; and on the afternoon of July 2, 1884, it was introduced to the London public at the Prince's Theatre. *Admiral Guinea* was produced at an afternoon performance at the Avenue Theatre, in London, on November 29, 1897; and *Beau Austin* was produced at the Haymarket Theatre, in London, on November 3, 1890, with Mr. Beerbohm Tree [later Sir Herbert

Tree] in the title part. I can find no record, in my notes, of the first performance of *Macaire;* but this piece, also, has been produced in public. Stevenson, however, never witnessed a performance of any of his plays, and was never even privileged to see a scene of his enacted in rehearsal.

The only one of these four plays which exhibited any indication of vitality in the theatre was the first, and perhaps the poorest, of them all,—*Deacon Brodie.* In 1887 this piece was presented in several cities in America,—the tour opening at Montreal on September 26; but its comparative success must be ascribed less to its own merits as a melodrama than to the very interesting acting of Edward John Henley, the brother of Stevenson's collaborator.

Deacon Brodie, which was elaborated from an early draft made by Stevenson himself, was completed by Stevenson and Henley in 1880, but was subsequently revised and rewritten. *Admiral Guinea, Beau Austin*, and *Macaire* were all composed in 1884 and 1885, during the period of Stevenson's residence at Bournemouth. His health, at that period, was at its very lowest ebb; most of his time was spent perforce in bed; and his main motive in embarking on the collaboration was merely to enliven the intervals of his lingering in the " land of counterpane " by a playful exercise of spirits in the company of a spirited and eager friend. There is ample evidence that Henley took their joint task much more seriously; but neither of the two collaborators had established a professional relation with the theatre.

As Stevenson looked back upon these plays, he clear-sightedly looked down upon them. In July, 1884, he wrote frankly to Sir Sidney Colvin,—" and anyhow the *Deacon* is damn bad "; and in March, 1887, he remonstrated with Henley, in the following terms, for sending copies of their joint plays to their literary friends:— " The reperusal of the *Admiral*, by the way, was a sore blow; eh, God, man, it is a low, black, dirty, blackguard, ragged piece; vomitable in many parts—simply vomitable. . . . *Macaire* is a piece of job-work, hurriedly bockled; might have been worse, might have been better; happy-go-lucky; act-it-or-let-it-rot piece of business. Not a thing, I think, to send in presentations."

II

These dictates of self-criticism—destructive as they are—have been, in the main, accepted by posterity; for, even among ardent Stevensonians, the plays of Stevenson and Henley have found very few apologists. A recent writer, Mr. Francis Watt, in his interesting book entitled *R.L.S.*, has gravely stated [page 249] that " the plays were too good to win a popular success "; but this is an opinion that will be at once distrusted by any habitual frequenter of the theatre. Plays do not fail because they are too good: they fail because they are not good enough in the right way.

The most illuminative criticism—in fact, the only finally authoritative criticism—of the plays of Stevenson and Henley is the opinion of Sir Arthur Pinero, delivered in his lecture to the members of the Philosophical Institution of Edinburgh at the Music Hall in Edinburgh on Tuesday, February 24, 1903. This lecture—entitled *R. L. Stevenson: the Dramatist*—has been printed only privately in England, because Sir Arthur has an ineradicable habit of reserving the limelight for his plays and keeping out of it himself; but it has recently been published in this country, in an edition limited to three hundred and thirty-three copies, by the Dramatic Museum of Columbia University.

Since, however, this thoroughly authoritative paper is still unknown to the generality of readers, it may be profitable to summarize its most important points. The first of these is that "One of the great rules— perhaps the only universal rule—of the drama is that you cannot pour new wine into old skins. . . . The art of the drama is not stationary but progressive. . . . Its conditions are always changing, and . . . every dramatist whose ambition it is to produce live plays is absolutely bound to study carefully, and I may even add respectfully—at any rate not contemptuously— the conditions that hold good for his own age and generation." The second important point is Sir Arthur's statement that "*dramatic* talent" is of service in the theatre only as "the raw material of *theatrical* talent. . . . Dramatic, like poetic, talent is born, not made; if it is to achieve success on the stage, it must be developed into theatrical talent by hard study, and generally by long practice." Almost equally suggestive is Sir Arthur Pinero's distinction between what he calls the "strategy" and the "tactics" of play-making. He defines *strategy* as "the general laying out of a play " and *tactics* as " the art of getting the characters on and off the stage, of conveying information to the audience, and so forth." His fourth important point is that fine speeches, and fine speeches alone, will not carry a drama to success; for Sir Arthur makes a clear distinction between " the absolute beauty of words, such beauty as Ruskin or Pater or Newman might achieve in an eloquent passage," and " the beauty of dramatic fitness to the character and the situation."

III

In the light of these four principles, Sir Arthur Pinero has examined the plays of Stevenson and Henley; and, at each of the four points, he has found the plays defective. Stevenson's work in the drama was anachronistic; and the models that he imitated not only were outworn but also were unworthy. Stevenson never took the trouble to develop into theatrical talent the keen dramatic talent he was born with. He never taught himself the tactics of modern play-making, and did not even appreciate the good points in the strategy of the melodramatists he chose to imitate. And, finally, Stevenson never managed to unlearn the heresy that fine speeches, and fine speeches alone, will carry a drama to success.

Sir Arthur's explanation of Stevenson's fourfold failure as a dramatist is equally acute. He finds that Stevenson failed to take the drama seriously, that he worked at it " in a smiling, sportive, half-contemptuous spirit," that he " played at being a playwright " and " was fundamentally in error in regarding the drama as

a matter of child's play." And, in a very interesting
parallel, Sir Arthur has pointed out the close resemblance between Stevenson's own plays and those typical
examples of Skelt's Juvenile Drama that are celebrated
with such a gusto of memorial eloquence in that delightful essay in *Memories and Portraits* called *A Penny
Plain and Twopence Colored*. "Even to his dying
day," Sir Arthur adds, "he continued to regard the
actual theatre as only an enlarged form of the toy
theatres which had fascinated his childhood . . . he
considered his function as a dramatist very little more
serious than that child's-play with paint-box and paste-
board on which his memory dwelt so fondly."

This criticism of the plays of Stevenson and Henley,
delivered by the finest dramaturgic artist still living in
the world to-day, must be accepted as final; but a word
or two should be appended in explanation of Stevenson's
utter lack of preparation for the serious task of making
plays. Owing mainly to the accident of birth—for
Stevenson was born in a rigorous metropolis that refused to countenance the theatre—and owing also to
the accident of his continuous ill-health, he grew up
without ever going to the theatre; and his earliest impressions of the stage were confined, necessarily, to the
repertory of the toy-theatre that he has celebrated with
enthusiasm in the famous essay that Sir Arthur has
referred to. Stevenson's biographer, Mr. Graham Bal-
four, has stated [Volume I, page 161],—"Although
he had read (and written) plays from his early years,
had reveled in the melodramas of the toy-theatre, and
had acted with the Jenkins and in other private theatri-

cals, I find no reference to his having visited a theatre before December, 1874." At this date, Stevenson was twenty-four years old; and it is not at all surprising that an author who first visited the theatre at the age of twenty-four should show himself deficient as a dramatist when he casually undertook the task of making plays in his early thirties.

In view of these facts, its seems only fair that Henley, more than Stevenson, should be called to account for the manifest anachronism of their plays; for Henley was a magazine-editor, and ought presumably to have kept himself in touch with the fashions of the theatre in his day. But it is possible, of course, that Henley was deterred from theatre-going by his bodily infirmity,—an infirmity much more painful and disastrous than that which kept Stevenson isolated in his bed at Bournemouth. At any rate, the one thing which the two collaborators never understood was the fact that the technique of the theatre had advanced beyond remembrance of the period of those transpontine melodramatists that they so blithely imitated.

IV

What Stevenson needed most of all was a different collaborator,—not a man of letters like Henley, but a man of the theatre like (for instance) Mr. Henry Arthur Jones, whose famous melodrama, *The Silver King*, had already been produced in 1882. He needed a professional assistant, to translate into terms of theatrical talent the keen dramatic talent he was born with. A collaborator of this type has lately been accorded to him, through the enterprise of Mr. Charles Hopkins, the director of the Punch and Judy Theatre. *Treasure Island* has been dramatized by Mr. Jules Eckert Goodman,—a playwright whose sound theatrical talent has been developed to efficiency by hard study and by long practice. Mr. Goodman has so successfully transferred the rapture and the thrill of *Treasure Island* to the stage that the delighted spectator comes away from the performance with a feeling that can only be expressed by quoting Andrew Lang's ejaculation,—" This is the kind of stuff a fellow wants ! "

The magnitude of Mr. Goodman's accomplishment can be appreciated only if we take into account the special difficulties of his task. Nearly all the critics who, from time to time, had been consulted concerning the possibility of making a successful play from *Treasure Island* had reported in the negative ; and, among the many, the present writer is compelled to confess that he agreed with the majority. The special obstacles were three in number :—first, the utter lack of feminine interest in the story, which seemed to make the material dangerous for successful exploitation in the theatre ; second, the apparent necessity of shifting the action rapidly from place to place, and of doing this at least a dozen times without impeding the onrush of the action ; and third, the particular requirement, in the case of a story known and loved by absolutely everybody, of clinging close to the original material and inventing nothing new.

But these three difficulties have been swept away by Mr. Goodman. Despite the tradition of the theatre

that the public cares much more for actresses than
actors, the audience never seems to notice the absence
of any feminine interest in the narrative. Jim's mother
is, of course, the only woman in the story, and she
appears only inconspicuously, for a few moments in the
first act; but the play succeeds so well without a
heroine that a necessary inference is forced that love is
not, by any means, the only subject that can capture
the attention of the theatre-going crowd.

Mr. Goodman has arranged the narrative in ten different chapters of time and nine distinct pigeon-holes
of place; but the changes are so rapidly and easily
effected on the stage of Mr. Hopkins that the spectator
is never released from the enthrallment of the story.
The first act is, by far, the best, and this fact is a little
unfortunate for the play; but the fault is Stevenson's,
not Mr. Goodman's. Stevenson began his story in a
high tide of delighted composition; but, after drying
up in the early paragraphs of the sixteenth chapter,
he never entirely recaptured the zest of the initiation
of his narrative. Mr. Goodman's first act, which is
set, of course, in the Admiral Benbow Inn, is quite as
good as any first act has a right to be; for if the
theatre were often as enthralling as this, no self-
respecting person could ever find an evening off, to sit
at home and read *The Count of Monte Cristo*.

But Mr. Goodman's success is perhaps even more
remarkable in respect to the third difficulty that confronted him. He has made a coherent play without
inventing anything that was not set down for him in
the well-known and well-belovèd novel; and he has not

left out anything that even Andrew Lang would emphatically miss. The great bother about dramatizing books for boys is, of course, that every boy in the audience will at once become a critic and will insist on having the story served to him—in Mr. Kipling's phrase —" just so." When the present writer first attended the performance, a concentrated company of four boys sat in back of him. There was a scene on the deck of the *Hispaniola*, disclosing the well-known apple-barrel " standing broached in the waist." There were indications of impending mutiny, as the ragged members of Flint's old crew muttered darkling in the corners of the stage. Jim entered, strolling down the deck. " Get into the barrel," said one of the boys behind me. " Hurry up and get into the barrel, before they see you: hurry up and hide, or how can you overhear what they are going to say? " This comment convinced the critic that the play was undeniably successful; but it also seemed to point a finger at the greatest difficulty which the dramatist was overcoming.

While glancing at this little point of Mr. Goodman's meticulous exactitude, the writer may perhaps be pardoned for pointing out the fact that, though Stevenson's *Hispaniola* was a schooner, the ship disclosed upon the stage of the Punch and Judy Theatre was not a schooner but a square-rigged vessel. This variation is, however, easily forgivable; for Stevenson himself confessed that the *Hispaniola* ought really to have been a brig, and that the only reason why he made her a schooner was that [in August, 1874] he had cruised for a month in a schooner yacht, and that he had never actually been aboard a square-rigged ship at sea.

v

The success of *Treasure Island* on the stage has called attention to the fact that comparatively few of the tales of R.L.S. have enjoyed a similar transference to the theatre. Mr. T. Russell Sullivan's dramatization of *Dr. Jekyll and Mr. Hyde* has heretofore stood almost alone as an example of what may be done with the Stevenson stories on the stage; and this play derived its public popularity less from the inherent interest of the subject-matter than from the very remarkable acting of the late Richard Mansfield. Mr. Mansfield, who was accustomed to consider very highly his own perform-ance of Beau Brummel and to speak with an entirely becoming pride of his best achievements on the stage, told the present writer, not once but many times, that his performance of Jekyll and Hyde was little more than a matter of theatric mechanism, and expressed surprise at the continued favor of the public for the play. " It's nothing but clap-trap," said Mr. Mans-field, " yet they seem to like it as much as *Richard III*, in which I give a performance that is worth consider-ing." The fact remains, however, that the play died with Mr. Mansfield's death; and that its continuous vitality for many years was due more to him than to Mr. Sullivan or Stevenson.

It may be interesting to record the fact that Steven-son never witnessed Mr. Mansfield's performance in the dual rôle of his hero and his villain. At the first night in New York, in the Madison Square Theatre, on Monday evening, September 12, 1887, Stevenson's wife and mother saw the performance from Mr. Sullivan's box; but, on this occasion, the novelist himself was lying ill in Newport at the house of Mr. and Mrs. Charles Fairchild, and he never subsequently saw the play.

After Stevenson's death, Mr. Otis Skinner appeared in a dramatic version of *Prince Otto*,—made, if I remember rightly, by himself; but the piece was not successful. On April 22, 1917, the Morningside Players produced at the Comedy Theatre in New York an adequate dramatization of *Markheim*, by Zillah K. MacDonald. Mention must also be made of Mr. Granville Barker's dramatization of *The Wrong Box*, entitled *The Morris Dance*, which was disclosed at the Little Theatre in New York in February, 1917. This was a very vapid play; and it went down swiftly to a thoroughly deserved oblivion. I find among my notes no other records of plays made professionally from the tales of Stevenson, with the exception of a few scattered and unimportant one-act versions of various short-stories.

VI

It is a curious fact that the tales of Stevenson were, for the most part, left untouched throughout that period of the eighteen-nineties when there was a popular and insistent demand for dramatized novels,—the period when the indefatigable Mr. E. E. Rose used to dramatize three or four novels a year. The reason for this fact, however, will easily become apparent. It is true enough, as Sir Arthur Pinero has reported, that "dramatic talent Stevenson undoubtedly possessed in abundance." His tales are full of striking situations, in which the actors appear in postures which are vividly impressed forever on the eye of memory. But in two respects his novels, despite their emphasis upon the element of action and their vividness of visual appeal, have been singularly difficult to dramatize. In the first place, Stevenson usually neglected the interest of love and excluded women rigorously from his most exciting situations; and, in the second place, he was accustomed to allow his narratives to wander very freely in both space and time and to depend for his effect on a frequent chance of setting. How, for instance, could one dramatize *The Wrecker*, which keeps the reader traveling over more than half the habitable globe?; and how could one dramatize *Kidnapped*, which leads the reader to a world in which there seem to be no women?

These objections, though they appear to explain the fact that very few playwrights have attempted to transfer the tales of Stevenson to the service of the theatre, afford no reason why they may not be successfully transferred to the service of the new and growing medium of moving-pictures. *Treasure Island*, for example, would make a better moving-picture than a play. It may sanely be conjectured that, if Stevenson were living still [and it is a sad fact to remember that even now he would be only sixty-seven years old], he would probably devote his mind enthusiastically to the new craft of making moving-pictures. In his *Gossip on Romance*, he said,—" The story, if it be a story, should repeat itself in a thousand colored pictures to the eye. . . . There is a vast deal in life . . . where the interest turns . . . not on the passionate slips and hesitations of the conscience, but on the problems of the body and of the practical intelligence, in clean, open-air adventure, the shock of arms or the diplomacy of life. With such material as this it is impossible to build a play, for the serious theatre exists solely on moral grounds, and is a standing proof of the dissemination of the human conscience. But it is possible to build, upon this ground, . . . the most lively, beautiful, and buoyant tales."

The Master of Ballantrae might be made into a good play, though the dramatist would experience considerable difficulty in projecting the last act; but this concluding passage would afford the very best material for the moving-picture craftsman. *Kidnapped*, also, could easily be shown in moving-pictures, but could hardly be compressed into a play. Stevenson, in his stories, wrote mainly for the seeing eye; he was less concerned with character than with action and with setting; he exhibited events, harmoniously set in place and time, and he never disturbed the exhibition by psychological analysis. His literary style is perhaps his greatest glory; but, even if bereft of this, he would remain—to quote him once again—a master of " brute incident." While still alive, he failed in his efforts as a dramatist; but there seems to be no reason now why he should not enjoy a posthumous success as a master of the moving-picture play.

XX

THE PLAYS OF LORD DUNSANY

I

In 1914, a slender volume entitled *Five Plays*, by Lord Dunsany, was published unobtrusively in *The Modern Drama Series*, with an introduction by Mr. Edwin Björkman. Until that time, the name of Lord Dunsany had hardly been heard of in this country, although he had previously published, on the other side of the Atlantic, five volumes of imaginative prose,— *The Gods of Pegana* [1905], *Time and the Gods* [1906], *The Sword of Welleran* [1908], *A Dreamer's Tales* [1910], and *The Book of Wonder* [1912]. Since then, however, four of these five plays, and three other plays which have been written subsequently, have been afforded public presentations in this country; and, in the first week of December, 1916, it was possible to see no less than three of them professionally acted in New York.

This astonishing success in a country where the theatre still remains excessively commercialized is all the more remarkable because the author has never made the slightest effort to attain success in the commercial theatre. His first play, *The Glittering Gate*, was written in 1909 for the Abbey Theatre Players at the request of Mr. William Butler Yeats. His other plays have been written, at convenient intervals, to please no other person than himself. Lord Dunsany has never enjoyed, or suffered, any personal connection with the theatre of his day, either in London or in Dublin or in any other city. He has never asked a manager to produce a play of his. He has never even met the mighty magnates who control the theatre in England and America. Yet all his plays have been acted; and, wherever they have been produced, they have been greeted with golden encomiums from the critics and the public. Without the slightest effort on his own part to exploit his wares, without even any knowledge of the eager interest that he has stirred up in America [for the man is very busy elsewhere in the world], Lord Dunsany, in the first week of December, 1916, was more talked about than any other playwright in commercialized New York. The moral of this simple fact is merely this:—that merit counts, and that it is better for a dramatist to retire to a far place and write a great play than to hang about Times Square and dramatize the views of all the mighty managers concerning " what the public wants." In the theatre, as in life itself, there is always room at the top; and, if a man can write so great a play as *The Gods of the Mountain* or *A Night at an Inn*, he need not even make an effort to secure a hearing. All the ears of the world will yearn instinctively in the direction of his eloquence until it shall burst forth by invitation and fill the theatre with a sound like thunder or the noise of seven seas.

Of this mysterious and mighty warrior, who has

broken into our commercial theatre by assault, without so much as marshaling his forces to win a fight in which so many other men have failed, very little news has come to us except such information as may be gleaned from personal letters to half a dozen correspondents in this country.   Mr. Björkman has summarized the entire career of this admired author in six sentences which may be quoted now:

" Edward John Moreton Drax Plunkett, Lord Dunsany, is the eighteenth member of his family to bear the title which gives him a place in the Irish peerage.   He was born in 1878 and received his education at Eton and Sandhurst. In 1899 he succeeded his father to the title and the family estate in Meath, Ireland.   During the South African war he served at the front with the Coldstream Guards.   He is passionately fond of outdoor life and often spends the whole day in the saddle before sitting down at his desk to write late at night.   His work proves, however, that he is as fond of spiritual as of physical exercise, and that he is an inveterate traveler in those mysterious regions of the partly known or wholly unknown where the imagination alone can guide us."

To this somewhat meager chronicle a few facts may now be added.   At the outbreak of the great war, Lord Dunsany was not sent immediately to the front with the expeditionary forces.   Because of his experience under fire, he was retained in England to help in the gigantic task of training the raw recruits of Kitchener's army.   Meanwhile, he wrote to two or three people in this country that, if he happened to emerge from the war alive, his first act, after peace had been reconquered, would be to visit the United States, for a physical and spiritual renovation.

Lord Dunsany was wounded in the Dublin riots; and, when last heard from in 1916, he was waiting at Londonderry barracks to be released by the medical board and sent to the front in France. He seemed then to suffer from a premonition that he would not survive the war. In a letter to Mrs. Emma Garrett Boyd, a popular lecturer who has done a great deal to propagate the fame of Lord Dunsany in this country, he said:—" If I do not live to come to America, there is none who can tell you more about me nor with better understanding than my wife. I was wounded less than three weeks ago. The bullet has been extracted and I am healing up rapidly. I am also under orders for France as soon as I have recovered. Sometimes I think that no man is taken hence until he has done the work that he is here to do, and looking back on five battles and other escapes from death this theory seems almost plausible; but how can one hold it when one thinks of the deaths of Shelley and Keats?"

This is all that, even now, on this side of the ocean, is positively known of the personal career of a man, still under forty, who has written at least two of the greatest plays of modern times. Lord Dunsany may be killed to-morrow,—" somewhere in France "—a land that all of us would gladly die for; or, after certain months and years, he may appear to us in khaki, smiling, with a weariness about his lips but with a glory in his eyes. In either case, the mere fact does not matter. He is one with Shelley and with Keats. He has done enough already to secure meticulous attention from the extra clerks that have been hired, of necessity in these over-busy years, by the Recording Angel. He has written more than half a dozen plays that have touched his fellow-dramatists to tears and have caused them to rise up like gentlemen and cheer his name; and he may live or die in peace. His work, although unfinished, is complete; his plays may be examined, one by one, in chronological succession; and, after that, some effort may be made to estimate his message and approximate a judgment of his standing in the theatre of the world.

II

The definitive point should be considered at the very outset that all of the dramatic works of Lord Dunsany are one-act plays. The student should not be led astray by the unimportant fact that, in the published text of *The Gods of the Mountain*, the three successive scenes are headed by the captions, " The First Act," " The Second Act," and " The Third Act." Neither should the reader be deceived by the accident that the published text of *King Argimenes and the Unknown Warrior* is divided into two parts which are denominated " The First Act " and " The Second Act."

The purpose of a one-act play is to produce a single dramatic effect with the greatest economy of means that is consistent with the utmost emphasis; and, in all the compositions now before us, this purpose has been carefully maintained. Considered technically, *The Gods of the Mountain* is a one-act play in three successive scenes; and, in production, these scenes should be hurriedly disclosed upon the stage without any intermission. In *King Argimenes* also, the two scenes should be presented without any intermediary lapse of time, since they exhibit two projections of the same idea,— as if the dramatist should say, " Look now upon this picture, and on this ! "

Lord Dunsany is as exclusively an artist in the one-act play as Edgar Allan Poe was an artist in the short-story. The strong point, with both of these technicians, is the intensity with which they are able to focus the imagination on a single definite and little project of the panorama of experience. Each of them is willing to sacrifice in range what he is able to gain in terrible intensity. Poe was not a novelist; and Lord Dunsany has still to prove that he can write successfully a three- or four-act play. Both men can seize a big idea and see it steadily; but this is a very different endeavor from seizing a great handful of experience and trying hard to see it whole.

" THE GLITTERING GATE " [1909]

In *The Glittering Gate,* we are wafted to a Lonely Place, which shows the golden Gate of Heaven in a granite wall of great slabs that overhangs an abyss hung with stars. There are only two actors, Jim and Bill, both burglars, and both lately dead. Jim has been dead several months and has spent this time in opening innumerable beer-bottles which appear, as if by miracle, about him, and which turn out, one after another, to be empty. He has grown accustomed to the grim, sar-

donic Laughter of the Gods and has forgot the world.
Bill joins him, freshly killed, remembering the yearnings
of the life that used to be. Bill has brought along with
him the " nut-cracker " that he had held in his hand at
the moment when he was shot by a householder whose
premises he had invaded. Bill endeavors to drill open
with his " nut-cracker " the golden Gate of Heaven.
Jim—the tired soul—is little interested, until the gold
of the great gate begins to yield like cheese. Then both
of these dead burglars give their minds up to imagining
the glorious immensity of Heaven. Bill's mother will
be there, and also a girl with yellow hair whom Jim
remembers dimly behind a bar at Wimbledon. Slowly
the great gate swings open, " revealing empty night
and stars." Bill, " staggering and gazing into the revealed Nothing, in which far stars go wandering,"
says,—" Stars. Blooming great stars. There *ain't* no
Heaven, Jim." A cruel and violent laughter is heard
off-stage. As it grows louder and more sardonic, Jim
replies,—" That's like them. That's very like them.
Yes, they'd do that! " And, as the curtain falls, the
laughter still howls on.

" KING ARGIMENES AND THE UNKNOWN WARRIOR "
[1911]

King Argimenes and the Unknown Warrior is, perhaps, the least impressive of the plays of Lord Dunsany. King Argimenes has been conquered and enslaved
by King Darniak ; and we meet the hero suffering from
hunger in the slave-fields of his conqueror. In passing,

it may be interesting to note that the picture of hunger here presented was drawn from the author's memory of certain days in South Africa when Lord Dunsany and his soldiers sat hungry on the ground.

King Argimenes, digging in the earth, discovers the buried sword of some Unknown Warrior. The possession of this sword gives him courage to command. He slays, one by one, the six guards of the slave-fields, and arms with their weapons six of his fellow-slaves. Then he storms the armory of King Darniak and overturns the image of the God Illuriel. This play, which appears to be an allegory of the sense of power which is given to a man when he becomes possessed of the symbols of dominion, is effectively theatrical; but the outcome seems less inevitable than that of Lord Dunsany's other plays.

"THE GODS OF THE MOUNTAIN" [1911]

We come now to consider the greatest, if not the most effective, play of Lord Dunsany, *The Gods of the Mountain*. This piece was first produced at the Haymarket Theatre in London. Mr. Austin Strong, who saw and remembered this impressive presentation, was the stage-director of the first important production in America, which was shown behind closed doors by the Amateur Comedy Club of New York City in the fall of 1915. This production in every respect was masterly; and all who saw it will remember the occasion with credit to Mr. Strong and to the many other members of the Amateur Comedy Club who helped him to achieve a great projection of a great play. The subsequent

professional production by Mr. Stuart Walker, of the
Portmanteau Theatre, was inferior to that of the
Amateur Comedy Club, because the spacious grandeur
of the play was inevitably dwarfed by the diminutive
proportions of the Portmanteau stage.   But even a
second-rate production of this masterpece is more impressive than a first-rate production of nearly any
other play by any other modern author.

Three beggars are discovered, seated on the ground
outside a city wall, lamenting that the days are bad for
beggary.   To them appears the super-beggar Agmar,
from another city, accompanied by a faithful servant,
Slag.   Slag asserts that his master is a man of big ideas
and that he has come to captivate the city by his cun-
ning.   Agmar sends a thief into the town to steal green
raiment, and explains to the beggars that they will
enter the city as gods,—the seven gods that are carved
from green stone in the mountains of Marma.   " They
sit all seven of them against the hills.   They sit there
motionless and travelers worship them.   They are of
green jade.   They sit cross-legged with their right
elbows resting on their left hands, the right forefinger
pointing upward.   We will come into the city disguised,
from the direction of Marma, and will claim to be these
gods.   We must be seven as they are.   And when we
sit we must sit cross-legged as they do, with the right
hand uplifted."

When the thief returns, with green garments, the
other beggars wish to put them on over their rags; but
Agmar has a subtler plan.   They must not look like
beggars disguised as gods; they must look like gods

disguised as beggars. He tears the green garments into
strips and makes each beggar don a shred beneath his
rags so that the green shall show through only casually.
Thus arrayed, the beggars enter the city of Kongros,
and sit cross-legged in the Metropolitan Hall, in the
attitude of the gods of the mountain.

Agmar has caused a prophecy to be bruited abroad in
the market-place that the gods who are carven from
green rock in the mountain shall one day arise in
Marma and come to Kongros in the guise of men.
Many citizens now gather in the Metropolitan Hall and
wonder if these seven are indeed the gods of Marma.
Agmar never actually tells them that his men are gods;
but he threatens them with dire penalties if they doubt
revealed divinity. A sacrifice of food and drink is
brought, with due obeisance. The other beggars eat
hungrily; but Agmar refuses food and pours out a
precious bowl of Woldery Wine, as a libation, on the
ground. By this abstention he assures the citizens of
his divinity; and the seven beggars are enthroned as
gods.

But still there are citizens who doubt; and these
doubters send two dromedary men to go to the mountains of Marma and see if the carven gods have actually left their places on the mountain-side. Agmar and
his men are filled with fright when they learn of this
expedition; and they are all the more astounded when
the dromedary men return with the report that Agmar
and his followers must be indeed the gods, since the
ancient idols were no longer to be seen in their moun-
tain-seat at Marma. Then a frightened messenger

appears, falls prostrate at the feet of the seven beggars, and implores them not again to wander in the
evening, as they walked the night before, on the edge
of the desert, terrible in the gloaming, with hands
stretched out and groping, feeling for the city. " Master," cries the messenger to Agmar, " we can bear to
see you in the flesh like men, but when we see rock
walking it is terrible, it is terrible. Rock should not
walk. When children see it they do not understand.
Rock should not walk in the evening."

When this cringing messenger has crept away, Ulf,
the oldest of the beggars, cries aloud, " I have a fear,
an old fear and a boding. We have done ill in the sight
of the seven gods. Beggars we were and beggars we
should have remained. We have given up our calling
and come in sight of our doom. I will no longer let
my fear be silent; it shall run about and cry; it shall
go from me crying, like a dog from out of a doomed
city; for my fear has seen calamity and has known
an evil thing."

Then, off-stage, amid a horror of great silence, is
heard the headlong heavy tramp of stony feet. The
seven gods of Marma, carved of jade, stalk lumbering
upon the stage. The leading Green Thing points a
stony finger at each of the seven beggars, one by one.
" As he does this, each beggar in his turn gathers himself back on to his throne and crosses his legs, his right
arm goes stiffly upward with forefinger erect, and a
staring look of horror comes into his eyes. In this
attitude the beggars sit motionless, while a green light
falls upon their faces."

The gods go out. The citizens return. They find the seven beggars turned to stone. " We have doubted them," they cry. " They have turned to stone because we have doubted them." Then, in a great and growing voice, there comes a chorus, " They were the true gods. They were the true gods." It is thus that big religions are begun. The faithful soul invents the faith it feeds on.

To this simple and straightforward narrative,—so terrible, so beautiful, so true, so absolutely self-sufficient,—many critics have applied the academic adjectives " symbolical " and " allegorical." With criticism of this sort, the author is exceedingly impatient. In a letter to Mrs. Emma Garrett Boyd, Lord Dunsany has said:—" In case I shall not live to explain my work, I think the first thing to tell them [the American people] is that it does not need explanation. One does not need to explain a sunset, nor does one need to explain a work of art.

" Don't let them hunt for allegories. I may have written an allegory at some time, but if I have, it was a quite obvious one, and, as a general rule, I have nothing to do with allegories.

" What is an allegory? A man wants the streets to be swept better in his town or he wants his neighbors to have rather cleaner morals. He can't say so straight out because he might be had up for libel, so he says what he has to say, but he says it about some extinct king in Babylon, but he's thinking of his one-horse town all the time. Now, when I write of Babylon, there are people who cannot see that I write of it *for love of Babylon's ways*, and they think I'm thinking of London still and our beastly Parliament.

"Only I get further east than Babylon, even to kingdoms that seem to me to lie in the twilight beyond the East of the World. I want to write about men and women and the great forces that have been with them from the cradle up—forces that the centuries have neither aged nor weakened—not about people who are so interested in the latest mascot or motor that not enough remains when the trivial is sifted from them. . . .

"Take my *Gods of the Mountain*. Some beggars being hard up pretend to be gods. Then they get all they want. But Destiny, Nemesis, the Gods, punish them by turning them into the very idols that they desired to be.

"First of all there you have a very simple tale told dramatically, and along with that you have bound, without any deliberate attempt of mine—so far as I know—a truth, not true to London only or to New York or to one municipal party, but to the experience of man. That is the kind of way that man does get hit by destiny. But mind you, that is all unconscious though inevitable. I am not trying to teach anybody anything. I merely set out to make a good work of art from a simple theme, and God knows we want works of art in this age of corrugated iron. How many people hold the error that Shakespeare was of the schoolroom! Whereas he was of the playground, as all artists are."

" THE GOLDEN DOOM " [1912]

In *The Golden Doom*, the playful aspiration of a little boy becomes inextricably intertangled with the destiny of a mighty monarch. The piece is set " outside the King's great door in Zericon, some while before the fall of Babylon":—and the reading of this simple stage-direction fills the ear with singing like that which Ibsen's Hilda heard in those inspired moments when she hearkened to the music of harps in the air.

This little boy comes to beg the King of Zericon for a hoop to play with; and, in the absence of the monarch, he addresses his petition to the King's great door,—a sacred door, which it is death to touch. When the sentries are not looking, this unthinking boy scrawls upon the iron door a little doggerel poem that is running in his mind,—using as a pencil a nugget of gold which he has fished up from the river near at hand.

This golden legend on the iron door is subsequently found and regarded as a portent. The King's great prophets are summoned to intrepret it. They read it as a doom from the stars. The King's pride has been too overweening, and he is marked for ruin. Therefore the King, to symbolize the sacrifice of all his pride, lays his crown and scepter humbly before the iron door and goes away bare-headed. The little boy comes back. His prayer to the King's door has apparently been answered. He regards the King's crown as a hoop, and the scepter as a stick to beat it with; and he frisks away, delighted with his toys. When the King returns, his sacrificial offerings have disappeared. " The gods have come," he says. " The stars are satisfied."

" THE LOST SILK HAT " [1913]

The Lost Silk Hat has not as yet been acted in New York; but it has been produced by Mr. B. Iden Payne at the Gaiety Theatre in Manchester and by Mr. Sam Hume at the Arts and Crafts Theatre in Detroit. It is written in a lighter vein than the other plays of Lord Dunsany. Before a house in London, a young gentleman, " faultlessly dressed, but without a hat," is standing, in a most embarrassing predicament. He has just said farewell forever to the young lady in the house; but, in accomplishing his tragic exit, he has left his top-hat in the drawing-room, " half under the long sofa, at the far end." Being a conventional young man, he cannot confront with equanimity the prospect of wandering about the streets of London without a hat.

A laborer, a clerk, a poet, stroll successively along the street. The young gentleman implores each of these in turn to ring the bell and to invent some subterfuge for recovering his hat. The laborer and the clerk regard him as insane and go their ways; but the poet lingers long enough to talk the matter over with him. The upshot of their conversation is that the young man eventually reënters the house, against the protests of the poet, who pleads that it would be much more fittingly romantic for the young man to go away to Africa and die; and that the young man, having been enticed once more within the dangerous precincts by the mere desire to recover his top-hat, nevermore returns from the toils of the young lady, to whom, once, in a dramatic moment, he had said farewell forever.

"THE TENTS OF THE ARABS" [1915]

The Tents of the Arabs was printed in the *Smart Set* for March, 1915, and was acted for the first time on any stage at the Arts and Crafts Theatre in Detroit, Michigan, on November 16, 1916, under the direction of Mr. Sam Hume.

The Tents of the Arabs is perhaps the least theatrical of Lord Dunsany's plays, but it is also the most lyrical in mood. It tells a very simple story of a camel-driver who wanted to be a king and a king who wanted to be a camel-driver, and how, because they had the luck to look sufficiently alike, they managed to change places in the world, so that each of them could be happy in the life of which the other had grown weary. There is no other mood more lyrical than that of longing—as Edgar Allan Poe pointed out in one of his acutest passages of philosophic criticism; and the longing of this fabled king who is weary of cities and desires evermore to wander over the illimitable desert is expressed by Lord Dunsany with incomparable eloquence. Thus, for instance, speaks the king: " O Thalanna, Thalanna, how I hate this city with its narrow, narrow ways, and evening after evening drunken men playing skabash in the scandalous gambling house of that old scoundrel Skarmi. O that I might marry the child of some un-kingly house that generation to generation had never known a city, and that we might ride from here down the long track through the desert, always we two alone, till we came to the tents of the Arabs. And the crown— some foolish, greedy man should be given it to his sorrow. And all this may not be, for a King is yet a King."

"A NIGHT AT AN INN" [1916]

On the night of April 22, 1916, three hundred people were gathered at the Neighborhood Playhouse, at 466 Grand Street, New York City, to attend the first performance on any stage anywhere in the world of a new and theretofore unpublished play by Lord Dunsany, entitled *A Night at an Inn*. The audience which crowded the Neighborhood Playhouse on this particular evening included less than half a dozen of those who, by professional connection, might have been expected to respond to the privilege of the occasion. Yet, when this great play by a great man was presented by the local company of Grand Street, it reached out and grabbed the casual auditors by the throat, and shook them, and thrilled them, and reduced them to a mood of inarticulate laudation.

To those of us who were present on that memorable evening, it appeared that *A Night at an Inn* was the most effective one-act play that we had ever seen. In the colder light of after-thinking, there seems to be no need to revise this judgment, except so far as to admit a reasonable rivalry on the part of *The Gods of the Mountain*, by the same author, and *Riders to the Sea*, by the dead but deathless poet, John M. Synge. One of these three is, assuredly, the greatest one-act play in the world; and the present writer will not quarrel with the choice of any critic for a verdict of uttermost supremacy among these three.

To tell in detail the story of *A Night at an Inn* would seem like the betrayal of a trust.   Basically, this one-act play is nothing more than a melodrama of the " shilling-shocker " sort; but it is so irradiated with imagination that the terrible theatric thrill of the immediate performance is survived by a memory that serenely satisfies the soul.   The theme of *A Night at an Inn* is identical with that of *The Gods of the Mountain;* but the later play is more terribly immediate in the medium of its appeal.   Though a romantic work, it has a realistic setting; and the imaginative horror of the narrative is brought so close to the audience that the action is accompanied by audible gasps and groans and a nervous gripping of the arms of all the chairs. To write a more effective play than this would seem, in fact, to be impossible.   *A Night at an Inn*, indeed, might be accepted without discussion as an answer to the academic questions, " What is a play? " and " What is, after all, dramatic? "

" THE QUEEN'S ENEMIES " [1916]

The Queen's Enemies was first produced at the Neighborhood Playhouse, in New York, on November 14, 1916.   It shows the author only at his second best; but the second best of such a man is better than the very best of most of our contemporary dramatists.

The story is a little reminiscent of *The Cask of Amontillado*, by Edgar Allan Poe,—an author whom Dunsany much resembles. A little Queen of ancient Egypt is annoyed by the fact that she has so many enemies. Therefore she invites them all to a banquet in an underground temple that is sacred to the Nile. They come—these mighty warriors—armed to the teeth, and accompanied by their retainers. The little Queen of Egypt is unarmed, and is accompanied only by a weakling female slave. She invites her guests to eat, to drink, and to be merry. The hostile warriors suspect the food, and feed it first to their subjacent slaves. They suspect the wine as well, and sedulously watch its effect upon their underlings. But the little Queen disarms their fear of being poisoned by partaking eagerly and freely of the proffered food and drink. The banquet begins to be successful. Light talk flows merrily around the board. Meanwhile, the Queen of Egypt and her attendant female slave edge their way gradually toward the only door. They make this door, dash through it, slam and bar it. Then the little, helpless Queen prays to the great god of the Nile. The river rises, and pours through a grating in the wall of the underground temple. In utter darkness, we hear the gurgles and gasps that mark the drowning of the incarcerated enemies of the little Queen. Then a sudden torch appears upon the outer stairs. The Queen ascends serenely to the upper air. She has no enemies any more; and she will sleep in peace.

III

That these eight one-act plays of Lord Dunsany are great works, no reader or observer will readily deny. There remains only for the critic the cold task of pointing out the various influences that have contributed, more or less, to their creation. Lord Dunsany is one of the most original dramatists of modern times. In an age of realism, he has dared to blow a brazen trumpet in celebration of the ceaseless triumph of romance. In a period when the majority of minds have worked inductively, he has dared to think deductively. He has invented facts to illustrate a central truth, instead of imitating actuality in a faint and far-off effort to suggest the underlying essence of reality. He has imagined and realized a world " some while before the fall of Babylon " which is more meaningful in utter truth than the little world that is revealed to the observer of a Harlem flat or of a hired room in Houston Street at the present hour.

But no artist, however original, is entirely devoid of predecessors. Lord Dunsany has derived his inspiration from Sophocles, from Maeterlinck, from the English Bible, and from John M. Synge. From Sophocles he takes the theme that forever tantalizes and invites his genius. This theme is the inevitable overcoming of the sin of pride, or *hubris*, by the primal power of *ananke*, or necessity. Like the ancient Greeks, Dunsany loves to show the tragic failing of a hero who has set his wits against the power of the God that rules the gods. In his greatest plays, he projects upon the stage a conflict between a super-man and a sort of idealized abstraction that may conveniently be called a super-god. In this conflict, the eternal law inevitably conquers the temporal rebellion. In this reading of the evermore recurrent riddle of destiny, Lord Dunsany agrees with Æschylus, with Sophocles, and with Euripides. Though never Greek in subject-matter, he is nearly always Greek in theme; and, in the spirit of his plays, Lord Dunsany has reminded us, more than any other modern writer, of the sheer augustness of the tragic drama of the Greeks.

In method, however, the plays of Lord Dunsany are related clearly to the early plays of Maurice Maeterlinck. Like Maeterlinck, Dunsany has the faculty of saying one thing and meaning many others. In this sense—and this alone—his writings are " symbolical." Before studying his collected plays, it would be well to re-read the famous letter concerning *The Divine Comedy* which Dante addressed to Can Grande della Scala. Most of what Dunsany writes must be read in three or four ways; and this is also true of the earlier works of the poet laureate of Belgium.

But the prose style of Lord Dunsany was derived from a source no less familiar than the Jacobean translation of the Bible. Mr. Björkman has reported him as saying, " For years no style seemed to me natural but that of the Bible; and I feared I would never become a writer when I saw that other people did not use it."

The indebtedness of Lord Dunsany to the prose style of the English translation of the Psalms of David may be indicated by the following quotation from *The Golden Doom:*—" Because if a doom from the stars fall suddenly upon a king it swallows up his people and all things round about him, and his palace walls and the walls of his city and citadel, and the apes come in from the woods and the large beasts from the desert, so that you would not say that a king had been there at all."

And sometimes, in sentences such as the foregoing, we hear a haunting echo of the voice of another Irish dramatist, untimely silenced,—the ever memorable poet, John M. Synge. Synge was richer than Dunsany in amplitude of outlook and variety of mood. But, like his only immediate successor in the theatre of the world, he saw life steadily more easily than he could see it whole. Lord Dunsany would cheerfully have died to write a masterpiece like *Riders to the Sea;* and Synge, who now is dead, would cheerfully have flung his hat into the air in recognition of such a masterpiece as *A Night at an Inn.* Both these men were natives of " John Bull's Other Island." The world of art owes much—oh, very, very much!—to this neglected outpost of European culture.

XXI

THE MOOD OF MAETERLINCK

In the *Blue Bird* of Maurice Maeterlinck, the little
boy who is the hero discovers the secret of seeing the
souls of things, and wanders through the present, past,
and future, seeing all things not as they actually seem
to unillumined eyes but as they really are in their
essential nature. This is the secret of M. Maeterlinck
as a poet: he too, like Tyltyl, sees the souls of things.
He removes veil after veil of the enveloping actual, to
reveal at last the palpitant and vivid real.

When Robert Louis Stevenson was a very little boy,
he drew a picture and showed it to his mother.
"Mamma," said he, "I have drawed a man. Shall I
draw his soul now?" This aspiration is fulfilled by
M. Maeterlinck. He knows that nothing really matters
in a man except his soul; and, in consequence, his characters are not people, but the souls of people. He
knows that life, which—in the phrase of Shelley—is
like a dome of many-colored glass, is merely a medium
through which the human spirit catches glimpses now
and then of the white radiance of eternity; and it is
only with these glimpses that his fables are concerned.
Reality is all he cares about; and he knows that actuality is merely an investiture which hides it from the

eyes of those who cannot see. To enter the sanctuary of his mind is to withdraw from the sound and fury of the actual world into a vasty silence that seems evermore eloquent with echoes; it is to ascend to an absolute awareness of the identity of truth and beauty; it is to be reminded of all the beauty we have ever known and all the truth we seemed to have forgotten; it is to bathe in Dante's Eunoè,—the river of remembrance; it is to attain that mood in which happiness and sadness are as one,—the mood of Botticelli's *Primavera*, whereon whoever looks must smile through tears.

In this mood, emotions think and thoughts are feelings, and the mind is conscious of an utter clarity. This clarity is mirrored in the style of M. Maeterlinck. His speech seems less like speech than like a sentient and tingling silence. It is so simple that the ear feels tender toward it. His sayings are like little birds that flutter home to fold their wings within our hearts.

To interpret the plays of M. Maeterlinck upon the stage requires an art that is kindred to his own,—an art that is true and beautiful and clear and simple,—an art that can dispense with the actual and concern itself solely with the real. Such an art was displayed by the Washington Square Players in their recent production of *Aglavaine and Sélysette*.

Aglavaine and Sélysette is the wisest and the loveliest of all the early plays of M. Maeterlinck,—the plays, that is to say, which preceded *Monna Vanna*. It expresses supremely the quintessence of an experience which occurs so frequently in actuality that it has been made the subject of innumerable plays by innumerable dramatists. One man loves two women, and is loved by both of them; furthermore, these women love each other: yet, though each of the three parties to this triangular relation is exalted by a holy and high affection for the other two, the situation is intolerable. Why should it be? . . . No poet yet has found the answer. As Aglavaine says to Sélysette, at the crisis of the play, " All three of us are making a sacrifice to something which has not even a name, and which nevertheless is much more strong than we are. . . . But is it not strange, Sélysette? I love you, I love Méléandre, Méléandre loves me, he loves you also, you love us both, and nevertheless we could not live happily, because the hour has not yet come when human beings can live in such a union." The hour has not yet come. . . . There are possibilities of spiritual intercourse so beautiful that the adventurous imagination knows they must be really true. " Such harmony is in immortal souls; but whilst this muddy vesture of decay doth grossly close it in, we cannot hear it."

Realism, which plays the sedulous ape to actuality, can merely imitate the trappings and the suits of an experience; but romance, which thrusts aside externals and plucks out the heart of a mystery, can communicate the wonder and the sting. Many realistic dramatists have told us all about this tragic triangle; but they have not told us what the tragedy was all about. They have told us everything except—everything. The advantage of the method of M. Maeterlinck is that he shows us not so much the experience itself as the essence of the experience. We are asked to assume that

Sélysette has the soul of a child and that Aglavaine is
experienced and wise. It is because they are so different that Méléandre loves them both; and it is for this
reason also that they love each other. Sélysette longs
to grow up and to learn; and Aglavaine desires to
mother her and teach her. Méléandre, hovering between the two, seeks eagerly to learn from Aglavaine
the wisdom that he may in turn bestow on Sélysette.
Yet all of this is told abstractly, as if this tremulous
and thrilling equipoise were a thing too delicate to be
expressed in the noisy terms of actuality. If a writer
were to describe the Venus of Melos as a naked woman
with no arms, he would express an apprehension of the
facts but would inhibit an imagination of the truth.

There is scarcely any narrative in *Aglavaine and
Sélysette;* and the five acts are almost totally devoid
of action, in the usual theatric sense. What is shown
is a delicately graded sense of the successive states of
the three souls that are involved in the experience.
When it has become completely evident that the situation
is intolerable, Aglavaine decides to go away. But the
tender little Sélysette forestalls her. She casts herself
from a tall tower; and, with her dying breath, she
piteously begs both Aglavaine and Méléandre to believe
that her sacrifice was merely an unpremeditated accident.

The Washington Square Players have done many
fine things; but their production of *Aglavaine and
Sélysette* is by far the finest thing that they have done.
Any touch of actuality in the production would have
marred the mood of essential reality in which the text

had been conceived. Reality is abstract; and the illusion of reality can be suggested only by means that are illusory. The various backgrounds for the successive scenes were suggested, therefore, by different arrangements of gray-green curtains, hanging tall, and played upon by lights that differed in intensity and quality. No built and painted scenery was employed, except in the single setting at the top of the tower, when Sélysette was disclosed leaning from a lofty window with her long scarf blowing largely in the wind. There was one particularly lovely scene, imagined in the castle park, in which the interlacing tracery of trees was vividly suggested by an interplay of mottled lights and shadows on the tall folds of the gray-green curtains. This successful experiment in imaginative scenic setting must be recorded as one of the finest achievements of its kind that has ever been exhibited in any theatre of New York.

XXII

EURIPIDES IN NEW YORK

Two thousand three hundred and thirty years ago, the citizens of Athens, to the number of twenty thousand, assembled in the Theatre of Dionysus on the southern slope of the Acropolis, to witness the first performance of *The Trojan Women* of Euripides. On the twenty-ninth of May, 1915, seven thousand representative citizens of New York assembled in the beautiful new stadium designed by Mr. Arnold W. Brunner and presented to the city by the munificence of Mr. Adolph Lewisohn, to witness a performance of the same tragedy, rendered eloquently into English verse by Professor Gilbert Murray. The play had not grown ancient in this interval. It appeared not as a dead thing, of interest only to archeologists who delve amid the graves of long-departed glories, but as a live thing, speaking to the men and women of this modern world with a voice as living as the voice of God. Hundreds who had come to the dedication of the stadium merely because it marked a civic celebration of unusual significance, hundreds also who, knowing nothing of Euripides, had been attracted to this performance merely by a wide-eyed curiosity, were touched with pathos at the parting between Andromache and Astyanax and sat weeping through the ultimate lament of Hecuba over the dead body of the little murdered boy. The effect of these scenes on the assembled multitude sustained the verdict of the great dramatic critic, Aristotle, who called Euripides " the most tragic of the poets." But a deeper thrill than this response of recognition to the grandest tragic art that the world has ever known swept through and through the seven thousand citizens who sat in serried ranks, tier above tier, in the wide curve of the stadium; for a poet, dead for more than twenty centuries, seemed to be speaking with peculiar pertinence of the crisis which confronts the world to-day. The name, Ilion, went ringing through his verses; but, as it echoed round the stadium, it seemed mystically to transmute itself into a kindred name, Louvain. This tragedy was written in a great crisis of human history. We stand to-day, once more, at such a crisis. Euripides is not only the most heartrending of all tragic writers; he is also one of the few authentic poets who have looked into the very mind of God and spoken to mankind with the ecstatic gift of prophecy. In *The Trojan Women*, he prophesied, two thousand three hundred and thirty years ago, the doom of military prowess in the ancient world; and now, with voice undimmed by all the intervening centuries, he is risen from the dead to prophesy the doom of military prowess in the world to-day.

To appreciate the peculiar timeliness of this immortal tragedy, we must inquire into the circumstances under which it was composed. During his dreamful and ambitious youth, Euripides had watched his well-belovèd Athens ascend to the highest pinnacle of culture that humanity has ever reached. Then, "drunk with sight of power," she deliberately resolved to embark upon the savage enterprise of conquering the world and imposing her own culture on unwilling peoples by force of arms. To this project the poet was opposed. He had served in the army for forty years, from the age of twenty to the age of sixty; he had fought for liberty, equality, fraternity, in hundreds of stirring combats, hand to hand; and, with all this vast experience behind him, he realized the vanity of war and longed at last for universal peace. But Athens was less wise; and, in his sixties, Euripides was doomed to witness the gradual giving-over of his city to a party hot for war and eager for dominion of the world.

In the year 416 B.C., the war-lords of Athens committed a great crime, the like of which was not repeated by any nation calling itself civilized until the year 1914 A.D. There was, in the Ægean Sea, a little island named Melos, which had steadfastly maintained neutrality through all the recent civil wars which had convulsed the mainland. Its inhabitants desired merely to be left alone; they imagined no military projects, and were contented to exist in peace on the products of their agriculture. But in this ill-omened year, the war-party that had seized control of Athens decided to annex this peaceful island. The Athenian envoys explained to the Melian senate that it suited their purpose that Melos should become subject to their empire. They announced their ultimatum in these words:—"We will not pretend —being sensible men and talking to sensible men—that the Melians have done us any wrong or that we have any lawful claim to Melos; but we do not wish any islands to remain independent—it is a bad example to the others. The power of Athens is practically irresistible: Melos is free to submit or be destroyed." This passage—strangely enough—has not been quoted from any recent speech of Chancellor von Bethmann-Hollweg; it has been quoted from the Greek historian, Thucydides, through the medium of Professor Murray. The Melians replied that right was right and wrong was wrong; and that, rather than accept the principle that might was right, they would prefer " to go down scornful before many spears." Once more, perhaps, the reader may need to be reminded that this answer is paraphrased from Thucydides, and not from Albert, king of the Belgians.

The Athenians crashed in, and had their way. They massacred the males of Melos, and sold the women and children into slavery. Then, elated with this easy victory, they prepared a gigantic naval expedition to subjugate a great, free people overseas,—the citizens of Sicily. It was precisely at this moment that Euripides, after several months of brooding, composed *The Trojan Women.* He was, at that time, sixty-nine years old. With an entire life-time of patriotic toil behind him, he perceived clearly that Athens had rashly started on the downward path; and he summoned all his powers to warn his well-belovèd city of the doom foretold to men who had unthinkingly assumed the burden of a crime so heavy as the crime of Melos. He chose for the subject of his tragedy the legendary fall of Troy,—a story which for centuries had been repeated as the greatest glory of the arms of Greece; but he told this old, heroic story in an utterly unprecedented way. Instead of lauding Menelaus and Agamemnon for the consummation of their ten-years' campaign for conquest, he summed up the tangible results of this campaign from the unexpected point of view of the women of Troy—because the burden of any offensive war falls heaviest upon the women of the vanquished. The fall of Ilion—which, for a thousand years before Euripides, had been trumpeted by poets as a theme for celebration —was seen by this clear-visioned prophet—with the imminent example of weak Melos burning in his eyes— to be, instead, a theme for lamentation and for grim foreboding of a Nemesis to be.

For this prophetic poet had perceived that, in his own day, his own Athens had surrendered to the sin of Pride—a sin with which the gods made men insane before destroying them; and, in this poignant tragedy, he sought to show his fellow-citizens that the glamor of military conquest is nothing but a sham, and that, whenever a mighty wrong succeeds in trampling down a worthy right, the only real glory is the glory of the glimmering of truth for those who suffer nobly for the right, and die in misery with souls still undestroyed. Before twenty thousand citizens of Athens, this veteran of many wars was bold enough to champion the cause of stricken Melos, and to cry aloud,—in words that may be quoted from a kindred poet,—" That way madness lies ! "

We know now that Athens failed to heed this prophet of the living God. Euripides was doomed to exile, and sent forth, in the winter of his years, to break bread with the barbarians of Macedonia, and, alone among their mountains, to write the *Bacchæ* and to die. Meanwhile, the expedition against Sicily set sail—and its sailing marked the doom of Athens. The Nemesis that lies in wait to punish those overweening mortals who surrender to the sin of Pride—the Greek word for which is *hubris*—overwhelmed, precisely as the poet had predicted, the greatest city of the ancient world. When Athens fell, the highest and noblest achievements of mankind fell crashing with her to oblivion. " Then I, and you, and all of us fell down,"—exactly as this prophet had foretold: and more than twenty centuries were destined to elapse before another nation dared to recommit the crime of Melos and to affront the anger of the gods.

Among the Greeks there was a fable that history would move in cycles and would repeat itself precisely in every thousand years. This fable was in the minds of many hundred citizens when, under the gray sky of the twenty-ninth of May, such words as these rang out from the voice of great Euripides:—

> " How are ye blind,
> Ye treaders down of cities, ye that cast
> Temples to desolation, and lay waste
> Tombs, the untrodden sanctuaries where lie
> The ancient dead; yourselves so soon to die! "

and again,

> " Would ye be wise, ye Cities, fly from war!
> Yet if war come, there is a crown in death
> For her that striveth well and perisheth
> Unstained: to die in evil were the stain! "

More than twenty centuries after Euripides was buried, there was dug up in the little isle of Melos an armless statue of the goddess Aphrodite which has become to millions of men and women of this modern age a living symbol of " the glory that was Greece,"—the glory that was sacrificed when Athens set her culture at the service of efficient barbarism.   Millions of people who are unaware that the fall of Athens must be dated from that rash moment when this city of all cities decided to violate the neutrality of a little island in the blue Ægean Sea, have bowed their heads in mere humility before that absolute expression of pure beauty— that utter culmination of all dreams of earth—which was rescued from this little island in some succeeding century.   Even the Parthenon is now a shattered ruin, standing lonely on a sun-parched hill, to remind us wistfully of all that Athens used to be; but the armless, radiant wonder in the Louvre speaks more eloquently still of the vision of a man of Melos, whose island was made desolate before his birth by the armies of some utterly unnoted war-lord who rashly sought to trample down the world, and only accomplished for his country an everlasting shame.

The many thousand people of New York who witnessed this revival of *The Trojan Women* were all a-thrill with recent memories of Louvain and Malines, of Rheims and Ypres,—and of the *Lusitania*.   This fact afforded a double meaning to the lines, which was analogous to that other double meaning which must have swept through the minds of the twenty thousand citizens of Athens who first listened to this tragic drama

two thousand three hundred and thirty years ago.
The brooding skies seemed rent with prophecy; and,
out of a vast silence, there seemed to come a voice,
ancient of days and hoary with omniscience, that cried
aloud, "Vengeance is mine, saith the Lord: I will
repay!"

The translation of Professor Gilbert Murray is beyond all praise. There is, in the German language, a
fitting symbol for this sort of work, which is incorporated in the word *Nachsingen*. Professor Murray
does not merely repeat the meaning of Euripides: in a
very literal sense, he " sings after " the great poet of
the Greeks. He writes almost as well as Swinburne;
and yet his writing is, at all points, faithful to his text.
Consider, for example, such a passage as the following,
in which Andromache, in *The Trojan Women*, is saying
farewell to her little martyred boy:—

> " Thou little thing
> That curlest in my arms, what sweet scents cling
> All round thy neck! Belovèd; can it be
> All nothing, that this bosom cradled thee
> And fostered; all the weary nights, wherethrough
> I watched upon thy sickness, till I grew
> Wasted with watching? Kiss me. This one time;
> Not ever again. Put up thine arms, and climb
> About my neck: now, kiss me, lips to lips." . . .

In staging this tremendous play, Mr. Granville
Barker ascended, at nearly every point, to the height
of his great argument. His method of production revealed a tactful compromise between the expectation

of the average modern audience and the expectation of the archeologist. He discarded the mask and the cothurnus; but he retained the formal evolutions of the chorus in the orchestra and the superior position of the three actors on the elevated stage. The stage itself —which was transportable from stadium to stadium— revealed a lofty wall, transpierced by the conventional three doors, and descending to the orchestra by the customary flights of steps. Upon this naked platform Mr. Barker contrived to recall a vivid reminiscence of all the pomps and glories of the ancient stage.

XXIII

ROMANCE AND REALISM IN THE DRAMA

I

THE purpose of all fiction—whether realistic or romantic—is to embody certain truths of human life in a series of imagined facts. The difference between the two methods is merely this:—the realist induces his theme from his details, and the romantic deduces his details from his theme.

In order to apprise us of the truth which he wishes to reveal, the realist first leads us through a series of imagined facts as similar as possible to those selected details of actual life which he studied in order to arrive at his general conception. He elaborately imitates the facts of actual life, so that he may say to us finally, "This is the sort of thing that I have seen in the world, and from this I have learned the truth I have to tell you." He leads us step by step from the particular to the general, until we gradually grow aware of the truths he wishes to express. And in the end, we have not only grown acquainted with these truths, but have also been made familiar with every step in the process of inductive thought by which the author himself became aware of them.

But the romantic artist leads us in the contrary direction,—namely, from the general to the particular. He does not attempt to show us how he arrived at his general conception. His only care is to convey his general idea effectively by giving it a specific illustrative embodiment. He feels no obligation to make the imagined facts of his story resemble closely the details of actual life; he is anxious only that they shall represent his idea adequately and consistently. He constructs his tale deductively: beginning with a general conception, he reduces it to particular terms that are appropriate to express it. " I have learned something in the world," he says to us: " Here is a fable that will make it clear to you." *

We have become so accustomed to the realistic method in modern art that the reader may need to be reminded that all fiction was romantic until three centuries ago. The reason why realism has arisen only recently in the history of art is that the direction of the world's thought was prevailingly deductive till the days of Francis Bacon. Bacon—the founder of modern philosophy and the precursor of modern science —was the first great leader of thought who insisted that induction was a safer and more efficient method than deduction in the search for truth. Realism is contemporaneous with modern science and other applications of inductive thought. Romance survives, of course, with scarcely an appreciable impairment of its

---

* The foregoing paragraphs are summarized from Chapter II of *Materials and Methods of Fiction*. The following application of the argument to the study of the drama is, however, new.

vigor; but it has lost the undisputed empery of fiction which it held in ancient and in medieval times.

It was not until the nineteenth century that the inductive method of revealing truth became predominant in all the arts,—though, in the single art of painting, it had been adopted as early as the seventeenth century by the great masters of the Netherlands. The drama was the last of all the arts to admit the new method of expression: indeed, the rise of realism in the drama did not begin till after 1850. The reason for this delay is obvious. Realism demands of the artist an ability to imitate details of actual life; and it was not until the second half of the nineteenth century that the physical equipment of the theatre had been developed to a point that made possible the exhibition of stage-pictures which could repeat the very look of life.

Realism was impossible on the platform-stage of the Elizabethans; and it was almost equally impossible on the apron-stage of the eighteenth century. It became possible only after the adoption of the picture-frame proscenium. A few of the Elizabethan dramatists revealed a temperamental tendency toward realism. This tendency, for instance, is apparent in such plays as Ben Jonson's *Bartholomew Fair*. In this record of the manners of contemporary London, Jonson was as realistic as any dramatist could be on a stage devoid of scenery; but he suffered the disadvantage of attempting a type of art with which his theatre, at the moment, was unprepared to cope. It was far easier for Shakespeare, in the same theatre, to suggest the atmosphere of the Forest of Arden by availing himself of the free conventions and easy assumptions of an essentially romantic stage.

When finally, however, in the latter half of the nineteenth century, the theatre was prepared, by the adoption of the picture-frame proscenium, to imitate details of actuality, the drama rushed at once to the contrary extreme; and a realistic method of present-ment was imposed upon all playwrights, regardless of their temperamental tendencies. When the theatre—which had been romantic ever since the days of Æschy-lus—became at last realistic, it became realistic with a vengeance. Romantic writers for a platform-stage—like Shakespeare—were encumbered with realistic scen-ery designed for a stage that made a necessity of its new-found virtue of imitating actuality. A totally illogical demand arose that every play should have the look of life; and this demand made the theatre as inhospitable to romantic writers as the earlier Eliza-bethan theatre had been inhospitable to realistic writers. It was just as difficult for Maeterlinck to write for Ibsen's stage as it had been difficult, three centuries before, for Jonson to write for Shakespeare's stage. In learning how to be realistic, the practitioners of theatric art had forgotten how to be romantic. The gain was compensated by an equal loss.

To dissolve this dilemma and to destroy this dead-lock, a movement toward a new stagecraft has very recently been instituted. The leaders of this movement are willing to leave the realistic stage alone as a medium of expression for realistic dramatists; but they demand that romantic dramatists should be released from the conventions of the recently developed realistic stage, and should be permitted to readopt the more summary and free conventions of those earlier periods in which the theatre was essentially romantic. They are willing to accord to Ibsen and Pinero the special advantages of the picture-frame proscenium; but they insist that Maeterlinck shall also be accorded the contrary advantages of the platform-stage of Shakespeare. If a writer of the present day prefers a Forest of Arden made of words to a Forest of Arden made of canvas trees and cotton rocks, these revolutionists against the recent tyranny of realism demand that he shall be allowed to have his way. If a realist must have actual water in an actual pitcher, let him have it; but if a romantic prefers imaginary water in a merely decorative pitcher, let him have it also;—here we have, in a single illustration, the program of the revolutionists.

The point of this revolt against realism in the theatre is, assuredly, well taken. The advocates of the new stagecraft do not demand the abolition of picture-frame productions of realistic plays; they demand only that romantic plays shall no longer be produced in a realistic manner. They insist that every writer shall be free to choose his method, and that an author who prefers to tell his truth in terms of fable shall not be forced to represent his truth in terms of fact. They do not advocate the suppression of realism on the stage; they merely advocate a restriction of the tyranny of realism over writers whose temperamental tendency is not realistic but romantic.

In the English-speaking theatre, the acknowledged

leader of this movement toward a new stagecraft is
Mr. Granville Barker,—an arch-realist in his own
plays, and an arch-romantic in his method of producing
the plays of writers other-minded than himself.

Mr. Barker's initial offering in this country was a
double bill composed of *The Man Who Married a Dumb
Wife*, by Anatole France, and *Androcles and the Lion*,
by Bernard Shaw. *La Comédie de Celui qui Epousa
une Femme Muette* is merely a dramatic anecdote
developed by M. France from two paragraphs of
Rabelais in which the medieval humorist outlined the
plot of a presumably imaginary comedy which he had
seen acted, in company with seven of his friends, at the
University of Montpellier. The point of the anecdote
is this:—A lawyer, married to a very beautiful woman
who is mute, invokes the services of a surgeon to untie
her tongue. After the operation, she becomes so volu-
ble and garrulous that he prefers to have her dumb
again; but, since the surgeon cannot nullify the operation, the lawyer is forced to accept the alternative of
being rendered deaf.

In *Androcles and the Lion*, Mr. Shaw has amplified
a familiar Latin fable and has embroidered it with satirical dialogue in his most light-hearted vein. Androcles,
a Greek tailor, is a keen lover of animals. Meeting a
lion in the jungle, who is suffering great pain from a
thorn in his paw, Androcles extracts the thorn and
wins the affection of a beast who might otherwise have
eaten him. This meek and gentle hero is a Christian;
and, because of his proscribed religion, he is later
doomed to be devoured by wild animals in the Roman

Coliseum. The beast to whom he is thrown, however, happens to be the very lion he had befriended in the jungle; and this lion, recognizing Androcles, refuses to attack him. The apparent miracle by which the hero tames the lion wins for Androcles the adulation of the Emperor and immunity from further persecution. This traditional fable is employed by Mr. Shaw as a framework for some of the wittiest and wisest dialogue that he has written in recent years.

Neither of these two plays attempts to imitate details of actuality; and, in producing them, Mr. Barker has discarded the conventions of the realistic stage. Before the curtain, he has built a wide apron, descending in terraced steps to the auditorium; and in this empty apron he has conducted a great part of the action. Behind the curtain, his scenery is merely summary and suggestive,—not detailed and photographic, like the scenery of the recent realistic theatre. His costumes are designed to be appropriate to a general decorative scheme; they are not designed to be exactly representative of the particular place and the particular time denominated in the action. Mr. Barker's Roman soldiers are not dressed like actual Roman soldiers of the third century, A.D.: they are merely dressed like people who might well enough be soldiers and might well enough be Roman. He suggests the immanence of the Eternal City by a pale monochromatic background with three round arches, and by a sweeping gesture of an actor toward the gallery which points out an imaginary Coliseum. For the purposes of a romantic play, this, surely, is a better method of investiture than a pictorial representation of the Coliseum on a back-drop and a solid imitation of the Arch of Titus in the foreground. In Mr. Barker's hands, the stage reminds us more of the reality of Rome, the less it is made to imitate that actuality of which we have been informed by archeologists. Two other conventions of the Elizabethan stage have been readopted by this revolutionist. He has resumed the Shakesperian device of the upper-room, or balcony, and thereby assails the eye from two levels simultaneously; and by obliterating footlights, and illuminating the stage entirely from above, he has destroyed that sharp distinction between the actor and the audience which was required by the picture-frame proscenium.

Before the advent of Mr. Granville Barker in America, the method employed by Mr. David Belasco in the production of his plays was invariably the method of the realists. He always achieved his effects by an agglomeration of actual details. For the last act of *The Governor's Lady*, for example, he merely bought a Childs' Restaurant, complete in all details, and, knocking out the fourth wall, set it up upon the stage. The incident enacted in this setting was untrue to life; but a false air of verisimilitude was accorded to it by the actuality of the environment.

This method served well enough for realistic plays; but Mr. Belasco was guilty of the error of applying this same method to the production of plays essentially romantic. The mystic moments of *The Return of Peter Grimm* were marred by a cluttering of unnecessary furniture upon the stage; and *The Darling of the*

Gods, for all its exactitude of scenery and costumes, was less Oriental in its atmosphere than *The Yellow Jacket*, which was produced upon a sceneless stage.

It is, therefore, especially important to record that Mr. Belasco has learned at last that realism is one thing and romance is another. His production of *Marie-Odile*, by Edward Knoblock, showed that even so staunch a realist had finally been converted to the new stagecraft. For this production, Mr. Belasco suppressed his footlights, extended his stage in an apron before the curtain, and obscured his picture-frame proscenium with simple hangings of a neutral tint. Thereby he destroyed that sharp distinction between the stage and the auditorium which was developed in the preceding period of realism. For the first time in his career—if we except his treatment of the dream-passages in *The Phantom Rival*—Mr. Belasco devised a setting that was simple and summary and suggestive, instead of actual, detailed, complex. The action of *Marie-Odile* took place in the refectory of an Alsatian convent during the Franco-Prussian war: yet there was nothing on the stage to indicate with any exactness the date or place of the story. The architecture was indefinite,—so indefinite that the observer could not even determine whether it was Romanesque or Gothic or Renaissance. The furniture was of the simplest; and not a single article of furniture or decoration was placed upon the stage that was not required by some exigency of the action. As a consequence of this suppression of superfluous details, the production of *Marie-Odile* made an appeal to the imagination that

surpassed in potency the appeal of any of the many
plays that Mr. Belasco had produced in the realistic
manner.

II

That spectacle and drama are two different things—
so different that they can never be successfully con-
joined—was clearly understood by the Elizabethans
three hundred years ago. When Ben Jonson wrote a
comedy or a tragedy, he produced it on a practically
sceneless stage; when he wrote a masque, he produced
it with the most sumptuous scenical embellishment.   In
the first instance, the play was the thing, and the
author would not permit his drama to be overlaid with
scenery; in the second instance, spectacle was the thing,
and the author, holding his dramatic talent in abeyance,
merely planned a sequence of processions, songs, and
dances that would afford a fitting theme for decoration.

It is absurd to assume that, because Shakespeare
produced *The Merchant of Venice* and *Hamlet* on a
sceneless stage, he knew nothing about scenery. As a
practical man of the theatre, he must have known all
that had been done, and all that could be done, on the
contemporary stage. He must have known, as scholars
know to-day, that the art of scenical embellishment had,
in his own sixteenth century, been developed to a very
high point in Italy; for his many friends who had returned from the conventional Italian tour of the time
must have told him of Italian opera. Anybody who
will take the trouble to examine the hundreds of en-
gravings of Renaissance Italian stage-sets still extant

will perceive that—except in the mere matter of lighting—no scenic artist in the world to-day can do anything that the Italians could not do, and did not do,
three centuries ago. Their scenic art was imported to
England by Inigo Jones; but, with a fine sense of the
fitness of things, the Elizabethan poets refused to spoil
their plays with spectacle, and reserved magnificence of
setting for their masques. The simple truth of the
matter seems to be that Shakespeare did not want
scenery in the last act of *The Merchant of Venice*,
because he wanted the audience to listen to his lines;
and that he did not want scenery in *Hamlet*, because he
wanted the spectators, at all times, to focus their attention on the leading actor.

Whenever a spectacle like *The Garden of Paradise*
is produced in New York at the present time, the
newspapers descant on the " unprecedented " expense
of the production. It is our American habit to measure
art in dollars and cents. *The Garden of Paradise* is
said to have cost $50,000. On February 3, 1633-4,
the Gentlemen of the four Inns of Court in London
presented before the King and Queen a masque by
James Shirley, entitled *The Triumph of Peace*. This
production cost £21,000. But money, in the first half
of the seventeenth century, was worth more than three
times as much as it is worth to-day; and it would cost
not less than £63,000 to produce *The Triumph of Peace*
on the same lavish scale at the present time. Since the
expense of a single performance of this masque of Shirley's amounted to more than $300,000, it is easy to
perceive that the expense of a spectacle like *The Garden*

of Paradise is not so " unprecedented " after all.   If
art must be measured in dollars and cents, we should
at least be willing to admit that our Elizabethan predecessors excelled us in the art of spectacle.

The text of *The Triumph of Peace* is still extant.   It
consists almost entirely of descriptions of the scenery,
the costumes, and the properties, and directions for the
dances and the grand processions.   The dialogue, quite
obviously, was not intended to be listened to.   There are
several songs, of course ; because music was essential to
a masque, and it was easier to sing words than to sing
do, re, mi, fa, sol.   These songs are beautifully written ;
for Shirley was so great a lyrist that it was easier for
him to write a good song than a bad one.   But it is
evident that the poet never for a moment regarded this
masque as a literary composition.   On the title page of
the original quarto, his name appears as the " inven-
tor " of the masque, and coincident credit is assigned to
Inigo Jones for " the scene and ornament," and to
William Lawes and Simon Ives for " the composition of
the music."

But when Shirley wrote a play—*The Traitor,* for
example—he presented it without adornment, on the
traditional inner-and-outer stage of the Elizabethan
theatre,—a bare platform, with only a summary hint
of scenery behind the arras.   When he wanted the public
to listen to his lines and care about his characters, he
was careful to avoid stage-pictures that would distract
attention from his poetry and from his drama.   Shirley
could " invent " a spectacle, and he could write a play ;
but he never attempted to do both things at once.   He

would no more have permitted an expenditure of $300,000 on the production of *The Traitor* than he would have allowed *The Triumph of Peace* to be repeated on a sceneless stage. He could make art either for the eye or for the ear; but he had common sense enough to know that people cannot, at the same time, and with equal eagerness, both look at pictures and listen to words.

XXIV

SCENIC SETTINGS IN AMERICA

I

ANYBODY who has studied Mr. Hiram Kelly Moderwell's instructive treatise on *The Theatre of To-Day* must admit that our American theatre, considered generally, is loitering at least ten years behind the times. This fact is somewhat disappointing to those of us who are habituated to believe that America is naturally the leader of the world in matters of mere enterprise. The phrase, " mere enterprise," is used advisedly; for though the drama is an art, the theatre is a business. Though we might be willing to admit that the backwardness of our drama is necessitated by a native ineptitude for art, it would be much more difficult to admit that the backwardness of our theatre is necessitated by a native ineptitude for business. This latter hypothesis would be a little staggering. America has always been supposed to be a country of good business men. We have proved that we can run such things as railroads, mines, and steel plants efficiently and well. Is it really possible that when it comes to running theatres, we are easily outdistanced, not only by the efficient Germans but also by the langourous Russians?

The facts appear to be incontrovertible. The best-conducted theatre in the world—according to the testimony of most investigators who have studied the matter at first hand—is the Art Theatre of Moscow; and, following close upon the heels of this leading institution, are the foremost theatres of Germany and Hungary. France, also, is close up in the running; but the American theatre is a manifest anachronism. What is the reason for our backwardness in this matter of mere enterprise?

The reason is not difficult to define; but it is extremely difficult to understand. It is merely that the men who control the theatre in America are not sufficiently interested in their own business to learn enough about it to make their methods up to date. Their conservatism—to dignify this strange inertia by a lofty word—seems curiously un-American. We are not accustomed to seeing our big business men defeated in a matter of mere business.

Suppose, for purposes of illustration, that an American business man has invested half a million dollars in the manufacture of mustard. Suppose, further, that he hears, from a returning traveler, that the Germans have found a way to manufacture better mustard at a smaller cost. What does he do? He immediately goes to Germany himself, or sends an emissary, to learn the new improvement in his business; thereafter, he revises his own methods of manufacture, in order to bring them up to date; and, by this means, he is soon enabled to undersell the world. This is the story of American business, as it is ordinarily recorded and commonly believed. If there was anything new to be learned about running railroads, Mr. Harriman learned it and put it immediately into operation; and, if there is anything new to be learned about the manufacture of steel, it is not likely to escape the eagerly acquisitive mind of Mr. Schwab.

This is the way in which Americans do business in every line—except the one line of the theatre. When word is brought from Europe that a great improvement has been made in the mechanism of the theatre, our American managers are not sufficiently interested to investigate the matter. As business men, they might save thousands of dollars by sending an emissary to Germany or Russia to study the innovation and import it to this country; but they prefer to remain ignorant of all advances that are made in the very business in which they are engaged.

This may seem to be an overstatement; but let us consider for a moment a single detail of the mere mechanism of the theatre. Everybody knows that it is desirable, for a multitude of reasons, to equip the theatre in such a way as to be able to supplant one stage-set with another in a few seconds. Throughout the last ten years, this purpose has been accomplished in Germany by three different devices,—namely, the revolving stage, or *drehbühne;* the sliding stage, or *shiebebühne;* and the rolling stage, or *wagenbühne.* Any American theatre-manager might study the respective merits of these three devices in a single day. Yet, in this country, we build theatre after theatre without installing any of these appliances for the rapid shifting of scenery. In all America, there are, as yet, only three revolving stages,—one in Oakland, California; and the other two at the Century Theatre and the Little Theatre in New York, both of which were projected by Mr. Winthrop Ames.

Take another matter of mere mechanism,—the matter of stage-lighting. In nearly every modern German theatre, the stage is bounded by a concrete cyclorama, which is used to reflect and to diffuse the light that ultimately irradiates the scene. There is only one theatre in New York which is provided with this new appliance,—namely, the Neighborhood Playhouse in Grand Street, which most of our American managers have never even visited.

During the last ten years, nearly every important producing manager in Europe has discarded the old method of illuminating the stage from a trough of footlights, and has adopted a new method of lighting from the top and from the sides. In New York, the new method of illuminating the stage was clearly exemplified in January, 1915, by Mr. Granville Barker; but thus far it has been adopted, in our American theatre, only by Mr. David Belasco. When the curtain rose upon the first performance of *The Boomerang*, on August 10, 1915, it was apparent that Mr. Belasco had removed the footlights from his theatre and had arranged to illuminate his stage from the top and from the sides. *The Boomerang* achieved a success which may be described without hyperbole as record-breaking; the play has been seen by hundreds of thousands of people; and Mr. Belasco has proved, by the sheer enjoyment of the public, that the new method of stage-lighting is more efficacious than the old. Yet, since the first performance of *The Boomerang*, no other American manager has adopted the new method of stage-lighting which Mr. Belasco has so successfully employed; and it may seriously be doubted that any of our other managers have even taken the trouble to study the devices by which Mr. Belasco has achieved his fine effects.

In the matter of stage-setting and stage-lighting, our American theatre is loitering many years behind the times. Speaking generally, our theatre is still lingering in the Victorian—or horsehair—period; as yet, it has scarcely felt the impress of that modern movement which is known as the " new stagecraft."

II

The movement known as the " new stagecraft " has been so long established on the continent of Europe that only in America can it literally be considered " new." It began, about fifteen years ago, as a protest against the ultra-realism of the preceding period. At the very end of the nineteenth century, the drama was prevailingly a realistic drama; the appliances of the theatre of that period were appropriately suited to the drama of the time; but realism was so thoroughly established in the drama that even those authors who preferred to write romantic or poetic plays were required to have their plays produced in a realistic manner. Inevitably, therefore, the " new stagecraft " began as a revolt against this utterly illogical requirement.

The theatre may appeal to the public in either of two ways,—first, by imitation of the actual, and second, by suggestion of the real. The first method is realistic, for it requires in the public a process of inductive thought; the second method is romantic, for it requires in the public a process of deductive thought. The apostles of the " new stagecraft "—while willing to leave to the realistic drama the methods of the realistic theatre— demanded that a new romantic theatre should be devised to cope with the requirements of a new romantic drama.

The subject is, in general, so large that only a single aspect can profitably be discussed in the course of the present chapter. Let us choose, for convenience, to examine the attitude of the apostles of the " new stage- craft " toward the one detail of scenic setting. The revolutionists insisted that romantic writers should be aided by an absolute release from the encumbrance of realistic scenery.

They demanded, first, that scenes which were not definitely localized by the dramatist in place and time should not be definitely localized by the superimposition of scenery and properties. In staging Shakespeare, for example, they insisted that scenes which were written to be acted on an empty fore-stage should be acted on an empty apron. But, secondly, they de- manded also that, in the scenery itself, the basis of appeal should be, not imitation, but suggestion.

For the detailed, pictorial scenery of the preceding period they substituted scenery which was summary and decorative. Instead of cluttering the stage with actual details, they contrived to suggest the desired scene by an appropriate design composed of lines and lights and colors. It was discovered, for example, that green curtains drooping in tall folds and illuminated with a light that never was on sea or land would suggest a better Forest of Arden than any imitative jumble of cotton rocks and canvas trees. It was discovered, also, that even for the uses of the realistic drama, a simple design of leading lines and elementary colors was more suggestive of the desired illusion of reality than a helter-skelter gathering of actual furniture and actual properties.

In two important particulars, the " new manner " of scenic setting proved itself superior to the old; for, first, it was more imaginative, and, second, it was more economical. The first point was particularly interesting to the audience; the second, to the manager.

People go to the theatre to enjoy *themselves:*—that is to say, their own participation in the play. They cannot really relish a performance until it ceases to seem to happen on the stage and begins to seem to happen in their own imaginations. A play, therefore, is effective in proportion to the extent to which it excites an imaginative contribution from the minds of those who see it. The old realistic scenery left the audience nothing to do, for everything had been already done upon the stage. The new suggestive scenery is more enjoyable, because it permits the spectators to create within their own imaginations an appreciable contribution to the total work of art.

Furthermore, the second great advantage of the decorative type of scenery is that it is considerably less expensive than the detailed, pictorial type of the preceding period. Here is a point which surely should appeal to our American managers, since they pride themselves on being business men. It is assuredly un-businesslike to perpetuate an old fashion when it costs much more to do so than it would cost to adopt a new fashion which is manifestly better.

III

Despite the inertia of the tired business men who control the great majority of our theatres, it is an interesting fact that, whenever the new type of scenery has been exhibited in America, it has been enthusiastically welcomed by the public. When Mr. Winthrop Ames imported Reinhardt's *Sumurûn*, the public was emphatically pleased; and an approval which was even more emphatic was accorded to Mr. Granville Barker's productions of *The Man Who Married a Dumb Wife* and *Androcles and the Lion*. Our public, as the phrase is, may not know anything about art, but it knows what it likes; and it likes the scenery designed by Bakst and Golovine for the Russian Ballet that recently has visited the leading cities of this country.

But our managers might reply that, in America, we lack the necessary artists to carry the new movement to success. This objection, if it should be made, would merely be a proof of ignorance. We have many fine artists, trained particularly for the work of scenic decoration; they are merely waiting for further opportunities to be employed. Setting aside Mr. Josef Urban, who, though resident in America, is an Austrian by birth, we have Mr. Livingston Platt, Mr. Sam Hume, Mr. Robert E. Jones, Mr. Robert McQuinn, Mr. William Penhallow Henderson, Mrs. O'Kane Conwell, Miss Helen Dryden, and many others, including the associated artists of the Washington Square Players, who have already shown what they can do whenever an opportunity has been accorded to them. Mr. Jones has studied with Reinhardt, Mr. Hume has studied with Gordon Craig, Mr. Platt has studied art in Bruges. All these artists are thoroughly prepared to design the new type of scenic settings.

The work of Mr. Urban is already well known in our theatre, because of the initiative of Mr. George C. Tyler; and he is now employed by managers so diverse in the intent of their productions as Mr. Erlanger, Mr. Ziegfeld, and Mr. Hackett. Mr. Jones was given his first chance by Mr. Granville Barker, and was subsequently retained by Mr. Arthur Hopkins; and Mr. Platt has been employed by that far-seeing manager, Miss Anglin. Mr. McQuinn was taken up by Mr. Dillingham and allowed to design the lovely scenery of several of his spectacles. But, despite these intimations of an ultimate triumph of the new art in our American theatre, nine-tenths of all our plays are still encumbered with the lumbering investiture of a fashion that is now a decade out of date.

XXV

THE NEW STAGECRAFT

I

In the movement known as " the new stagecraft "
there is really nothing new. The apparent innovations
of this movement arise merely from the resumption of
many conventions as old as the theatre itself, which
were injudiciously discarded less than half a century
ago. The purpose of " the new stagecraft " is to effect
a working compromise between the methods of the platform stage and the methods of the picture-frame stage,
so that the merits of both shall survive and their defects
be nullified. The intention of the leaders of this movement is not to erect a new ideal; it is merely to reconcile
two different ideals, each of which has shown itself to
be of service in the past. Shakespeare could write his
plays only for a platform theatre; Ibsen could write his
plays only for a picture-frame theatre; but, if the advocates of " the new stagecraft " can effect the compromise that constitutes their program, the playwright of
to-morrow will be allowed to write his plays for either
type of theatre, or for a combination of the two.

To appreciate this compromise, we must first consider separately the different merits and defects of both

233

factors to the intended reconciliation. The drama was produced upon a platform stage from the days of Æschylus until the second half of the nineteenth century.   Though the theatres of Sophocles, Plautus, Shakespeare, Calderon, Molière, and Sheridan differed greatly in detail, they remained alike in their essential features. In each of these theatres a full half of the stage was employed as a bare platform surrounded on three sides by spectators. For this projecting platform it is most convenient to employ the term " apron," by which it was denominated in the eighteenth century. Any scene in any play which did not have to be precisely localized in place and time was always acted in the apron. Within this universal ground, certain characters accomplished certain acts, immune from any questioning of " where " or " when." The actor in the apron was accepted frankly as an actor; his presence presupposed the presence of an audience; and he could address himself directly to the spectators who surrounded him on three sides. At the same time, each of these theatres provided also a " back stage "—distinguished from the " apron "—in which it was possible to localize events in place and time by some summary arrangement of scenery or properties. The background of this secondary stage might be merely architectural, as in the theatre of Sophocles; or it might be decorated with a painted back-drop and wings, as in the theatre of Sheridan. In any case, as in the theatre of Shakespeare, it could be employed for the exhibition of any set-piece of stage-furniture necessitated by the narrative. Withdrawn to the " back stage," the actors reduced themselves to component parts of a general stage-picture; they were no longer surrounded by spectators on three sides; and, to address the audience directly, they had to step out of the picture and advance into the " apron." The convention of the inner and outer stage, however, permitted the dramatist to alternate at will between eternity and time, between somewhere and anywhere, and between the employment of the actor as an orator or merely as a movable detail in a decorative composition.

The development of the picture-frame proscenium in the latter half of the nineteenth century signalized the advent of a different conception of the drama. The " apron " was abolished; and what had formerly been the " back stage " was brought forward, and expanded to include the entire domain available for acting. The whole was framed in a proscenium that gave it the aspect of a picture hung upon a wall. For the first time in its history of more than twenty centuries, the drama was conceived as a drift of moving pictures, assiduously localized in place and time. An inviolable boundary was drawn between the auditorium and the stage; and theatrical performances, which formerly had been projected, so to speak, in three dimensions, were now reduced to two. The drama became a thing at which the public looked, instead of a thing in the midst of which the public lived. The time-honored convention which had permitted the actor in the " apron " to address the audience frankly as an actor was swept away with the platform stage that had rendered this convention simple and natural; and, as a consequence of this revolution, the soliloquy and the aside were discarded. For the first time the drama became primarily a visual, instead of an auditory, art. Conviction was carried to the eye, by an arrangement of actual details behind the picture-frame proscenium, instead of to the ear, by the literary appeal of lines delivered from the "apron." The gardens of Portia's Belmont were no longer suggested by the poet's eloquence; they were rendered to the eye, and not the ear, by an artist other than the author. The drama, in other words, became essentially a special sort of painting instead of a special sort of literature.

This new concept of a play as a thing to be seen instead of a thing to be listened to was developed at a time when realism happened to be rampant in all the arts. Whatever traditional conventions of the theatre were anti-realistic were, in consequence, summarily discarded. The actor was no longer permitted to presuppose the presence of an audience; he was required to comport himself as if he were living in life instead of acting in a play. He could never address a public imagined to be non-existent: hence he could never utter a soliloquy or an aside. He was required at all moments to "see himself" (as actors say) as a component part of a picture, instead of addressing a gathered audience with ears to hear. This new convention of the theatre has been best defined by Mr. Henry Arthur Jones as the "eavesdropping convention,"—"the convention which charges playgoers half-a-crown or half-a-guinea for pretending to remove the fourth wall, and pretending to give them an opportunity of spying upon actual life, and seeing everything just as it happens."

The " eavesdropping convention " rendered an unprecedented service to the realistic drama; for realism is the art of inducing an apprehension of truth from an imitation of facts. For imitating facts, for localizing a story both in place and in time, for reproducing the very look of actuality, the picture-frame theatre was so superior to the platform theatre that, in a single generation, it drove its predecessor out of usage. But, while this sudden, overwhelming triumph of the pictorial, non-literary concept of the drama made easier the composition and production of realistic plays, it set unprecedented difficulties in the path of writers of romantic plays,—the sort of plays that refuse to be confined within set limits of place and time, and depend for their effect more upon the imaginative suggestion of their lines than upon the imitation of actuality in their investiture. Though a precise and accurate scenic setting behind a picture-frame proscenium was an aid to Ibsen, who wrote realistic plays, it was only an encumbrance to Shakespeare, who wrote romantic plays intended for a platform stage.

It occurred, therefore, to the advocates of that latest movement we are now examining that some compromise should be effected which, while rendering to the realists the manifest advantages of picture-frame production, should also reassert for the romantics the no less manifest advantages of production on a platform stage. They decided to readopt the " apron," with all the free conventions that depend upon its use; and, at the same time, to embellish the "back stage" with decorations sufficiently pictorial to satisfy the eye of a public grown accustomed to the visual appeal of the realistic drama.

In the English-speaking theatre, the most notable exponent of "the new stagecraft" is Mr. Granville Barker; and, for a further elucidation of this movement, we need only examine in detail the method of Mr. Barker's productions of the plays of Shakespeare. For these productions, Mr. Barker has constructed a new type of inner and outer stage. An "apron," several feet in depth, projects before the curtain, and descends in terraced steps to the floor of the auditorium. This platform is accessible from either side, by entrances made available by the suppression of the two stage-boxes of the theatre. Upon this "apron," in frank and utter intimacy with the audience, are enacted all scenes that are not precisely localized in place or time, or that do not demand the employment of set-pieces of stage-furniture. Such other scenes as require a pictorial environment are enacted on the "back stage," or on a full stage constituted by an imaginary obliteration of the boundary that separates this "back stage" from the "apron." The "back stage," disclosed behind the curtain, is framed in a rectilinear proscenium of gold. Whatever scenery is used is set within this frame, at the extreme rear of the stage. Mr. Barker's scenery is summary rather than precise, decorative rather than pictorial. It attains its effect not by imitation of the actual but by suggestion of the real. It is so simple that it can be shifted in a few seconds; and, by virtue of this fact, the decorative aspect of the " back stage " can be altered at any moment without interrupting the continuance of the dramatic narrative. No footlights are employed on Mr. Barker's platform: the stage is illuminated from above by artificial light, just as, in the Elizabethan theatre, it was illuminated from above by natural light. His performances seem to be rendered not in two dimensions but in three; and a person seated in the orchestra is made to feel more like a participant in the business of the play than a mere spectator of what is going on.

II

It is an axiom that the structure of the drama in any period is conditioned by the structure of the theatre in that period; for, to get his work before the public, the dramatist must make his plays in such a fashion that they will fit the sort of theatre that is ready to receive them. He cannot plan his plays for an unknown theatre of the future; and, if he is wise, he will not plan them for some forgotten theatre of the past. The problem of making a play for the Theatre of Dionysus in Athens was very different from the problem of making a play for the Little Theatre in New York; and this difference in the fundamental problem accounts for all the myriad minor points of disagreement between the dramaturgic craft of Sophocles and the dramaturgic craft of Mr. Galsworthy.

It would be utterly unfair to Mr. Galsworthy to produce *The Pigeon* before twenty thousand spectators in an open-air auditorium carved out of the sunlit hollow of a hill; and it would be almost equally unfair to Sophocles to produce *Œdipus the King* on a tiny stage before three hundred people seated in a roofed and lighted drawing-room. The dramaturgic craftsmanship of any play can be appreciated only when the play is produced with some approximation to the physical conditions of the type of theatre for which it was originally fashioned.

This point is so absolutely obvious that even to mention it in passing might appear to be unnecessary, were it not for the fact that the dramaturgic art of Shakespeare has suffered sorely from a lack of recognition of this fundamental principle. Shakespeare was undeniably a great dramatist, and, at his best, he was probably the greatest of all time; but he was a dramatist of the sixteenth century, and not of the seventeenth or the eighteenth or the nineteenth or the twentieth. He fashioned his plays to fit a type of theatre which was legislated out of existence by the Roundhead Parliament of 1642; and, ever since the restoration of the English stage in 1660, his plays have been hashed and harried, in an effort to make them fit a more modern type of theatre for which they had never been intended.

The physical conditions of the Globe Theatre on the Bankside have been explained so frequently in recent years that they need not be expounded in the present context. The essential fact to be inculcated is that the Elizabethan theatre afforded to the dramatist the utmost liberty in handling the categories of time and place. No scenes, in any way, were definitely localized except such scenes as were set upon the full-stage, with a summary background of furniture and properties. Shakespeare never pigeon-holed a scene in either place or time unless he needed to; and, whenever it was really necessary to anchor an incident in actuality, he re-enforced the effect of his meager scenery by describing the desired setting elaborately in the lines. The custom of his period required him to rely with greater confidence on the appeal to the ear than on the appeal to the eye.

Furthermore, Shakespeare could change his place and change his time as often as he wished, by the simple expedient of emptying his stage and then repeopling it with other characters. Because of this advantage, he could build his plays not in five acts, nor in four or three, but in an uncounted sequence of scenes. The arbitrary division of each of Shakespeare's plays into five acts, with which the modern reader is familiar, was imposed upon the playwright by his eighteenth-century editors, who, knowing nothing about the Elizabethan theatre and assuming that every good play must be constructed in five acts, presumed to cut up Shakespeare's narrative in the interests of a falsely founded theory. There is every reason to suppose, however, that the plays of Shakespeare were originally acted, from the outset to the end, without any intermission; for otherwise it would be impossible to understand the famous phrase in the prologue of *Romeo and Juliet* about " the two hours' traffic of our stage." In this connection, it may be interesting to point out that, though the narrative structure of the Elizabethan drama differs radically from that of the contemporary play, it coincides almost exactly with that of the contemporary moving-picture. Our moving-pictures, with their swift facility for changing time and place, and their equipment for the easy exhibition of a story in an uncounted sequence of scenes, have carried us back to the freedom and amplitude of narrative that was enjoyed by Shakespeare.

This freedom and amplitude have been sacrificed by the modern theatre for the sake of an assiduous definition of details in place and time. Our modern plays are no longer constructed in an uncounted sequence of scenes: they are arranged—less fluently but much more solidly—in three or four acts, in accordance with a careful time-scheme and with the uttermost economy of place. Each act is anchored heavily in actuality, by realistic scenery, realistic furniture, realistic properties, and artificial lighting that is suited realistically to the time-table of the narrative.

Great plays have been written for this modern theatre by the meditative giant of the north, and by a host of Ibsen's tall successors in nearly every nation of the breathing world; but the merit of these plays has been totally different, in its technical basis, from the merit of the plays of Shakespeare. To produce *Hedda Gabler* or *The Thunderbolt* in the Globe Theatre on the Bankside, in accordance with the customs of the Elizabethan stage, would be to rob these modern plays of all their meaning. And, similarly, to produce the plays of Shakespeare in accordance with the customs of our modern realistic stage, with its picture-frame proscenium and its meticulous arrangement of a story in little labeled pigeon-holes of place and time, is to clip the wings of one accustomed to soar through an illimitable void.

Toward the close of the nineteenth century, when realism was rampant in the theatre, an immense indignity was done to the dramaturgic craftsmanship of Shakespeare. In this period, those passages which Shakespeare had airily devised to be acted on the fore-stage, " out of place, out of time," were presented on a stage encumbered with realistic scenery which pinned them down to a definite place and a definite hour. The leader of this momentary heresy toward a realistic presentation of an essentially romantic dramatist was the great actor, Sir Henry Irving. In Irving's production of *Romeo and Juliet*, when Mercutio spoke his dying quip, saying humorously that his wound was " not so deep as a well nor so wide as a church door," he waved his right hand and his left at an actual well and an actual church door which were standing on the stage. By this exhibition of the actual, the audience was imperiously prevented from imagining the real.

The method of Sir Henry Irving, which was supported in America by the late Augustin Daly, was maintained until his death by Sir Herbert Beer-bohm Tree. Sir Herbert, in producing the platform plays of Shakespeare, drowned the stage with realistic scenery, assiduously localizing incidents which were meant to be unlocalized in either place or time. Like Daly, and like Irving before him, he cut and rear-ranged Shakespeare's text in order to make it fit the modern realistic stage, and sacrificed the swift sweep of the Elizabethan narrative in order to reduce it to conformity with the conventions of the Victorian theatre.

If any lasting service can be done to Shakespeare, this service should take the form of a rehabilitation of his own familiar art upon the stage. The only way in which his art can fairly be restored to its pristine freshness and its pristine vigor is by a presentation of his plays with due regard to the conventions of the sort of theatre for which they were originally fashioned. We should resolve henceforward to produce the greatest of the great Elizabethans as an Elizabethan dramatist, and not as a Victorian dramatist or as a competitor of Mr. Galsworthy in the traffic of the contemporary stage. To produce a play of Shakespeare's with modern realistic scenery is just as absurd as to present the Prince of Denmark in a top-hat and a morning coat or to exhibit Julius Cæsar with a wrist-watch and a khaki uniform. Just as a good servant knows his place, a good play should be permitted to demonstrate a knowledge of its time.

A vigorous move in the right direction was made in 1916 by the Drama Society in its notable production of *The Tempest*, under the direction of Mr. Louis Calvert and Mr. John Corbin. This production was planned in accordance with conditions which approximated the liberties and limitations with which Shakespeare was confronted.

This play must be produced on an Elizabethan stage or not at all. Its requirements are utterly at variance with the conventions of the realistic theatre; and this is the main reason why, in recent years, *The Tempest* has rarely been produced. The story is spun of " such stuff as dreams are made on." The incidents occur, as in a dream, " out of place, out of time." To anchor this fantastic narrative in actuality, according to the method of Augustin Daly or Sir Herbert Tree, is to force it to compete unfairly with the modern realistic drama. But Mr. Corbin and Mr. Calvert chose wisely to afford this Elizabethan relic the advantage of a production in accordance with the chief requirements of the Elizabethan stage.

When the curtain rose, it disclosed a counterpart of the stage of Shakespeare's theatre; and on this stage the entire text was spoken, without interruption and without rearrangement. No cuts whatever were made, except for the excision of a few words and a few lines here and there which, to the oversqueamish modern ear, might sound indelicate. Yet the performance was run through in a little over two hours, because there were no intermissions, except for a single interval of fifteen minutes, which was introduced arbitrarily to afford the restless modern auditor an opportunity for a smoke in the lobby. The narrative gained greatly from this continuity. The fantastic story of *The Tempest* demands a drifting fluency of narrative; and to interrupt the text with many intermissions, as Augustin Daly did, is to release the auditor irrevocably from the spell of Prospero's enchantment.

The Elizabethan drama was more imaginative than ours, for the simple reason that the Elizabethan stage demanded from the spectator a greater and more conscious contribution of imaginative receptivity. The modern dramatist says, " Two and two make four," and the modern auditor agrees with him, saying to himself subconsciously, " I've often thought that very thing myself." Herein we see the source of the appeal of Pinero and Galsworthy and Shaw. But the Elizabethan dramatist said, " You see this orange? . . . Let us now pretend it is the twirling world; and let us next imagine that we blink like thronèd stars upon that mutable and restless planet "; and the Elizabethan auditor took wings, and made himself a god by contemplation of an orange. Herein we see the source of the appeal of Shakespeare.

The ship scene with which *The Tempest* opens is ineffective on the modern stage, because no mimic shipwreck can compete with actuality; but it is very effective on the rehabilitated Elizabethan stage, because it casts all actuality aside and appeals to the desire of the audience to contribute an imagination of the real. In presenting such a narrative, it is more difficult, and less effective, to rock the stage than to suggest a rocking of the mind by a helter-skelter of the lines.

By virtue of these principles, and by virtue also of the fact that the actors were excellently chosen, the recent exhibition of *The Tempest* was genuinely entertaining. This fact seems all the more remarkable when we remember that *The Tempest* is a bad play and by no means a monumental poem. Of dramatic merit it is almost void, and in literary merit it sinks considerably below the works of Shakespeare's prime. This may seem a shocking thing to say at a time when Shake-speare is being lauded loudly for his very faults; but, some time or other, when the atmosphere is not bethundered with unthinking plaudits, it might be well for some critic of the drama to condemn the exposition of the story in the crude and tedious narrative of Prospero to Miranda, and for some critic of poetic art to condemn the decadence of the author's verse in that later period when he trod upon the heels of Fletcher in the new and devastating habit of terminating lines with adjectives and prepositions and conjunctions.

XXVI

THE LONG RUN IN THE THEATRE

WE have become so accustomed to the long run in recent years that we are likely to forget that this factor in the conduct of the theatre was utterly unknown until the last half century. Euripides often wrote a play which was intended to be acted only once, and then contentedly went home and wrote another; yet many of his tragedies are likely to be remembered longer than *Within the Law*. When Shakespeare first produced *Hamlet* at the Globe Theatre in 1602, we may be certain that he never expected it to be played so many as a hundred times—not a hundred times consecutively, but a hundred times in all, before it was finally discarded and forgotten. Molière never even thought of running a single comedy throughout a season, however popular the comedy might be. In theatrical memoirs of the eighteenth century, we often read of a tragedy that took the town by storm and was acted for as many as ten consecutive nights, or of a comedy that proved itself so popular that it had to be repeated no less than twenty times during the course of the year. So recently as 1863, in our own country of America, Lester Wallack's *Rosedale*, which broke all preëxistent records for popularity, was acted only one hundred

and twenty-five times during the first twelve months of its career. Yet nowadays, in New York, a play is commonly regarded as a failure unless it runs at once for at least a hundred consecutive performances.

The development of the long run in the last fifty years has been undoubtedly determined by the growth of modern cities to a population of more than a million; it seems, in consequence, a natural phenomenon; but our present familiarity with the long run should not lead us to neglect to ask whether a system which permits *Peg o' My Heart* to run consecutively for three years is really more salutary to the drama than the system which inspired the composition of such plays as *Othello*, *Le Misanthrope*, and *The School for Scandal*.

Nobody denies that the long run is a bad thing for the actors, except for the fact that they are thereby assured of continuous employment at a stated salary. It is a bad thing for the " star " performers, because any histrionic composition is likely to become perfunctory if it is repeated for more than a hundred consecutive exhibitions; but it is a much more devastating thing for the minor actors, who—condemned to spend a year in repeating inconsiderable " bits "—miss the needed opportunity for experience and training in a wide variety of parts.

From the financial point of view, the long run is a good thing for the author, since it permits him to make a fortune from a single play—a consummation that was never possible at any previous period in the history of the drama. Thomas Heywood, a successful Elizabethan playwright, was paid three pounds for his best play, *A Woman Killed with Kindness;* and, allowing for the increase in the purchasing power of money in the last three hundred years, this sum would now amount to about seventy-five dollars. On the other hand, it may reasonably be conjectured that Mr. Roi Cooper Megrue will earn at least one hundred thousand dollars with *Under Cover,*—a play which, despite its many merits, is not likely to be remembered for three centuries.

But, though the theatre is now—as Robert Louis Stevenson remarked—a " gold-mine " for the author, the long run is disadvantageous to the dramatist from another—and perhaps a more important—point of view. Under our present system, the author is condemned to try for a long run, whether he wants to or not; for scarcely any manager is willing to produce a play that does not seem likely to run for at least a hundred nights. To seize an illustration from the analogous art of the novel, our present system in the theatre condemns all our authors to emulate Harold Bell Wright or Gene Stratton-Porter, and forbids them absolutely to emulate George Meredith or Henry James.

Whether or not the long run is a good thing for the manager is a question more difficult to answer. Under our present system, the average manager produces five new plays in the course of a season. He hopes that one of these may run a year; and he expects, from the profits of this one production—whichever it may be—to liquidate the losses of the other four, and thus to finish the year on the right side of the ledger. Any play which does not, almost immediately, show signs of settling down for an entire season's run is summarily discarded within a period that varies from two weeks to six weeks from the date of the original performance.

This system—to borrow an analogy from the game of roulette—is similar to the system of backing five successive single numbers and hoping that one of them may win, instead of playing more safely with a series of five even chances on the red and black. One of the most intelligent of our American theatrical managers said recently to the present writer, " Our theatre business is not a business at all; it is only a gamble." The main trouble with the business of our theatre at the present time is that it is utterly unbusinesslike.

There are two ways of embarking on a money-making enterprise. One way—the sound, commercial way—is to manufacture one hundred articles and to sell them at a profit of two dollars each. The other way—the dangerous and gambling way—is to manufacture one hundred articles, to sell one of them at a profit of four hundred dollars, and to sell the other ninety-nine at a loss of two dollars each. From the first of these hypothetical transactions, the business man will earn a profit of two hundred dollars; from the second, he will earn a profit of two hundred and two dollars; but everybody will agree that the first transaction is " business " and that the second is " only a gamble."

If our theatre business at the present day is " only a gamble," it is because our managers have made it so, by trying always for long runs. The main trouble with our commercial managers appears to be that they are not sufficiently commercial. They try, over and over again, to hit upon " the one best bet," instead of investing their money more conservatively.

Let us imagine for a moment that all the publishers in America, with two or three exceptions, should decide to-morrow never to print another book outside that field of fiction that is always expected to be " popular." Let us suppose, also, that each of our publishers should decide to issue five novels in the course of the next twelve months, in the hope that one of the five might achieve a sale of one hundred thousand copies; and let us imagine, further, that if any of the novels so issued should seem, within the first month of its career, to be unlikely to attain an ultimate sale of one hundred thousand copies, the publishers should determine to remove it summarily from circulation, destroy the plates, and burn the manuscript. Every author would protest at once that all the publishers had gone insane; and the reading public would clamor loudly against the discontinuance of all books of poetry, biography, history, criticism, scholarship, and science. Yet this hypothetical and almost unimaginable situation in the world of books is precisely the situation that confronts our dramatic authors at the present time in the world of plays. They must write a " best seller " or nothing: they must write a play that seems likely to run a year, or they must not write a play at all.

When every manuscript is judged by its likelihood to achieve a season's run, it follows that many great manuscripts must be rejected. Of such a piece as *The Weavers* of Gerhart Hauptmann, our gambling American managers have been saying for twenty years, " It's a great play, of course; but there isn't a cent of money in it." What they mean, really, is that there isn't a hundred thousand dollars in it; but the distinction remains unapparent to the gambling mind. *The Weavers* has lately been produced at an abandoned theatre in New York; it has run for more than two months, and it has paid its way: but this sort of success has come to seem a sort of failure to the mind that is fixed forever on a season's run. Why bet at all—the gamblers seem to say—unless you have a chance of winning thirty-five for one? But anybody who has ever systematically played roulette will be likely to protest that " that way madness lies."

There are many great plays which might be produced for one month at a total cost of twenty thousand dollars—including all the necessary expenses both of the proprietor of the theatre and of the proprietor of the production—and which, during that period, would be certain to attract to the box-office at least twenty-two thousand dollars. A surplus of two thousand dollars in a single month is considered a very good profit in any other business; but, in the gamble of the theatre, our managers persist in losing many times that sum in the hope of ultimately winning one hundred thousand dollars at a single cast.

What we really need is a system which will permit our managers to present a play for six weeks only, with the expectation of reaping a reasonable profit of not less than ten per cent. on each production, but with no intention of running any single play throughout an entire season.   This sound and businesslike and sensible system has been adopted by the Washington Square Players; and it is reassuring to record that the productions which have been offered to the public by this organization have been registered among the most interesting enterprises of recent years.

XXVII

THE NON-COMMERCIAL DRAMA

There is no reason why the critic should feel a greater patience for the uncommercial drama than is commonly evinced by the theatre-going public; but the non-commercial drama is another thing entirely. Any protest against commercialism in the theatre should be based upon a clear distinction between these very different alternatives. Many good plays may be classed as non-commercial; but no play that is utterly uncommercial can logically be considered good.

There is a sense in which all art is of necessity commercial. Art makes things which need to be distributed; business distributes things which have been made: and each of the arts is, therefore, necessarily accompanied by a business, whose special purpose is to distribute the products of that art. The sentimental tradition that a sincere artist should be a bad business man is lacking in essential sanity. History has recorded a few instances of great painters and great poets who have starved to death or wearied out their lives in penury because they failed to realize the commercial value of their products; but if the public must sentimentalize over these tragical exceptions, it should weep more because the artists were lacking in common sense than because the world was lacking in appreciation. A man who can make great things that his contemporaries will not buy should be able also to make great things that his contemporaries will buy: and a failure to cope with this alternative is not to be regarded as a sign of genius.

In a special sense, the drama is of necessity the most commercial of the arts. A play must be produced in a theatre; and theatres cost money. In any large city —and any city that aspires to become a producing center of the drama must be large—a theatre, because it must be situated in a generally accessible district, must occupy ground that is very valuable; and the mere continuance of its existence demands a large expenditure for rent. A play, also, must be presented by a company of actors; and this necessity demands a large expenditure for salaries. Furthermore, the production of a play requires the collaboration of many other artists in addition to the author and the actors; and these collaborators—the stage-director, the designer of the scenery and costumes, the musicians, the electricians, and many minor functionaries—must also be paid for their services. To sum the matter up, it costs much more to launch a play than to launch a poem or a picture. This cost is paid by the theatre-going public; and the public that pays the cost has a reasonable right to reject any project that it deems unworthy of its patronage.

Any theatrical production for which the theatre-going public summarily refuses to defray the cost must be classed as uncommercial; and to insist on planning uncommercial plays must be regarded as a failure in dramatic art. In an art whose necessary aim is to interest the public, there is no virtue in denying the right of the public to determine whether or not it has been interested. If a man has entered a target competition and has missed the mark, the question whether his failure has resulted from aiming too low or from aiming too high is merely secondary: the point is that he has missed the target.

But there are many plays which, properly projected, can pay their way, without reaping, let us say, a larger interest on the investment than would have been afforded if the capital had been employed in any other enterprise. These plays should be classed, not as uncommercial drama, but as non-commercial drama; and the difference is obvious.

A non-commercial play may be defined as a play that is produced more for the love of the production than for the love of the financial profit that may possibly result from the investment. All business may be divided into good business and bad business. Dismissing bad business as uncommercial, good business may further be subdivided into big business and small business. Small business may be defined as that which yields less than ten per cent. on the investment; and big business may be defined as that in which a yield of less than ten per cent. is regarded as a failure.

The trouble with the prevailing theatre system in America to-day is not that this system is commercial; for, in any democratic country, it is not unreasonable to expect the public to defray the cost of the sort of drama that it wishes, and that, therefore, it deserves. The trouble is, rather, that our theatre system is devoted almost entirely to big business; and that, in ignoring the small profits of small business, it tends to exclude not only the uncommercial drama, but the non-commercial drama as well.

Whether or not the government of the United States can succeed in proving legally the existence of a theatre trust, everybody knows that the theatre system of this country is controlled by less than twenty men. These men have organized our theatre-business as a big business; and in none of their productions can they rest contented with a profit of less than ten per cent. Any play that does not realize this profit is summarily discarded as a failure; and four failures out of every five productions must be paid for by the overwhelming profits of the single fifth production. Thus, plays that might earn a profit of two hundred dollars per week are killed off to make room for other plays—which are frequently less worthy—that may earn a profit of two thousand dollars per week. In the frantic gamble of big business, large losses must be offset by larger gains.

It is this system of big business—which demands that any play, to earn the privilege of a continuance of its existence, shall reap a profit of several hundred per cent. of the original investment—that weighs so cruelly upon the author in America to-day. It is reasonable to demand of the dramatist that he shall sufficiently appeal to the theatre-going public to draw a yield of ten per cent. on the investment required to produce his play; but it is not reasonable to demand that a yield in excess of this percentage shall be regarded as a condition precedent to the continuance of his production. Any project that demands a profit of more than ten per cent. is not business, but gambling; and a gambling proposition is just as uncommercial as a non-commercial proposition.

To give the dramatist a proper chance to earn his living in America, we must break the power of the theatre trust. A review of recent judicial decisions in this country affords small hope that this effect can be attained by any governmental process. The only thing to do is to prove, by actual experiment, that small business can still be done in our theatres, quite irrespective of the dictates of the less than twenty men who have decreed that, in all our theatre-business, there shall be no alternative between big business and no business at all.

While discarding the uncommercial drama—that is to say, the sort of drama that cannot pay its way—as not worth fighting for, we must fight for the existence of the non-commercial drama—that is to say, the sort of drama that can earn a profit of from five to ten per cent., but is incapable of earning more.

XXVIII

THE PUBLIC AND THE THEATRE

I

A STUDY of the public is an indispensable detail of the study of the drama; for the public, in conjunction with the actors and the author, constitutes a corner of that eternal triangle upon which, as a fundamental basis, the edifice of the drama must be reared. If some Mæcenas, endowed with an exacting taste and an all-commanding pocketbook, should desire to enjoy a better drama than is ordinarily offered in the theatre of to-day, he might spend his time and money in the search for finer actors or for nobler authors, but he could accomplish his intention much more easily and quickly by collecting and delivering to the theatre a finer and a nobler audience. It has frequently been stated that the public always gets as good a drama as it deserves, since the managers, in order to make money, must give the public what the public wants; and this somewhat cynical theory is true to this extent,—that the public never gets a better drama than it concertedly requests. To improve the quality of the supply, it is necessary, first of all, to improve the quality of the demand. Though the drama is an art, the theatre is a business; and it does not pay to cast pearls before people who are lacking in intelligence and taste.

One of the main troubles with the theatre in America to-day is that it suffers tragically from a lack of constant patronage by people of intelligence and taste. Our supply of plays is not determined by the demand of our most cultured public, but only by the demand of a public that is by no means representative of the best that is thought and felt in this country at the present time. Any study of this problem must begin and end in the city of New York; for it is an unfortunate fact that our theatre is so constituted that the rest of the country is allowed to see only those plays which have previously made money in the metropolis. The exceptions to this statement are of the kind that only prove the rule. Attempts have been made, in recent years, to institute " producing centers " in certain other cities—Chicago, Los Angeles, and Boston, for example—but even plays produced originally in these cities have seldom been sent on tours through the country until they have been labeled as " successes " by the people who frequent the theatres in New York. As conditions stand at present, a metropolitan verdict is the only one that counts; and an author or an actor, in order to reach the rest of the country, must first secure the privilege of being booked throughout the circuits of the smaller cities by passing a favorable examination in New York. Thus—except for the admirable work that is being accomplished here and there in little independent theatres—the destiny of the drama in this country is still decided by the people who habitually pay to be amused in the tiny circle that is centered in Times Square. The question, then, becomes of prime importance whether these people are adequately representative of America, either as it is or as it yearns to be: and to this important question the answer is, emphatically, " No."

Any one who makes a practice of attending every play that is exhibited in the metropolis needs only to look about him in the orchestra to see at a glance that the success or failure of an offering is not determined by an audience that is representative of America or even of New York. The audience is recruited mainly from that artificial region that is known, in the language of the theatre, as Broadway,—a region in which real people do not live, and cannot live, because it is lighted only by electric lamps instead of by the sun and moon and stars.

The prospect would be hopeless if the public of Broadway were the only public in New York that the theatre might appeal to; but this is not the case. There are very many people of intelligence and taste—people of the sort who welcome eagerly the best that is thought and said through the medium of any of the arts— who have ceased to attend the theatre in New York because the theatre, for the most part, has ceased to give them the sort of stimulus that they desire. It is easy enough for any student of this problem to meet these people face to face, for their patronage of art is an active and a public exercise. Whenever the *Ninth Symphony* of Beethoven is played by a great orchestra in Carnegie Hall, the enormous auditorium is crowded to the roof by people who would also patronize the theatre if the theatre would afford them a commeasurable exaltation. A cultured and appreciative public pays six dollars a seat at the Metropolitan Opera House to hear the finest singing in the world; and whenever Nijinsky dances, the same public assembles in thousands to enjoy the spectacle. Yet music and dancing are arts less democratic than the drama—less popular in their appeal—and a more specific culture is required for the due appreciation of them. An afternoon stroll through the galleries of the various art-dealers on Fifth Avenue will also bring the student face to face with still another public composed of people who are quick to welcome the best that can be thought and said in terms of art. These people, who love painting and sculpture, would also love the theatre if the theatre should set out to woo them in the mood of beauty and of truth; and the teeming thousands who annually study the exhibits in the Metropolitan Museum of Art might crowd the galleries of any theatre that should successfully appeal to them.

The tragic fact of the matter seems to be that these thousands and thousands of people, who patronize music and painting and sculpture and dancing and all the other arts, have ceased to patronize the theatre. People of the same class, twenty years ago, attended every production at Daly's or the old Lyceum and exercised an active influence on the traffic of the stage; but nowadays, for the most part, they stay at home and permit the destiny of the drama to be determined by a mob of other people who are inferior in intelligence and taste.   They behave like educated voters on Election Day who remain away from the polls and allow some vulgar politician to sneak into a great office by default.

The way in which this cultured public was alienated from the theatre may now be studied, in retrospect, as a dismal fact of history.   Daly's audience was not dispersed by Daly's death, and the retirement of Daniel Frohman from active management was not a cause but a result of the disaster.   The catastrophe occurred about a dozen years ago, at the time of the great struggle between trust and counter-trust for supreme control of all the theatres in America.   During the course of this long struggle—which resulted ultimately in a no less devastating deadlock—the theatre became entirely commercialized, and the cathedrals of the drama were pulverized by the artillery of business.   At that period, the cultured public of New York—the public which, in the preceding decade, had supported Daly's Theatre and the old Lyceum—renounced regretfully the theatre-going habit; and the theatre of to-day still suffers from the fact that it is very difficult to reëstablish a faith which has been wantonly destroyed.

The sins of the fathers are visited upon the children; and the managers of to-day are forced to suffer for the crimes committed in the theatre by the managers of a dozen years ago.   The status of the drama has been steadily improved in recent years.   A new generation of managers, led by such men as Mr. Winthrop Ames, Mr. John D. Williams, and Mr. Arthur Hopkins—to mention only a few of those who are now appealing for consideration of the drama as an art—has greatly improved the product of our theatre; but this new array of managers has not yet succeeded in winning back the concerted support of that cultured public which renounced the theatre-going habit in the dark days of a dozen years ago.

The immediate problem at the present time is to find an effective method of convincing the cultured public that ten or a dozen of the round number of two hundred plays that are now produced every season in New York are genuinely worthy of the patronage of people of intelligence and taste. The best public must be won back to the support of the best drama; and this public must be organized and delivered so effectively that once again—as in the days of Daly's Theatre—it will become impossible for a really fine production to fail for lack of patronage.

One of the main difficulties of the situation is the decadence of dramatic criticism in New York. Dramatic criticism may be defined—in the terminology of Matthew Arnold—as " a disinterested endeavor to learn and propagate the best that is known and thought in the theatre of the world." This endeavor was at least attempted twenty years ago; but, during the last decade, the majority of our most influential newspapers have ceased to treat the drama as an art and have chosen, rather, to regard the theatre merely as a function of Broadway.

Thus the editing of our theatre for an inferior public is fostered by the fact that the dramatic columns in our newspapers are edited for the same public and confine themselves, for the most part, to an utterly uncritical endeavor to estimate in advance the success or failure of an undertaking in the theatre. They print a guess that a certain play will run a year, or else they print a guess that the production will be carted to the storehouse in a week. In other words, they judge the offerings of art according to a standard which is determined merely by the taste of an uncultivated audience.

The point is not that our individual dramatic critics are lacking in discernment. Nearly half a dozen of the writers who are employed at the present time to report the doings of the theatre in New York are endowed sufficiently, in education and in taste, to distinguish a work of art from a product of commercial manufacture; but the general attitude of our public press—considered as a whole—obscures their individual efforts " to learn and propagate the best that is known and thought in the theatre of the world." Even these writers are required to devote as many columns—or nearly as many—to the consideration of inconsiderable offerings as they are permitted to devote to the ten or twelve productions every year that really count. They are condemned, nine-tenths of the time, to write news about nothing; and, when *Pierrot the Prodigal* appears, their eloquent praise of the production remains unheeded by ears that have been previously deafened by other columns of praise devoted to some commercial fabric that seems sure to run a season,—like the highly-heralded *Turn to the Right!*, which, though popular and entertaining, is a badly constructed play and cannot be considered seriously as a work of art.

That our newspapers, for the most part, have ceased to treat the drama as an art, is a fact that can be easily established by a study of their pages. Whenever a new opera is produced at the Metropolitan Opera House, it is analyzed in detail by an expert who interprets its defects and qualities to an audience of cultured readers; exhibitions of painting or of sculpture are studied carefully by scholars who talk about art in terms that receive respect from an initiated public; but new plays, in the same newspapers, are merely written up amusingly as items in the general doings of the day. The policy of our newspapers toward music and painting and sculpture is scholarly and critical; but, with one or two exceptions, their policy toward the drama is merely reportorial. They treat the theatre mainly from the standpoint of its value as a fountainhead of news.

Now, art is art, and news is news, and never the twain shall meet. It is one thing to inform the cultured public of the fact that a visit to *Pierrot the Prodigal* affords an adventure to the spirit that may be classed with the unforgettable experience of traveling all the way to Nîmes to come suddenly around a corner and see the tiny Roman temple sitting lonely and eternal in the midst of time; and it is another thing entirely to inform the public of Broadway that *Turn to the Right!* is a " knock-out." The same newspaper cannot successfully sustain an attitude toward the theatre which shall be reportorial and an attitude toward the drama which shall be critical. Art is not news; because news wears a date upon its forehead and art does not. News, at the most, may be worthy of a nine days' wonder; but art, at its best, is a wonder for all time.

By editing their dramatic columns for the unculti-vated public of Broadway, instead of for that finer public that desires to learn and to enjoy the best that is known and thought in the world and is eager to patron-ize any exercise of art where art may be discerned, our newspapers make it very difficult for people of refine-ment to keep actively in touch with the best that is being done in the theatre of America. These people— and their name is legion—hang back from the support of even so superlative a thing as *Pierrot the Prodigal* because so often in the past they have been disillusion-ized by patronizing inferior productions that had been grossly overpraised.

This leads us to consider the great harm that has been done by the persistent over-advertising of inferior productions. The decadence of dramatic criticism is all the more dangerous at a time when the theatre is required to endure the insidious assaults of a system of mendacious puffery. It would scarcely be an exaggera-tion to state that the greatest foe of the contemporary drama is the contemporary press-agent. This func-tionary is employed to beat a big drum in front of every theatre and to tell the public that every play presented is a masterpiece. The weakness of the press-agent arises from the fact that, in the nature of things, he can't fool all the people all the time; but the tragedy of his position arises from the fact that, by fooling some of the people some of the time, he prevents nearly everybody from believing him, on some subsequent occasion, when he happens to come forward with the truth.

A perusal, at any time, of the advertising pages in the Sunday newspapers might lead to the impression that each of the forty plays then current in New York was the greatest play of the twentieth century; but this impression would be speedily corrected by a visit to the plays themselves. The trouble of the matter is that it would cost a cultured theatre-goer no less than one hundred and sixty dollars, and forty evenings of priceless time, to find out for himself that all these advertisements were nothing but mere lies; and, after this expensive experience, he might feel indisposed to risk another four dollars and another evening to see a masterpiece like *Pierrot the Prodigal*. The efforts of many press-agents to lure him to attend inferior productions are more than likely, in the long run, to result in keeping him away from a production which he would be very glad to patronize.

The method by which the press-agent manages to advertise a bad play as if it were a good play is just as simple as it is dishonest. Suppose that so cultured and reliable a critic as Mr. Walter Prichard Eaton, in reviewing a hypothetical farce entitled *The Straw Hat*, has written something like the following:—" The theme of *The Straw Hat* is traditional; the plot is mechanical; the dialogue is dull. One or two moments in the second act, however, are made mildly amusing by the acrobatic antics of a knockabout comedian."

The press-agent will seize upon this notice and print the following extraction from it in the next edition of the Sunday newspapers:—"'Amusing.'—Walter Prichard Eaton." By this procedure, people of intelligence and taste who subsequently see the play are led to believe that Mr. Eaton is an idiot; and when this distinguished commentator, at a later date, implores the public to patronize so beautiful a thing as *Pierrot the Prodigal*, a certain number of his readers will remember *The Straw Hat* and hug their money in their pockets.

A study of the psychology of theatrical advertising must lead to the opinion that the lies of the press-agent are the sort of blunders that are worse than crimes. Every lie that is printed to puff a bad play cuts down the attendance at the next really good play that is presented.

This is, perhaps, the biggest lesson that our managers have still to learn:—that, in the long run, it pays to tell the public that Mr. John Galsworthy is a greater man than Mr. James Montgomery, and that *The Thunderbolt*—which did not make any money in America—is a greater play than *Cheating Cheaters*—which was very popular. The persistent practice of press-agentry alienates more people from the theatre than it attracts; and the overadvertising of inferior productions makes it very difficult to secure the patronage of works that are superior by people of intelligence and taste.

II

There seems to be a general assumption—on the part of editors and managers and publishers—that the reading and theatre-going public is made up, for the most part, of fools.

Several years ago, the present writer was invited to prepare a series of instructive articles for a magazine whose circulation amounted to a million copies every month. " Remember, first of all," remarked the editor, " that our magazine is planned to appeal to the women-folk of Muncie, Indiana. Don't use any words that the women-folk of Muncie would not be likely to understand; don't refer to any authors that they haven't heard of. Write down to them. Don't talk above their heads." The answer was, of course, inevitable. " Have they read Sir Thomas Browne? Have they seen the lovely little jewel-box of Nîmes? Do they know the difference between Savonarola and a brand of soap? " " I'm afraid not," said the editor, and sighed. At this point, I retreated from the office, with a dignified adieu—for that was many years ago, and I accepted the editor's opinion of the public of Muncie, Indiana. But I know better now.

The fact is that many editors and publishers and managers assume a state of imbecility in the general and public mind. Their advice to authors, nearly always, is couched in some such phrase as this,—" Be careful, *do* be careful, not to talk above their heads! " That other danger of talking *underneath* the heads of the public is a matter that they seldom seem to think of! It never occurs to them, apparently, that the public may know more than they know themselves, and that the public may care more about the calling of high matters than they themselves have ever learned to care.

No author who really is an author can ever be successfully advised to " write down " to the public. The only reasonable thing to do—as every author knows— is to " write up " to the public; for every artist who has mystically listened to the elusive but imperious insistence of the harmony of words knows that nothing can be gained by a deliberate destruction of the predetermined pattern, and that everything is to be gained by a frank and free appeal to all the ears of all the world that are capable of hearing. As Lincoln said, in an apostolic moment, " You can't fool all the people all the time." Why not, therefore, take a chance and trust them?

Many, many years ago [for this was long before the period of moving-pictures] the present writer attempted to compose, in collaboration with a man who has since become a noted poet, a melodrama of the type designed to appeal to the public of Third Avenue. It was called *The Mad Dog*—if memory is not at fault —and the villain was a wicked doctor whose special business in life was to assault the lives of heroes and of heroines by inoculating them with germs of hydrophobia. But, after the first act had been sedulously planned, the poet said, one evening,—" The trouble with this job is that we haven't learned how not to laugh about it. Owen Davis doesn't laugh: Theodore

Kremer never laughed in his life. For Gawd's sake, let's be serious!" And then we tried—very, very hard—to be serious; but, after many weeks, we discovered that this consummation devoutly to be wished could not be achieved by merely taking thought. We did not know how not to laugh: we could not capture the mystic secret of "writing down" to the public of Third Avenue. We discovered, incidentally, that such masterpieces as *Bertha, the Sewing-Machine Girl* or *Chinatown Charlie, the King of the Opium Ring* can be written only by authors who are as certain of their mission and their message as Mr. Percy MacKaye; and we learned also that the only way to do a job successfully is to care about it, and to care about it absolutely. *The Mad Dog*—needless to say—was never written; but it served its momentary purpose in the scheme of things by teaching two young authors that the general and public mind is not a thing to be despised.

Why should it be despised, when so often—so very, very often—it has shown a disposition to stand up and to salute the momentary passing of anything at all that may be looked upon as offering an intimation of immortality? The heads of the public loom far higher than our managers or editors or publishers imagine. The problem is not how to talk down to them, but how to talk up to them! The only proper aspect for the author is the attitude of any of those favored saints of Perugino's painting, who look upward at they know not what, and smile, and wonder, and believe, and—in consequence—convince.

For nearly twenty years our theatre has been hampered by the fact that it has been commercially controlled by a little coterie of managers who—lacking education, lacking culture, lacking taste—have neglected to perceive the simple fact that, in these respects, the heads of the public have towered higher than their own. They have approached the public not humbly and with due respect, but arrogantly and with the sort of scorn which accompanies incompetence. They have based their business on a bland assumption that the people who support the theatre have no brains.

But, recently, there have been many unquestionable indications that the dominance of the American theatre is passing rapidly from those managers whose habit has been always to look down upon the heads of the public to a younger and a newer group who have adopted the more salutory habit of looking up to heads which they mystically hope to find somewhere in those higher regions which have remained, for such a long time, unexplored. In all their undertakings, these new managers have been actuated by a motive which may be defined—in philosophic terms—as " a daring to believe "; and this daring has been appreciated and rewarded by a public which enjoys the quite uncustomary feeling of being approached with that degree of courtesy which arises from respect.

XXIX

A DEMOCRATIC INSURRECTION IN THE THEATRE

I

A PERSON living in England in the period of Shakespeare, or in France in the period of Molière, would have considered himself cheated by the people who controlled the theatre if he had never been permitted to see a play of Shakespeare's or of Molière's; yet such an inhibition is imposed upon the public by the people who control the American theatre at the present time. We are living in the midst of a great period of dramatic productivity—one of the very greatest since the drama first emerged in Europe two thousand and four hundred years ago. During the last twenty-five years great plays have been delivered to the world by dramatists as different in message and in method as Ibsen, Strindberg, Hauptmann, Sudermann, Schnitzler, Donnay, Hervieu, Brieux, Rostand, Maeterlinck, Heijermans, Echegaray, D'Annunzio, Tchekoff, Pinero, Jones, Shaw, Synge, Galsworthy, and Barrie. These twenty men have written at least a hundred plays which will hold a permanent and honored place in any ultimate history of dramatic literature; and during the same period scores and scores of exceptionally worthy pieces have been written by other dramatists, including at least a dozen native-born Americans. In sheer productivity of dramatic authorship of prime importance, the present age undoubtedly exceeds the period of Molière and probably exceeds the period of Shakespeare. Yet very rarely is the public of New York, and almost never is the public of any of our smaller cities, permitted to see a performance of any of the great plays of the present age. Generally speaking, the theatre-going public of America might just as well be living in a period when no great plays were being written. The fact is that, in this country, the current theatre lamentably fails to fulfil its proper function of purveying the current drama.

The reason for this failure is that, though the drama ought to be a democratic art, the constitution of our theatre at the present time is not popular, but oligarchic. Nine-tenths of all the theatres in America are controlled by fewer than half a hundred men, and only a minority of these men are really interested in employing the theatre to purvey the current drama. The majority merely find themselves by accident in the theatre-business, and their chief object is to make as much money as they can. In consequence, they seldom produce a play which does not seem likely to run continuously in New York for at least half a season, and they rarely send to any of our lesser cities a play which has not already reaped the profits of a long run in the metropolis.

Of course, in a city like New York, a larger public can be found for a silly or a vulgar show than for a play that requires from its audience an appreciable amount of intelligence and taste. The naked legs of sportive chorus-girls will always appeal to more people than the naked souls of Ibsen's heroines. But, in theory, at least, the theatre ought to be a public-service corporation; and shall no service be performed for the mighty minority who care more about the human mind than the human members?

To this question the managers reply that they give the public what the public wants, and point to the testimony of the box-office to back up the assertion. This argument would be incontrovertible if the only public in America were the public that every evening flickers moth-like around the white lights of Broadway, seeking momentary entertainment with no forethought and no afterthought. But New York is not America—and Broadway is not New York. There are thousands and thousands of people who are eager to learn the best that is known and thought in the drama of the present period. In any particular community these people may stand in the minority; but, considered as a whole, they constitute a larger legion than is dreamt of in the philosophy of our oligarchic managers. A single enterprising organization, the Drama League of America, has already tabulated the names and addresses of a hundred thousand people who are willing and eager to patronize any great play that may be set before them. What can these people do to win the privilege of seeing the best plays of the present period adequately acted on the stage? As conditions stand at present, there is only one answer to this question. They must get together and produce these plays themselves. By a general and democratic insurrection, they must counteract the control of a public-service corporation by an oligarchy that has not given them the service they desire.

The only apparent impediment to such a revolution is the economic problem. If our millionaire managers cannot afford to show the American public the best that is known and thought in the drama of the present period, how can this great purpose be accomplished by people without capital?

But the oligarchs who now control our theatre risk more than is required—in the hope of winning more than is decreed. They waste enormous sums of money, for rent, for scenery, for salaries, which a democratic theatre could easily afford to save. It costs at least thirty thousand dollars to raise the curtain on a new show at the Winter Garden; but any little group of lovers of the drama can raise the curtain on a wise and lovely play, like Barrie's *Alice Sit-By-The-Fire*, for instance, at a total cost, for rent, for scenery, for salaries, of less than five hundred dollars.

There is, first of all, the cost of rent. Metropolitan managers count always on the patronage of the casual theatre-goer—the person who, after a good dinner, wishes merely, as the phrase is, to " go to the theatre," and does not choose deliberately to see a special play. Hence, to catch this drifting patronage, the theatres must always be located in immediate proximity to the best hotels and restaurants. A theatre so situated must occupy a large parcel of very valuable real estate; and the normal rent of such a site necessitates a very heavy overhead charge that must be assumed as a burden by any play produced in such a theatre.

To diminish this excessive burden of expenditure, two means are possible and practical. First, the theatre may be reduced in size; or, second, it may be moved away from the most expensive district of the city. The first of these adjustments accounts for the advent of what is called " the little theatre," and the second for the advent of what is called, in Paris, the *théâtre à côté*, or the theatre on the side.

Since fewer people wish to patronize great plays than wish to patronize a Winter Garden show, it is entirely practical to house them in a smaller auditorium, and thereby to save, in a city of considerable size, an initial expenditure of many thousands of dollars for real estate. It may also logically be assumed that those people who really want to see great plays will be willing to travel an extra quarter of an hour for the privilege of doing so. It is entirely practical to save several thousand dollars more by placing the democratic theatre in a less expensive district of the city than that which is adjacent to the best hotels and restaurants.

Turning to the economic problem of scenery, it must be said at once that the advantage lies heavily upon the side of a democratic insurrection. The suggestive and decorative type of scenery which in recent years has been developed in Germany and Russia under the inspiring influence of Gordon Craig is not only much more artistic, but much less expensive than the realistic scenery of the Victorian period which is still retained

by the gambling oligarchs in their desperate endeavor
to give the public what they think the public wants.
Now that the way has been shown by the new great
artists of the theatre, any one with half an eye for line
and color can make a set so inexpensively that men
accustomed only to big productions would doubt the
evidence and would insist on paying more money for
something less artistic and less beautiful.

In the third place, an enormous saving may be made
in salaries by the simple expedient of producing plays
with casts of amateur or semi-professional actors.
Even though it be immediately granted that an actor
who commands a salary of three hundred dollars a week
is likely to be a better artist than an actor who is
willing to work for thirty dollars a week—or an actor
who is willing to work for nothing at all—it must still
be stated, on the other side, that those who really love
the drama would rather see a great play only adequately acted than see great acting in a silly
play.

To sum up the situation, it appears that the thousands and thousands of people in America who wish to
see the great plays of the present period adequately
acted on the stage must start a democratic theatre
of their own, in opposition to the theatre of the
oligarchic managers; and it appears, further, that this
project is economically feasible by the elimination of
superfluous extravagance in the expenditure for salaries, for scenery, and for rent.

The soundness of this theory has already been tested
and proved. In several of our cities, semi-professional

companies in little theatres on the side have already put
the Broadway managers to shame. The most signal
success of this sort is that of the Washington Square
Players in New York. This organization was incorporated by a little group of lovers of the drama who
desired to stimulate and to develop new and artistic
methods of acting, producing, and writing for the
American stage. From the very outset, the constitution of the company was democratic, and it welcomed
to its membership any actor, artist, or author who was
sympathetic with its aims. The project of the Washington Square Players has been to produce new plays
by American writers and important plays by foreign
dramatists which would not otherwise have been granted
a hearing in New York.

During the first season, which began on February 19,
1915, and in which the company played only two or
three evenings a week, ten one-act plays by American
writers were produced and four by foreign authors.
During the second season, which began on October 4,
1915, and lasted till the end of May, 1916, the company played every night and every Saturday afternoon.
During this period ten new plays by American writers
were produced, and eight by foreign authors.

In one season and a half, these thirty one-act plays
—ten by European dramatists and twenty by American—were adequately set before the public, and the
charge for tickets was limited to fifty cents and one
dollar. The reader may wonder how it has been possible to produce so many plays, at such a small charge
for admission, without any endowment to begin with,

and without rolling up any deficit during a season and a half.

The Washington Square Players contrived to diminish the excessive cost of rent, at the outset of their undertaking, by locating in a little theatre on the side— the Bandbox Theatre, in Fifty-seventh Street, east of Third Avenue. The excessive cost of scenery was easily eliminated by relying on the artist-members of the organization to supply summary and decorative settings for the love of doing so. The scenic settings exhibited by the Washington Square Players were far and away the most artistic that were exhibited in any theatre in New York in 1916; yet these settings cost, upon the average, a little less than fifty dollars each.

Again, the democratic organization of this company made possible a great saving in salaries. The leading actors were paid only thirty dollars a week; most of the performers received only ten dollars a week; and many of the minor parts were played without remuneration by amateurs of independent means who were seeking an opportunity for practice on the stage. No royalties were paid to any of the authors. The American playwrights contributed gladly their one-act plays, and all the foreign plays produced were out of copyright.

This detailed examination of the budget of the Washington Square Players reveals one or two conditions which are not ideal; but the general conduct of the organization has been of enormous service to all lovers of the drama in New York. The acting which has been exhibited at the Bandbox for fifty cents has been, in general, inferior to the acting which has been exhibited on Broadway for two dollars; but the scenic settings have been undeniably superior, and the choice of plays has been much more satisfactory. Taking into consideration every element of possible enjoyment, it may be said without reservation that this company has conducted one of the most interesting theatres in New York.

The valuable work which has been accomplished at the Neighborhood Playhouse, in the heart of that great district of plain living and high thinking which the patrons of the theatres along "The Great White Way" are accustomed to refer to as " the slums," must be considered in a slightly different category. This exquisite little playhouse was presented to the Henry Street Settlement by the Misses Irene and Alice Lewisohn. The initial item of rent was thereby canceled from the ledger. Many interesting plays have been produced by a well-trained company of amateurs, composed mainly of working people who live in the neighborhood; and there is, therefore, no expense for salaries. The scenery and costumes are designed and executed by the art classes of the Settlement. Though always adequate and often exceptionally beautiful, they are very inexpensive. The Neighborhood Players have thus been enabled to present, at a charge for tickets limited to twenty-five and fifty cents, a large number of unusually worthy plays, and have established a living theatre in a district which had been totally neglected in the past.

But the work which has been done in the metropolis by such organizations as the Neighborhood Players and the Washington Square Players is not, by any means, unique; it is important mainly as an indication of a general and democratic insurrection which has found expression also in many other cities of this country. Here and there and everywhere, people who demand good plays are taking the matter into their own hands and producing them themselves.

In Chicago, for example, one of the most interesting institutions at the present time is the Little Theatre, which is conducted by Maurice Browne. When this theatre was founded, Mr. and Mrs. Browne deliberately limited their own salaries to the living wage of fifteen dollars a week, and by this economy were able to make productions which have been talked about beyond the seas.

Excellent work has also been accomplished at Mrs. Lyman Gale's Toy Theatre in Boston. It was here that Livingston Platt was afforded his first opportunity to exercise his exquisite art in designing scenery and costumes. Mr. Platt has subsequently been employed by Margaret Anglin to design the sets for her Shakespearean repertory and her productions of Greek tragedies. But it should always be remembered that it was at the Toy Theatre that Miss Anglin discovered this gifted artist.

The next step which must be taken in furtherance of the democratic insurrection will be the erection of a chain of little theatres in various cities, so that an interchange of plays and companies may be effected between one city and another. Already there are indications that this next step will soon be taken. In

Philadelphia, for instance, a movement is on foot to erect an Art Alliance building in Rittenhouse Square which shall house under a single roof all the art societies of the city. This building is to contain a theatre which shall always be available, at a minimum of cost, for any adequate performance of the better sort of drama. In Buffalo, also, there is a movement to erect a similar Art Alliance building containing a little theatre. When these two institutions are established, it should be a simple matter to arrange an interchange of worthy plays between Buffalo and Philadelphia.

It is important, also, that some mention should be made of the only municipal theatre in the United States, which is situated in Northampton, Massachusetts. The Academy of Music in that city, a beautiful and well-appointed building, was erected and owned by the late Edward H. R. Lyman; and at his death he bequeathed it to his fellow-citizens. Throughout the season, eight performances a week are given, with a weekly change of bill, by a resident stock-company, under the direction of Jessie Bonstelle and Bertram Harrison. The majority of the plays presented are pieces which have already been successful in New York. However, under the patronage of a public-spirited citizen, Mr. George B. McCallum, special matinées are given every month by the Northampton Players in a comfortable little theatre in his house, and these matinées are devoted to classical examples of the contemporary drama.

If Northampton, a city of only twenty thousand inhabitants, can maintain a municipal theatre, there is no reason why the theatre should not be established in other cities as a public institution. If the Washington Square Players can develop in a season and a half the most interesting theatre in New York, there is no reason why a similar undertaking should not succeed in any other city.

It is the small towns of this country that suffer most at the hands of the oligarchs who conduct the theatre-business. Only third- or fourth-rate productions of unimportant plays whose only title to remembrance is that once, when they were acted by a first-rate company, they made money in New York, are sent out to the one-night stands; and, if the people in these towns really want to see the best contemporary plays, they must produce them themselves.

It has been proved already that this undertaking is not impossible. In any community of ten thousand citizens there must be at least ten people who can act and at least five who can design scenery and costumes. Artistic ability is more widespread than many people know; and wherever a democratic theatre has been started, its ranks have soon been crowded by applicants of adequate ability.

To see great plays in the American theatre, our public needs only to deserve to see them; but this deserving must express itself not passively, but actively. We must no longer rest contented with an oligarchic conduct of what ought to be a public-service corporation. We must demand a drama of the people, by the people, for the people; and we must toil for it until we get it.

II

There are many indications which tend to show that a newer and a nobler chapter in the history of the American theatre is shortly to be opened, and that the only fitting caption for the chapter that is being closed and set away forever must be " The Passing of Broadway."

The meaning of " Broadway "—like the meaning of " Bohemia "—is less important when the word is used to designate a geographical location than when it is employed to indicate an atmosphere and attitude of mind. Broadway—upon the map—is nothing but a narrow, winding, and unlovely thoroughfare; but the Broadway attitude of mind—a narrow, winding, and unlovely attitude—is a phenomenon that calls for careful study. A mood is more important than a street, even as the law of gravitation is more important than a falling apple. Thus the word " Broadway " takes on a larger meaning when it ceases to suggest a place and begins to be employed as the outward and visible embodiment of an idea.

The Broadway attitude of mind is the attitude of a little group of never more than fifty thousand people that swarm and flutter in a futile circle around that tiny point upon the map which marks the intersection of Broadway and Forty-second Street. The life of this little group of people is not related logically to the life of that great city which envelops and ignores it; and it is even less related to the life of America at large. America is one thing; New York is something different; and Broadway—as Mawruss Perlmutter might be imagined to remark—is "something else again."

The denizens of Broadway lead a life that is utterly artificial. They begin the day's experience with a heavy and exceedingly expensive dinner at some glittering hotel or restaurant. Then they buy tickets for some " show " that is recommended to them by an agency. After sitting through this " show "—which, as chance may fall, they deem to be a " knock-out " or a " flivver " —they finish out the difficult adventure with supper and a dance at some noisy and meretricious cabaret. These people never notice the sun and moon and stars, because their life is lighted with a million incandescent lamps; but the Great White Way, which tempts their feet to wander, is nothing but a tinsel imitation of that starry track which sweeps across the unimpeded and immeasurable sky.

The population of Broadway is temporary and un-stable. The people of New York do not participate, in any noticeable number, in the puny flutterings of this tiny inner circle. Broadway does not attract them. People of any standing in New York society have homes or clubs to go to; and they do not have to entertain their friends at a public and ill-mannered restaurant or cabaret. They do not even have to go to the theatre— if their purpose be to kill an evening—unless the theatre offers them a spectacle that is unusually worthy of at-tention. The Broadway populace is made up mainly of transient visitors from other cities who are trying, rather desperately, to " see New York," because they do not live there. They " see New York " by visiting a show or two and a hotel dining-room or two, and their subsequent impressions of the daily life of the metropolis are founded on the evidence of these adventures.

These people are not natives of New York, and neither are they representatives of America at large. They have ceased to be representative of Omaha or Oshkosh because, for the moment, they have divorced themselves in mood from their traditional locality and embarked upon a holiday adventure. They are in an artificial state of mind. People from Peoria who spend fantastic sums of money for the privilege of sitting at adjacent tables in a restaurant and regarding each other as " typical New Yorkers " do not constitute a public that is representative of anything that can reasonably be related to the reality of life at large.

For nearly twenty years our theatre has been edited to entertain this trivial and transient population. Commercial and non-commercial travelers enjoying a temporary sense of playing hookey from their homes have set the tone of taste for our American productions. Those enterprising managers who, at the outset of the present century, organized the theatres of America into a gigantic trust and a scarcely less gigantic counter-trust, were men whose vision of this country was limited to the tiny circle that is centered in Times Square. They convinced themselves that the surest way of making money in the theatre was not to produce plays about the life of America for the public of America, nor even to produce plays about the life of New York for the public of New York, but to produce plays about the life of Broadway for the public of Broadway.

Because of this predisposition of the managers, our playwrights have been required to conform to a standard of taste that has been extremely stultifying. To earn the privilege of making an appeal to America at large, they have been required, first of all, to secure a Broadway production and to achieve a Broadway success. If an author has imagined something too simple and too beautiful and true to fit the comprehension of the fifty thousand flutterers who swarm around Times Square, he has been denied the privilege of talking to a saner and serener public.

It would not be fair to say, or to suggest, that Broadway has given nothing to the theatre that has been worth while. Broadway cares little about beauty and rather less than little about truth; but it takes a lively interest in cleverness, and it has a well-developed sense of humor. Several of our Broadway plays have been very good plays of their kind; and in the person of one man at least—the celebrated Mr. George M. Cohan—Broadway has developed a dramatist of quite extraordinary talent. Several other playwrights—Mr. Winchell Smith, for instance—have done artistic work while following the formula laid out by Mr. Cohan; but the trouble is that these artists of Broadway were soon surrounded by an over-eager legion of subsidiaries, until our stage was flooded with second- and third-rate imitations of the Cohan type of play.

Half a dozen years ago, a big majority of all the plays that ran for more than a hundred nights in New

York were plays in which the Broadway attitude of mind was formulated for the entertainment of the floating population of Times Square. But a definitive feature of more recent seasons is the triumph of a new tendency in the American theatre which foretells the final passing of the devastating dominance of the Broadway attitude of mind. A new group of producing managers—led by such men as Mr. Winthrop Ames, Mr. Arthur Hopkins, and Mr. John D. Williams—has successfully assaulted the long-standing and hitherto apparently impregnable position of the Broadway magnates. These men have quietly and modestly unfurled a flag that bears the simple, but unconquerable legend—" Beauty is Truth, Truth Beauty." Instead of seeking what the public wants, they are seeking what the public needs; and the public has risen up and praised them for their insight and their enterprise. These managers —whose vision is by no means circumscribed within the limits of the tiny circle that is centered in Times Square—have been supported strongly by many sturdy little groups of insurrectionists—like the Washington Square Players and the Portmanteau Players—who have insisted, from the very outset of their activities, that the proper thing to ask about a play is not whether the people of Broadway will like it, but whether the people who do not like Broadway will like it.

XXX

LITERATURE AND THE DRAMA

I

ONE reason for the regrettable divorce between American literature and American drama is that our leading novelists and our leading playwrights live in different worlds and rarely meet each other. In France, where every playwright is a man of letters and every man of letters understands the theatre, it would be impossible for a leading dramatist, like the late Paul Hervieu, not to know a literary leader, like M. Anatole France. It may safely be assumed, without inquiry, that M. Brieux and M. Paul Bourget are acquainted with each other, and that each of them appreciates the other's art. But, in America, it may just as safely be assumed that Mr. George M. Cohan has never met Mr. William Dean Howells and that Mr. George Broadhurst is not personally acquainted with Mrs. Edith Wharton. Our leading literary writers do not understand the theatre, and several of our most successful playwrights are unfamiliar with our literature. They live, as has been said, in different worlds.

The world of our American novelists is immeasurably broader and deeper than the world of our American playwrights. In the entire history of our theatre, there is no dramatist who has at all approached the world-significance of Hawthorne, or Mark Twain, or Mr. Henry James. If America can make great literature, if it can give to the world a Walt Whitman and a Bret Harte, why should it be impossible for America to make great drama? The answer is that our men of the theatre have not yet learned to live as sanely and to work as honestly as have our men of letters.

It is a curious and interesting fact that, whereas nine-tenths of all our leading playwrights live in New York and write about Times Square for the entertainment of the metropolis, the majority of our novelists live elsewhere and write about some little section of America for the edification of America at large. The main reason why our literature is better than our drama is that art must be planted in the soil and grow up as a miracle of nature bursting into flower and fruit, and that there isn't any soil in Times Square, but only paving-stones. Our American literature has discovered America, in all its variety and multiplicity. Our novelists have written faithful and illuminating records of life in Maine and Massachusetts, in Georgia, Tennessee, and Louisiana, in Illinois and Indiana, in Arizona and California; but our playwrights, for the most part, have written records of America only as America is seen from the point of view of Broadway and Forty-second Street. Our drama is metropolitan, and therefore un-American; for what do they know of America who only know Broadway?

Many years ago, Mr. Augustus Thomas started out

with the adventurous idea of writing a series of plays that should be localized in different states; but, after having dealt with Alabama, Missouri, Arizona, and Colorado, he " discovered " the philosophy of Bishop Berkeley and renounced his self-appointed task of observation to embark upon the mystic seas of abstract speculation. Just for a handful of culture he left us; and no successor has arisen to strive earnestly to make the map of our American drama coextensive with the map of our American literature.

The average American novelist who attains distinction lives for many years in the locality where he was born, studies the people about him, and interprets their peculiarities to the world at large. His work is alive because it is local; and—despite the paradox—it is national because it is provincial. But the average American playwright who attains distinction moves to New York in his early twenties, becomes associated with the theatre, and thereafter interprets only the thoughts and feelings of Broadway to the public of Broadway. He ceases to be national by becoming metropolitan; he ceases to see over the footlights into the illimitable domain of life.

This is the reason why our American drama shows such a paucity of *genre* studies, although the intimate depiction of localities has always been a strong point in our American literature. Our novelists, who study life, know nothing of our theatre; and our playwrights, who study the theatre, know nothing of our life. This antithesis may overstate the facts, but it is based upon a sound distinction. Hawthorne, who could not make a play, was so familiar with the little town of Salem, Massachusetts, that when he wrote about it in *The Scarlet Letter* he achieved a contribution to the literature of the world; but Mr. William Gillette, who can make plays, has never studied any aspect of American life as thoroughly as Hawthorne studied the life of colonial New England.

When we try to make a *genre* play in America, we usually have to call into collaboration two different artists who do not really understand each other—a novelist, who understands the life to be depicted, and a dramatist, who understands the exigencies of the stage. The first supplies the material, and the second supplies the method of the play. The result is a hybrid product which, though ceasing to be literature, has not attained the dignity of drama. It is as if the material for *Hindle Wakes* had been supplied by a novelist from Manchester and the play had been built and written by a London dramatist who had never been in Lancashire. If ever we are to have a real drama of New Orleans, it must be written at first hand by a playwright as familiar with life among the creoles as Mr. George W. Cable: it must not be dramatized from one of Mr. Cable's stories by a playwright who has never ventured south of Philadelphia. If we could bring all our novelists to New York and put them through a practical course in theatrical construction, and if, at the same time, we could exile all our playwrights from New York and put them through a practical course in living and in observation, we might eventually bring about a marriage between American

literature and American drama, and create a real and
true dramatic literature.

II

In recent years, the locus of the best dramatic creation in the British Isles has been shifted from London
to the provinces.   Remarkable and richly human plays
have come from Lancashire (like Stanley Houghton's
Hindle Wakes), from Yorkshire (like Githa Sowerby's
Rutherford and Son), from Wales (like *Change*, by J.
O. Francis), from Scotland (like Graham Moffat's
Bunty Pulls the Strings), and from Ireland, where half
a dozen worthy dramatists have spurred each other on
to a very ecstasy of productivity; but, in the same
period, scarcely any richly human plays have come from
London playwrights writing about London life.   Thus,
although the British theatre is still centered of necessity in the metropolis, the British drama has lately
found its most fruitful source of genuine inspiration
elsewhere.

The practical reason for this change is not difficult to
find.   The greatest drama is called into being by the
greatest theatre; and the two greatest theatres in the
British Isles at present are the Abbey Theatre in Dublin and the Gaiety Theatre in Manchester.   In both of
these institutions—for they are worthy of that dignified
and lofty word—the repertory system is maintained,
and every encouragement is offered to new authors to do
their very best, regardless of commercial consequences.
The London theatres, like the theatres of New York,
acknowledge the existence of new playwrights only after

their existence has been proved; but both Miss Horniman and Lady Gregory go out into the highways and hedges, and find new playwrights, and compel them to come within the theatre.   Thus Miss Horniman discovered Stanley Houghton, encouraged him to write his masterpiece, and made him famous throughout the world, at an age when it would have been extremely difficult for him to compel a recognition of his worth in the metropolis.

But, regardless of how and why the change has been effected, it must be said emphatically that this shift in the dramatic locus of the British Isles has been a good thing for the British drama.   It has brought the British drama closer to the soil, made it more real and more sincere, freed it almost utterly from artifice, and in making it more local has made it in the deepest sense more national.

A peculiarity of modern progress has been a leveling of natonal distinctions in the life of the biggest cities in the world.   Immediate communication by telegraph and constant travel by rapid transit have caused great cities to conform to a compromise of custom that is not national but cosmopolitan.   Life, on any of the higher levels of society, no longer differs greatly in London or New York, in Paris or Berlin, in Petrograd or Rome. The seeker after traits that are definitively national must plunge into the provinces.   To see France the traveler must keep away from Paris, and to see England he must turn his back on London.   New York is now the least American of American cities, for the very reason that it has become the most cosmopolitan.   A metropolis, acquiring international importance, ceases to be national.

The greatest drama of any nation must always be a national drama; and this is only another way of saying that, in this present period, the greatest drama must tend more and more to be provincial. A truly English drama must now be sought for, not so much in Mayfair nor in Belgravia, as in Lancashire or Yorkshire or some other of the rural counties. Hence the field that Miss Horniman has staked out for the rising writers of provincial Manchester is a field in reality more fertile than that cosmopolitan and trampled tract that is offered to the London dramatist.

This fact is of emphatic interest to those of us who are seriously concerned with the development of a native drama in America. The chief difficulty that impedes the progress of the American drama at the present time is the fact that nearly all our plays are written in New York and written from the New York point of view. New York is not America: New York is not even—as has been said before—American: to see America only as it is superficially and superciliously seen in the metropolis is not to see America at all. For a true interpretation of what is most definitively national in our national life, we should look to the provinces; and this we have not done, except in a few extraordinary compositions like *Children of Earth*, by Alice Brown. Many of our plays—the majority, perhaps—are set in little cities; but in these plays we do not genuinely study the life of little cities, we merely transfer to a different locality the life that has been studied in Times

Square.   Mr. George M. Cohan's practice is a case in point.   Such plays as *Hit-the-Trail Holliday*, *Broadway Jones*, and *Get-Rich-Quick Wallingford* are set in provincial towns; but nearly all the characters behave as Times Square people would behave if transported to a little city, and not at all as natives of a little city would behave.   Our playwrights tread the narrow lane that is bounded by the buildings of Broadway; but they do not fare beyond the precincts of Manhattan Island, to settle down and look about with open eyes, until they can achieve the miracle of discovering America.

XXXI

A SCHEME FOR A STOCK COMPANY

My Saturday morning course in the Contemporary Drama at Columbia University is attended by a hundred and fifty students, of both sexes, whose ages range from seventeen to sixty. They come from many different sections of the country, and may be regarded as fairly representative of the sort of public that is particularly interested in the contemporary theatre. Every now and then, before I bring up for discussion some unusually popular and celebrated play—such as *The Second Mrs. Tanqueray*, or *Candida*, or *Mrs. Dane's Defence*, or *Alice Sit-By-The-Fire*—I ask the class to tell me how many of its members have seen the piece in question; and I am always staggered and disheartened when only five or six hands go up in the entire room. More than nine-tenths of these particularly interested students of the stage have never actually seen these notable and standard plays, because they did not happen to be living in New York in those seasons when these pieces were first set before the public. It is only reasonable to suppose that the plight of my students is not at all exceptional, and to assume that there are thousands of other people in New York who, though seriously interested in the best that has been thought and said in the contemporary drama, have missed their only opportunity for seeing several of the most celebrated plays of recent years.

It is only in the English-speaking theatre that great plays are utterly withdrawn from currency as soon as they have come to be regarded—as least in a restricted sense—as classical. Our theatre is astonishingly wasteful. It tosses away to undeserved oblivion the best plays of the best playwrights it has called into its service. The theatre is conducted otherwise in all the countries of continental Europe. If a great play happens to be written by a Frenchman, a German, a Russian, an Italian, a Norwegian, or a Spaniard, it is not thrown carelessly into the scrap-basket as soon as its initial run has been completed; it is permanently preserved, as a part of the dramatic repertory of the nation that has produced it. For many years, it will be acted ten or twenty times a season; and then, for half a century, it will be acted three or four times every year; for any play which, at the outset, has come into the theatre trailing clouds of glory and displaying intimations of immortality is a play that no continental nation can willingly permit to be forgotten.

But, in the English-speaking theatre, the career of a great play is very different from this. At the outset, it may perhaps be acted for an entire season in London or New York; the next year, it may be sent " on the road " in the United States or on a tour of " the provinces " in England; and, subsequently still, it may be acted fitfully by half a hundred cheap stock com-

panies in little towns: but after that, the play is thrown
away and never acted any more.

Since the modern English drama was inaugurated by
Sir Arthur Pinero in 1893 [the date of the initial production of *The Second Mrs. Tanqueray*], at least a
hundred plays have been written in the English language that are worthy of being seen and studied again
and yet again; yet nowhere in the English-speaking
world does there exist a theatre that is dedicated to the
endeavor to keep these plays before the public.

Something, manifestly, should be done to remedy
this " great refusal " of our theatre to recognize and
reverence the accomplished fact of greatness.   Some
Villon should arise, to chant a tragical ballade demand-
ing an answer to the question, " Where are the plays of
yesteryear? " . . . *Man and Superman, The Mollusc,
Mid-Channel, Michael and His Lost Angel, Hindle
Wakes, The Admirable Crichton*—why should plays so
eminent as these be left to gather dust upon the shelf
when they might be gathering applause behind the footlights?

The answer is that neither in England nor in America does there exist a national theatre—like the Théâtre
Français—which has been chartered to perpetuate the
milestones and the monuments of the dramaturgic
genius of the nation.   Our people, furthermore, are
singularly lacking in the instinct for conservation.   In
America, at least, we have no past; and this is probably
the reason why we overvalue the present and bet too
heavily upon the future.   We lose our breath in chasing
the elusive light of novelty, and lack serenity to settle

down and contemplate the landmarks of the road that
we have traveled.

It has been proved in practice that the repertory
system—which works easily and economically in the
national and municipal theatres of France and Germany—cannot be imposed successfully upon the public
of New York. Our people are not accustomed to a
change of bill from night to night; they expect the run
of any play—however long or short its period—to be,
at least, continuous; and the experience of Mr. Winthrop Ames at the New Theatre, and Mr. Granville
Barker at Wallack's, and Miss Grace George at the
Playhouse, convinced all three of these experimenting
managers that any change of program between a Monday and a Saturday was disconcerting and discouraging to the ticket-buying public. People who came to
the box-office with money in their hands to buy tickets
for a certain play would go away again when they
discovered that another piece was to be given on the
night in question. But no experimental manager has
yet discovered an objection to a frequent change of
program, provided that the run of each successive
play shall be continuous, and provided also that the
date for each successive change of bill shall be clearly
and emphatically impressed upon the public.

We have not had a first-class stock company in New
York for more than a dozen years. Is there any ir-
remediable reason why such a company should not be
organized at present, for the specific purpose of recalling to the attention of the theatre-going public a series
of great plays by great authors—all of which have been

written since 1893 [and therefore in conformity with the conventions of the contemporary theatre], and all of which have been written by British or American authors [and therefore in conformity with standards of taste to which our theatre-going public is accustomed]; is there any real reason why a stock company, that should never present a single play which had not already been approved by the public and praised by every critic as a masterpiece, should fail to be supported by the thousands and thousands of people who are interested eagerly in studying the best that has been thought and said in the contemporary drama?

First of all, it would be necessary to rent a theatre outright for a season of thirty weeks, beginning in October. Perhaps some semi-abandoned playhouse that is not so very distant from the center of the theatre district—like the Garrick, for example—might be secured at a rental that would be comparatively low. Next, it would be necessary to assemble a well-balanced company of experienced professional actors. The acting should be of a high order of excellence; and there should be no dallying with beginners or with amateurs. That it is not by any means impossible to collect the sort of company that I have in mind was proved by Mr. Winthrop Ames in his experiment at the New Theatre and again by Miss Grace George in her more recent experiment at the Playhouse.

During the season of thirty weeks, precisely fifteen plays should be produced, and each play should be performed two weeks, and two weeks only, regardless of its comparative success or failure. The entire program of fifteen plays to be presented should be announced before the beginning of the season, and subscriptions should be asked for on the strength of this announcement. Every item on the list, without exception, should be a play originally written in the English language, since 1892, by some author of acknowledged excellence—a play, moreover, which ran for many weeks or months when it was first produced, and is now regarded by a consensus of both popular and critical opinion as a masterpiece according to its kind.

These requirements are high; but it is by no means difficult to find plays that fulfil them. Here, for instance, is a list of fifteen plays, of many kinds, that might be offered as the program for the initial season:— *The Second Mrs. Tanqueray* and *The Gay Lord Quex*, by Sir Arthur Pinero; *Mrs. Dane's Defence*, by Henry Arthur Jones; *Candida* and *Man and Superman*, by George Bernard Shaw; *The Admirable Crichton* and *Alice Sit-By-The-Fire*, by Sir James Matthew Barrie; *The Mollusc*, by Hubert Henry Davies; *The Silver Box*, by John Galsworthy; *Don*, by Rudolf Besier; *Hindle Wakes*, by Stanley Houghton; *The Easiest Way*, by Eugene Walter; *The Truth*, by Clyde Fitch; *The Witching Hour*, by Augustus Thomas; and *The Poor Little Rich Girl*, by Eleanor Gates.

This list has been written rapidly and almost at random; and it would be very easy to draw up several other programs of fifteen well-remembered plays that would be equally attractive. If a stock company of experienced and well-known actors should offer to produce these fifteen plays [or fifteen other plays of equal interest] in thirty weeks, would it be very difficult to secure subscriptions for the season on the strength of this announcement? The public would be assured in advance that every play would be worth seeing, and that every play would be well acted; and the management would be certain in advance that every play would be reviewed with critical approval by a press that could be counted on, for once, to be unanimous.

Every encouragement should be offered to induce the theatre-going public to subscribe for the entire season of fifteen plays. Thus, the seats in the orchestra might be sold to subscribers for a dollar and a half and to non-subscribers for two dollars, the seats in the balcony might be sold to subscribers for a dollar and to non-subscribers for a dollar and a half, and the seats in the gallery might be sold to subscribers for twenty-five cents and to non-subscribers for fifty cents. Season tickets for the balcony and gallery, admitting the purchaser to one performance of each of the fifteen plays, should be offered in blocks of ten or more, at even cheaper rates, to students of our colleges and schools and workers in our social settlements.

If I am right in thinking that my own students at Columbia are not exceptional but representative, and that there are thousands of people in New York who are eager for an opportunity to make acquaintance, or renew acquaintance, with the acknowledged masterpieces of our modern English drama, it would not be difficult to secure sustained support for a season of fifteen plays of the quality that has been indicated by the tentative list which I have ventured to suggest. The force of habit is as strong in theatre-going as it is in every other exercise of energy; and I believe that these people would soon acquire and enjoy the habit of sitting in the same seat, on the same evening, every other week, to see an adequate performance of a play whose merit is known to be unquestionable.

A considerable amount of the working capital of this hypothetic institution would be furnished by subscriptions—after the plays had been selected, and the company had been engaged, and a prospectus [announcing both plays and company] had been published. But, of course, the major portion of the capital would have to be supplied by some commercial manager who believed in the idea, or borrowed from certain public-spirited citizens of the type concerned in the directorate of the Metropolitan Opera House. An initial investment of not less than one hundred thousand dollars would be necessary, in order that the director of the undertaking should be able, at the outset, to lease a theatre for thirty weeks and to engage a company of experienced actors for the same period. I believe, however, that the first season would return a profit of at least ten thousand dollars, or ten per cent. on the original investment; and I believe, also, that the percentage of profit would be increased in subsequent seasons.

In the first place, it is cheaper to lease outright a semi-abandoned theatre for a period of thirty weeks than to secure admission to an active theatre, and to continue tenure, for the same period. In the second place, the rate of royalty that has to be paid to a great author for a great play which is more than three years old is considerably less than the rate of royalty that has to be paid to an inconsiderable author for a new play that may turn out to be devoid of merit. By a blanket arrangement that could easily be made with the agents who have been deputed to represent the authors, the fifteen plays enumerated in the list which I have ventured to suggest could be produced at a fixed royalty of two hundred dollars a week; and this is much less than the royalty that has to be paid for any new play that is not an arrant failure. In the third place, a considerable saving could be made in the matter of adjusting the salaries of the actors. Many excellent performers who customarily demand two hundred dollars a week for their services would be willing to join the sort of company I have in mind at a salary of one hundred dollars a week. Any actor who might join this hypothetic company would be assured of thirty weeks of continuous employment, instead of the usual two weeks; he would be assured of an entire season on Broadway; and he would also be assured of a certain opportunity, within a single season, for playing fifteen different parts, each written by an author of acknowledged eminence, before the eyes of every manager and critic in New York. In view of these three inducements, which would be absolutely guaranteed, there is scarcely an experienced actor in the profession who would not willingly accept a considerable diminution in his customary salary. The reason why many actors demand a salary of three or four hundred dollars a week is merely that, after they have rehearsed for nothing for three weeks, the play may fail and they may be summarily discarded from employment, with only two or three weeks' pay for five or six weeks' work. These same actors could be signed up, at half-salary, for a metropolitan season that was guaranteed to last for thirty weeks.

The expense for scenery in the sort of theatre that has been suggested would be extremely slight. In most cases, the very scenery that was employed in the original American productions of the plays could be rescued from the storehouse at a merely nominal expenditure for transportation. Furthermore, the current cult of scenery, which has perhaps been overemphasized in recent seasons, would be properly subordinated to a recognition of the primary importance of the contributions of the author and the actor.

Two reasons have actuated the suggestion that a change of program should be made not weekly but fortnightly. In the first place, it has frequently been indicated [as in the case of *Candida*] that a great play, whenever it may be revived, can crowd the theatre in New York for at least sixteen performances. In the second place, it is desirable to avoid any overworking of the actors. An established play—in which the " business " has already been worked out and recorded —can easily be rehearsed and acted by a company of experienced performers within the short time of a single week. If a fortnightly change of bill should be established, the actors would not be required to rehearse at all during the first week of the run of any play: they would begin rehearsals of the subsequent production only at the outset of the second week of the play that was being currently performed in public.

A permanent stock company of no more than a dozen artists would suffice for the casting of most of the plays that would be listed in the program. Other actors might be engaged, as guests, from time to time, to supplement the cast of any particular production. Though the entire list of fifteen plays should be promised to subscribers in advance, and no renegation of this program should afterward be countenanced, it would not be necessary to establish in advance the order in which the various plays should be exhibited. By such a reservation, it might be possible [for instance] to arrange a date for the promised two weeks' run of *Candida* at a time when Arnold Daly did not happen to be acting in any other play. Mr. Daly might then be invited, as a guest of the permanent stock company, to resume, for that particular fortnight, his original rôle of Marchbanks. This principle has been established for many years in the municipal theatres of Germany; and it has recently been exemplified in New York by the gracious gesture of the Washington Square Players in inviting Mary Shaw to resume her original rôle of Mrs. Alving in their revival of Ibsen's *Ghosts*.

In suggesting a rather random list of fifteen plays for presentation in the course of the initial season of this hypothetical stock company, I have not attempted to arrange them in the order of production. The season, of course, should open with a pleasant comedy; and, thereafter, plays of serious complexion should alternate with plays of lighter mood. But it is only at one single little point that my own mind, in this regard, has already been made up. I should like to see the season terminated by an eloquent performance of *Alice Sit-By-The-Fire*, the masterpiece of Barrie—so that the almost intolerably lovely speeches of Alice in the final act should seem to serve as a sort of valedictory to the public after many months of beautiful endeavor; and I should like to hear these speeches read once more—as they were read of old—by another great guest who would be welcomed by the company and by the theatre-going public,—Ethel Barrymore.

XXXII

WHAT IS WRONG WITH THE AMERICAN DRAMA?

At a meeting of the Authors Club of New York on the evening of April 9, 1914, Mr. William Archer delivered an informal address, during the course of which he asked an exceedingly significant question concerning the current American drama. He stated that he had visited this country several times during the course of the last fifteen years, and that, on each occasion, he had been impressed by the vivacity of invention, the alertness of observation, and the zest of entertainment in our popular American plays; but that, whenever he had returned to New York after an absence of only two or three years, he had discovered with surprise that nearly all the current American plays had been written by new writers, and that the playwrights whose work he had admired only a short time before had apparently been relegated to oblivion. He regarded our continual discovery of new writers as an evidence of an extraordinary fertility in native talent for the theatre; but he considered our apparent failure to develop the writers whom we did discover as an evidence of a scarcely explicable prodigality. " Why is it," he inquired, " that each new generation of American

312

playwrights seems to endure only two or three seasons?
Why is it that so many men of talent, who have written
one or two promising plays, are supplanted by other
men of talent before they have had time to fulfil their
promise? What becomes of all your playwrights? Why
do you throw them away, instead of helping them to
develop their ability?"

This inquiry is extremely difficult to answer. In the
first place, it may be stated that our theatre-going
public seems to set a higher value on invention than on
imagination. This fact was clearly felt by the late
Clyde Fitch; and to satisfy the public craving for invention, he nearly always devoted his initial acts to
exploiting some novel device of theatrical dexterity.
His audience desired him to be clever; and, responsive
to the sense of this demand, he tossed out a sop of
cleverness before proceeding to the imaginative business
of his play. But the history of nearly all considerable
artists teaches us that they begin with invention and
then slowly ripen to imagination,—they commence with
cleverness and ultimately rise to simplicity and serenity.
It is not surprising, therefore, that the most vivid
invention, the most captivating cleverness, should be
displayed in the first or second plays of writers of
ingenious talent. A new idea is most likely to be
advanced by a new man. This is probably the reason
why the American public, with its avidity for clever
invention, prefers the ingenuity of new authors to the
matured imagination of writers who have risen above
the initial exercise of cleverness.

In the second place, it should be stated that the

American public goes to the theatre merely to be entertained, and that it finds more entertainment in a shifting of the point of view toward life than in a deepening of the vision of life from an established point of view. Thus far, no incentive has been offered to our playwrights to grow up. Our public does not ask that a man shall meditate upon our life until he is able to say something about it that is valuable; it asks merely that he shall point an unexpected finger at some aspect of our life that has not previously been exploited on the stage. In setting this premium on sheer originality, it votes in favor of new writers at the expense or older and wiser men, and tosses aside Augustus Thomas, who is trying to expound a philosophy of life, in favor of Bayard Veiller, who gives it news.

Only twenty years ago, it was commonly complained that a new playwright could not get a hearing in America. Nowadays any playwright can get a hearing, providing only that he come forward with something that is new. This premium that is set on novelty is perhaps the greatest cause that inhibits the development of serious drama in America. A mature playwright, who has grown to take a greater interest in life than in the theatre, is seldom likely to deal with novel subjects or to present them in a novel way. Great themes are never new; and an artist with something to say about life is rarely willing to overlay his message with the distractions of inventive ingenuity. As a result of the public demand for cleverness, we are now confronted with a situation which makes it easy for new playwrights to display their inventions, but makes it comparatively difficult for the same writers a few years later to secure a favorable hearing for the more imaginative works of their maturity.

Until this situation is changed, we shall never succeed in developing a national drama in America. Until we devise some system for distinguishing between new playwrights who are merely clever and new playwrights who are likely to progress from invention to imagination, until we devise some method for nurturing the comparatively few writers who seem inherently capable of an ultimate achievement of dramatic art, until we learn to throw away the merely entertaining craftsmen as soon as they have entertained us but never to throw away an author of real promise, and until we learn to laud imagination more than we applaud invention and to set a premium upon the man who secures his incentive from life itself instead of from the theatre, we shall not be rewarded with a national drama in America. The familiar statement that the theatre-going public gets what it deserves is true, at least, to this extent:—that no public ever gets a national drama until it deserves it.

As Mr. Archer stated, we have more than enough playwrights of sufficient talent to achieve a national dramatic literature, if only the conditions of our theatre were such as to foster the development of their ability instead of to cut it off at the very outset. The reason why we produce so few American plays of any genuine importance is not that we lack the men to write them, but that as yet we lack the conditions to demand them. Great dramatists are made, not born.

Dramatic talent is born; but dramatic genius is developed only when dramatic talent is fostered by inspiriting theatrical conditions. No plant can come to flower unless it can take root in fertile soil; and the reason why so many of our playwrights are never heard from after their first two or three plays is that they are sown as seed by the wayside and fall on rocky ground.

The responsibility for the present dearth of American dramatic art must be divided between the public, the managers, the critics, and the playwrights themselves; and we may most clearly analyze the situation by approaching it successively from the points of view of these four factors.

First of all, it must be frankly stated that the public of America, considered as a whole, is not at all interested in the drama. It is enormously interested in the theatre; but that is another matter altogether. Throughout his recent book on *The Foundations of a National Drama*, Mr. Henry Arthur Jones has insisted on the prime importance of dispelling the confusion between the drama and the theatre which persists in the popular mind. The drama is an art of authorship; and the theatre entertains the public by the exhibition of many other matters than the art of authorship. Mr. Jones has pointed out that the theatre has often flourished in periods when the drama was dead. Thus, in England in the early nineteenth century, there was no British drama of any consequence, but the British theatre prospered by exhibiting the acting of such great performers as Mrs. Siddons and the Kembles, Kean and Macready. Sir Henry Irving, who did great things for the British theatre, did absolutely nothing for the British drama, since he never produced a play by a contemporary author of importance. Likewise, Edwin Booth and Richard Mansfield, who led the American theatre for two successive generations, accomplished nothing whatsoever for the American drama.

The drama, to repeat, is an art of authorship; and the American public of to-day, considered as a whole, cares nothing for dramatic authorship. It goes to the theatre merely to be entertained; and it does not care in the least whether it is entertained by musical comedy, vaudeville, moving-pictures, or what are quaintly called legitimate plays. It groups all these heterogeneous exhibitions together, and decides that certain offerings —without regard to class—are "good shows" and certain others are not.

Since the American public is not interested in dramatic authorship, and cares only for what it is willing to consider a "good show," it would scarcely be fair to blame our theatrical managers for devoting most of their attention to non-dramatic forms of entertainment, such as musical comedies, vaudeville, and moving-pictures, nor even for insisting that the legitimate plays they do produce shall be so planned as to compete commercially with these other types of "what the public wants." Thus we perceive that the growth of the American drama is actually impeded by the popularity of the American theatre. The fact that a million Americans go to the theatre every night is of no assistance to our playwrights; it is, instead, a hindrance to them, since, in spending their time and money for forms

of entertainment that are mainly non-dramatic, these
million people are preventing themselves from developing any interest in the drama.

The reason why Mr. George M. Cohan is the most
popular playwright in America to-day is that he has
succeeded in inventing a type of legitimate comedy that
can hold its own against the drastic competition of
musical comedy and vaudeville and moving-pictures.
His plays unite the rapid, dashing plot of kinetoscopic
exhibitions with the low-comedy characterization of
vaudeville turns and the general air of inconsequential
sprightliness that pervades the best musical comedies;
and *Get-Rich-Quick Wallingford* or *Seven Keys to
Baldpate* are denominated " good shows " by the same
people who always go to see Gaby Deslys and never go
to hear John Galsworthy. Mr. Cohan is an artist of
the theatre; and he must be very highly praised for his
dexterity in managing to meet the public on its own
ground with plays that, none the less, may be admired
by people of intelligence and culture. But it seems
unfortunate that the Cohan formula should be accepted
at the present time as the most reliable talisman to
success in the American theatre.

Is there a single manager in America who is willing
to forego the emoluments that result from wholesale
dealing in popular theatric entertainments, in order
to foster the development of an American dramatic
literature? . . . Have we a single manager who is willing to work for a national achievement, as Lady
Gregory has worked in Dublin, as Miss Horniman has
worked in Manchester, as Mr. Granville Barker has

worked in London? Without the managerial efforts of
Lady Gregory and Mr. Yeats, the world would never
have heard of John M. Synge; without the managerial
efforts of Miss Horniman, the world would never have
heard of Stanley Houghton; and without the managerial efforts of Mr. Granville Barker, the world would
never have heard of Bernard Shaw. It is, perhaps,
enough to ask this question. It would be, of course,
embarrassing to answer it.

Our managers, following our public, seem to care
only for the theatre and not at all for the drama. Perhaps, for the sake of clearness, it may be desirable, at
the present point of our discussion, to define what is
meant by " the drama." We can find no better definition than one which has been offered by Mr. Henry
Arthur Jones. According to this good and faithful
servant of all that is noblest in the contemporary
theatre, the purpose of the drama is (1) to represent
life and (2) to interpret life, in terms of the theatre.
Mr. Jones admits that only a few great dramatists
have succeeded in *interpreting* life in terms of the
theatre; but he insists that no writer should be dignified with the name of dramatist unless he has at least
succeeded in *representing* life in terms of the theatre.
According to this formula of criticism, we should, in
estimating any drama, inquire (1) whether the author
has set forth a representation of life, and (2) whether
he has also revealed an interpretation of life. A play
that passes the first test is a drama; a play that also
passes the second test is a great drama; but a play that
does not pass either test is not a work of dramatic art

and can be considered only as a passing entertainment.

How often are these simple tests applied by the men who are employed by our newspapers and magazines to inform the public of what is going on in the theatres of America? . . . This question brings us face to face with one of the most important causes of the dearth of public appreciation of the drama in this country. Our so-called organs of opinion, instead of endeavoring to lead the public, are content to follow it; and, instead of establishing departments of dramatic criticism, they are content to conduct departments devoted merely to gossip of the theatre. With less than a dozen exceptions, the newspapers and even the magazines of this country treat the theatre as " news " and refuse to recognize the drama as an art. When the late Stanley Houghton came forward with *Hindle Wakes*, a work of dramatic art in which he told the utter truth about an important phase of life which for centuries had always been lied about in the theatre, did any of our newspapers trumpet this rare and wonderful achievement in its headlines? . . . Did any of our editors deem it important to declare that a new dramatist had emerged in Manchester who was able to set forth both a truthful representation of life and a piercing interpretation of it? . . . No, indeed; our newspaper reviewers merely stated, as a piece of news, that *Hindle Wakes*, though meritorious, seemed scarcely likely to enjoy a long run in New York. In other words, it wasn't a " good show "; and the public, prejudiced against it by the faint praise of the papers, permitted the piece to be withdrawn without a hearing.

It seems scarcely an exaggeration to state that there is no dramatic criticism in America,—that there is no concerted effort on the part of those who edit the theatrical pages of our publications to assist the public to distinguish between the drama and the theatre and to cultivate an appreciation of the drama which shall be clearly set apart from the enjoyment of non-dramatic types of entertainment. Our so-called " dramatic critics " [with less than a dozen exceptions in the whole United States] are not critics but reporters. They give greater publicity to the fact that Miss Billie Burke looks well in pink pajamas than to the fact that Miss Eleanor Gates has written a work of art in *The Poor Little Rich Girl*. The fancy and the wisdom of Miss Gates are considered less important as a piece of " news " than the pajamas of Miss Burke; and, as a result of this sort of propaganda, our potential dramatists are required to compete not only against musical comedy and moving-pictures but also against the lay figures in a haberdasher's window.

It will be seen, therefore, that the comparatively few playwrights in America who are honestly ambitious (1) to represent life truly, in order (2) to interpret life nobly, are condemned to struggle single-handed against the embattled negligence of the public and the managers and the theatrical reviewers. The public does not want to be told the truth; it wants to be amused. The managers do not want dramatic art; they want " what the public wants." The theatrical reviewers are not interested in the drama; they judge the value of a play in proportion to the number of nights it seems destined to run in the metropolis, and consequently consider *Peg o' My Heart* a more important work than *The Pigeon.* Need we wonder any longer why so many of our playwrights succumb to this embattled negligence and never fulfil the promise of their earliest endeavors?

But our playwrights themselves cannot be entirely absolved from blame for the present dearth of dramatic art in America. Too many of them, even from the very outset, write with an eye to the theatre instead of with an eye to life. They derive their inspiration from the wrong side of the footlights. Instead of trying to express what they think that life is like, they are contented to express what they think a play is like. Instead of following Hamlet's advice and imitating nature, they imitate each other. If one of them writes a play about the underworld that makes money in the theatre, a dozen others hasten to write plays about the underworld,—not because they are really interested in the underworld or have anything to say about it, but because they are merely interested in making money in the theatre. This enervating circle revolves until it has exhausted its transient popularity; and, the next season, the same playwrights are chasing each other around another circle. Thus, instead of moving on and getting anywhere, our playwrights merely exhaust themselves in running Marathons around a track which returns continually to the starting-point.

Another point to be considered is that the American drama at the present time seems to be hovering in a state of transition between that initial period during which it was made up of mere theatrical machinery and discussed no topics of serious importance to the public, and that still future period during which it will ascend to the revelation of permanent realities of life. Meanwhile, it is devoted mainly to an exhibition of the events of the hour and a discussion of the topics of the day.

Our most successful playwrights, for the moment, are those who hold their noses close to their newspapers. They gather what is being talked about in the daily press and set it forth upon the stage before a public that naturally wants to see what it has been reading of for many months. As one topic after another is promoted to the first pages of our journals, it also comes forward in our theatres and assumes the center of the stage. Several seasons ago, the favorite subject for discussion in our drama was the iniquity of big business; later on, it was the methods used by malefactors to evade our laws; and still later, it was, for a time, the white slave traffic. An interest in these public evils having previously been worked up in the press, our playwrights took advantage of the occasion to show the public what the public had been reading about.

There is no surer avenue than this to immediate success within the theatre; and yet it is scarcely necessary for the critic to point out that in thus allying their work with journalism our playwrights are withholding it from literature. One of the most serious handicaps to the development of a national drama that shall have some value as literature is the craze of our theatre for keeping, as the phrase is, up to date. In this endeavor to make our work, at all costs, timely, we label our plays as belonging to the vintage of a particular season; whereas in the best plays of our British contemporaries—like *Mid-Channel*, for example, or *Don*, or *What Every Woman Knows*—there is nothing to indicate precisely the year when they were written. But Time is sure to take revenge on all things timely; and these British plays will still seem new a dozen years from now, whereas our dated efforts will be out of date, like the journals of yesteryear, fit only to make soft padding under carpets.

In the interesting preface to his published play, entitled *The Divine Gift*, Mr. Henry Arthur Jones remarks, " No play that has lived has set out to tackle the latest newspaper and political problems in the spirit and by the methods of the social reformer. If I may whisper a caution to young and aspiring playwrights, I would say, ' Never choose for your theme a burning question of the hour, unless you wish merely for a success that will burn out in an hour. If you wish your plays to live, choose permanent themes and universal types of characters.' "

These words of the sagacious mentor of the modern British drama sum up one of the chief drawbacks of our American drama at the present time. It deals with types of character that are local instead of being universal, and discusses themes that, instead of being permanent, are merely temporary. Our playwrights think too little of the ultimate aim of art and too much of the immediate aim of social reform. Reform is the only enterprise that annihilates its own existence by success; and, when once a current topic has been settled, there can arise no reason for reopening discussion of the point. The more successful our journalistic plays may be, the more quickly must they go to a grave of their own digging. But a drama that expounds the great recurrent problems of humanity may remain as immortal as the human race itself.

On the other hand, however, in these years while we are waiting for the great American drama that is to be, it is surely better that our playwrights should attack the social problems of the hour than that they should discuss no problems whatsoever. Our theatre has advanced far from that initial period when it merely discoursed sweet nothings to awaken easy tears. The newspaper is nearer to life than the picture story-book; and it is but another step from the newspaper to the novel. If we are merely lighting candles that will burn out in an hour, we are at least casting a momentary light upon some problems that, for the moment, are in need of illumination; and, in even discussing so sordid a topic as the white slave traffic on the stage, we have moved nearer to the mood of literature than our Victorian predecessors stood when they exhibited a matinée-hero plucking the petals of a daisy and murmuring, " She loves me," and " She loves me not." Though some of us may not particularly like what our playwrights are at present discussing in the theatre, it is at least a reassuring sign that they are discussing something.

What, then—to sum up the entire situation—must we still accomplish in America, before we shall deserve to develop a national drama to which we shall be able

[in the florid language of political platforms] to
" point with pride "?   First of all, we must educate a
considerable section of our public to distinguish between the theatre and the drama, and to value the art
of the drama as something distinct from, and better
than, such types of ephemeral entertainment as musical
comedy and vaudeville and moving-pictures.   Having
educated a special public to patronize dramatic art, we
must organize this public and be able to deliver it to the
support of every play in which life is represented truly
in the endeavor to interpret life nobly.   These two
tasks—the task of educating the public to recognize
dramatic art, and the task of organizing the public to
support it—have already been undertaken by the
Drama League of America; and this society has thus
far done its work so well that it no longer seems quixotic
to expect that, within the next ten years, a strong and
potent interest in the drama (as distinguished from the
theatre) will be developed in America.

In the second place, we must discover and encourage
and support a few managers who will be willing to make
a living wage by catering to the growing interest in
the dramatic art, instead of gambling to win or lose
large fortunes by catering to the prevailing taste for
entertainment of a type that has no real relation to the
drama.

In the third place, we must organize a vigorous demand for dramatic criticism in America.   While permitting our newspapers and our magazines to report
non-dramatic entertainments as they report baseball
games, while allowing our editors to extract the fullest

" news value " from the pinkness of Miss Burke's pajamas, we must also demand that contributions to the great art of the drama shall be explained and interpreted by experts in the noble art of dramatic criticism. In other words, we must insist that our so-called organs of opinion shall consider the art of the drama as seriously as they now consider the art of painting and the art of music. We do not permit our newspapers to treat Rembrandt or Wagner as subjects for feeble merriment; and we must likewise cease to allow them to treat Ibsen as a joke.

In the fourth place, we must encourage our playwrights to endeavor to represent life truly and to interpret life nobly, by rewarding them with fame and money whenever they succeed in either of these difficult endeavors. We must convince them that the playing of the game itself is more than worth the burning of the candle at both ends. The present writer now recalls a conversation with the late Clyde Fitch, which occurred about ten years ago, in which Mr. Fitch complained because *The Truth*, which he regarded as his best play, had failed in New York, at the same time when *Sapho*, which he regarded as a work of no importance, was still playing to twelve thousand dollars a week in one-night stands in Texas. " Is there anybody in this country," he inquired, " who cares to have us try to do our best? " . . . It is an encouraging sign that, whereas *Sapho* has now been tossed aside, *The Truth* has recently been revived in New York by Mr. Winthrop Ames,—one of the very few American managers who care about the drama as an art. This revival demonstrated that *The Truth* was worthy of its title, and that the man who wrote it was capable of representing and interpreting the life he saw about him in America. But Clyde Fitch was not destined to live until this sincere and able work was accorded, at a belated date, the recognition which it deserved when it was first disclosed. At present we can merely wonder if our public and our managers and our reviewers would so negligently have allowed themselves to throw away this dramatist, if they had known, at the moment when he wrote *The Truth*, that he was doomed to die at the early age of forty-four.

INDEX

INDEX

NOTEWORTHY DRAMA BOOKS

Clayton Hamilton's PROBLEMS OF THE PLAYWRIGHT

This is probably even more interesting than the author's popular *Theory of the Theatre* or than his *Studies in Stagecraft* and is somewhat longer and more varied than either of its predecessors. It represents the best of his work for several recent years. $1.60 net.

Constance d'Arcy Mackay's THE LITTLE THEATRE IN THE UNITED STATES

An intensely interesting book on the most promising development in The American Theatre, by a high authority. She tells of nearly sixty of these little theatres, including something of their repertory, and has interesting supplementary discussions of The New Theatre, The Northampton Municipal Theatre, Repertory, etc. With illustrations of buildings, scenery, etc., and full index. Uniform with the author's "Costumes and Scenery for Amateurs." $2.00 net.

Arthur E. Krows's PLAY PRODUCTION IN AMERICA

With numerous and unusual illustrations and full index. $2.25 net.

Dramatic Mirror: "Any would-be playwright or actor should not proceed until he has read and 'carefully digested' this book. There is not a detail in the realm of writing a play or in the art of acting that is not made plain and valuable . . . full of vital information.

Richard Burton's BERNARD SHAW: The Man and the Mask

By the author of "How to See a Play," etc. *With Index*. $1.60 net.

Archibald Henderson, author of the standard biography of Shaw, calls Dr. Burton's book—"The best introduction to Bernard Shaw in print. No other book gives an analysis and study of each play . . . genius of simplicity of expression and effectiveness in interpretation."

Otto Heller's Lessing's MINNA VON BARNHELM

An illuminating introduction and notable translation. $1.25 net.

Independent: "Admirable translation in idiomatic English, yet true to the spirit of the original."

Christian Register: "Accurate and readable. . . . Professor Heller may be congratulated."

Jonathan Hubbard in the Baltimore Evening Sun: "His invaluable translation . . . Lessing's dramatic masterpiece and Germany's greatest comedy."

☞The Publishers will send free on application their DESCRIPTIVE LEAFLET OF DRAMA BOOKS.

HENRY HOLT AND COMPANY
PUBLISHERS   NEW YORK

By Clayton Hamilton

STUDIES IN STAGECRAFT

CONTENTS: The New Art of Making Plays, The Pictorial Stage, The Drama of Illusion, The Modern Art of Stage Direction, A Plea for a New Type of Play, The Undramatic Drama, The Value of Stage Conventions, The Supernatural Drama, The Irish National Theatre, The Personality of the Playwright, Where to Begin a Play, Continuity of Structure, Rhythm and Tempo, The Plays of Yesteryear, A New Defense of Melodrama, The Art of the Moving-Picture Play, The One-Act Play in America, Organizing an Audience, The Function of Dramatic Criticism, etc., etc. $1.60 net.

Nation: "Information, alertness, coolness, sanity and the command of a forceful and pointed English. . . . A good book, in spite of all deductions."

Prof. Archibald Henderson, in The Drama: "Uniformly excellent in quality. . . . Continuously interesting in presentation . . . uniform for high excellence and elevated standards. . . ."

Athenaeum (London): "His discussions, though incomplete, are sufficiently provocative of thought to be well worth reading."

THE THEORY OF THE THEATRE

THE THEORY OF THE THEATRE.—What is a Play?—The Psychology of Theatre Audiences.—The Actor and the Dramatist.—Stage Conventions in Modern Times.—The Four Leading Types of Drama: Tragedy and Melodrama; Comedy and Farce.—The Modern Social Drama, etc., etc.

OTHER PRINCIPLES OF DRAMATIC CRITICISM.—The *Public* and the Dramatist.—Dramatic Art and the Theatre Business. —Dramatic Literature and Theatric Journalism.—The Intention of Performance.—The Quality of New Endeavor.— Pleasant and Unpleasant Plays.—Themes in the Theatre.— The Function of Imagination, etc., etc. 4th printing. $1.60 net.

Bookman: "Presents coherently a more substantial body of idea on the subject than perhaps elsewhere accessible."

Boston Transcript: "At every moment of his discussion he has a firm grasp upon every phase of the subject."

THE GERMAN DRAMA OF THE NINETEENTH CENTURY

By GEORG WITKOWSKI. Translated by PROF. L. E. HORNING.

Kleist, Grillparzer, Hebbel, Ludwig, Wildenbruch, Sudermann, Hauptmann and minor dramatists receive attention. 12mo. $1.00.

New York Times Review: "The translation of this brief, clear and logical account was an extremely happy idea. Nothing at the same time so comprehensive and terse has appeared on the subject."

HENRY HOLT AND COMPANY
PUBLISHERS   NEW YORK

PLAYS BY THREE AMERICANS

Beulah M. Dix's ACROSS THE BORDER

A dream play suggested by the present war. $1.00 net.

Clayton Hamilton: "The best of all recent plays inspired by the European War . . . highly imaginative, powerful and touching."

Beulah M. Dix's ALLISON'S LAD and Other Martial Interludes

These one-act episodes of olden wars include *Allison's Lad, The Hundredth Trick, The Weakest Link, The Snare and the Fowler, The Captain of the Gate, The Dark of the Dawn.* All the characters are men or boys. $1.35 net.

Percival Wilde's DAWN and Other One-Act Plays

Dawn, The Noble Lord, The Traitor, A House of Cards, Playing with Fire and *The Finger of God.* 2nd printing. $1.25 net.

Percival Wilde's CONFESSIONAL and Other Short Plays

Confessional, The Villain in the Piece, According to Darwin (2 acts), *A Question of Morality* and *The Beautiful Story.* $1.25 net.

The Independent: "The subjects are those of most interest today, the treatment is fresh and sincere, and the author shows a keen sense of dramatic values."

PLAYS BY GEORGE MIDDLETON

EMBERS and Other One-Act Plays

Including *The Failures, The Gargoyle, In His House, The Man Masterful* and *Madonna.* 3rd printing. $1.35 net.

TRADITION and Other One-Act Plays

Including *On Bail, Mothers, Waiting, Their Wife* and *The Cheat of Pity.* 3rd printing. $1.35 net.

POSSESSION and Other One-Act Plays

Including *The Groove, The Black Tie, A Good Woman, Circles* and *The Unborn.* 2nd printing. $1.35 net.

NOWADAYS

A Comedy of American Life To-day. 4th printing. $1.20 net.

THE ROAD TOGETHER

A four-act play of married life. $1.20 net.

New York Tribune: "He is America's only serious contribution to the international drama of the period . . . one constantly reflects how much better it acts than it reads, and it reads exceedingly well."

☞ For fuller information send for the publisher's DESCRIPTIVE LIST OF DRAMA BOOKS to

HENRY HOLT AND COMPANY

PUBLISHERS   IX '17   NEW YORK